Daring to Be Good

Thinking Gender

Edited by Linda Nicholson

Also published in the series:

daring to be
good

Essays in Feminist Ethico-Politics

edited by

Bat-Ami Bar On and Ann Ferguson

Routledge *New York and London*

Published in 1998 by
Routledge
29 West 35th Street
New York, NY 10001

Published in Great Britain by
Routledge
11 New Fetter Lane
London EC4P 4EE

Copyright © 1998 by Routledge
Printed in the United States of America on acid free paper.
Book design by Charles B. Hames

Library of Congress Cataloging-in-Publication Data
Daring to be good : essays in feminist ethico-politics / edited by
    Bat-Ami Bar On and Ann Ferguson.
        p. cm. — (Thinking gender)
Includes bibliographical references and index.
ISBN 0–415–91554–6 (hardcover : alk. paper).
ISBN 0–415–91555–4 (pbk. : alk. paper).
    1. Feminist ethics. I. Bar On, Bat-Ami, 1948–   . II. Ferguson, Ann.
    III. Series.
BJ1395.D37   1998
170'.82–dc21   97–28333
                                                             CIP

Contents

Acknowledgments

We wish to thank the former philosophy editor at Routledge, Maureen MacGrogan, and the Thinking Gender series editor, Linda Nicholson, for their words of encouragement, helpful suggestions, yet the space to develop the book autonomously. We are grateful as well to the other editors, copyreader, and indexer we worked with at Routledge in writing this book. We particularly wish to acknowledge the work of our excellent authors, without which this book would not exist. Finally we thank our loved ones and supportive friends for nourishing us while the book project was underway.

Bat-Ami Bar On and
Ann Ferguson

Introduction

Bat-Ami Bar On and Ann Ferguson

At the beginning of the second wave of the European and American women's movements there was a sense that feminist issues were easy to identify: they were those that all women had in common, e.g., reproductive rights or violence against women. But since then there has been an explosion of problems taken as feminist, and the early choices have been criticized as falsely universalizing, privileging some while excluding other groups of women (cf. Jaggar, 1994; Moraga and Anzaldua, eds., 1981). In addition, Western women's movements have gravitated toward the kind of political action that centers demands for change on public policy, thus reinscribing a particular mainstream notion of the political. This is a notion that presupposes the state as a site of politics, the view that interests are what motivate politics, that human subjects compose one of the foundations of politics, and that women as a group are a proper kind of political subject (Butler, 1992). But recently, important critiques of essentialist identity politics and other foundational political concepts have led us to focus on the questions of what constitutes a "feminist" and a "political" issue, with special attention to the place of ethics in feminist thought. Thus in this book, we ask how ethical problems connect to and are distinguished from political problems in academic feminist thought.

What makes this question particularly complicated is that ethics and politics have been split in Western thought since the beginning of modernity. Ancient Greek philosophy distinguishes between ethics and politics yet posits them as implicated in each other so much that the ideas of the just or good individual and the just or good polis are either investigated together, as in the *Republic*, or when separated, as in the case of Aristotle, it is still with the understanding of their interdependence. Medieval philosophers, like Augustine, make a little more of a distinction between ethics and politics, distinguishing what is owed to God and what to an earthly sovereign. Nonetheless, they still idealize the connectedness of value and power, as in, for example, the theory of the divine right of kings. It is only with the rise and development of classical liberal thought, as represented by Machiavelli, Hobbes, Locke, Hume, Hutcheson, and Adam Smith, that a sophisticated separation between ethics and politics is worked out (MacIntyre, 1981; Larmore, 1987; Poole, 1991).

The formation of nation-states and the growth of capitalism and free markets stimulated Adam Smith's ideology of an "invisible hand" of the market, which was supposed to coordinate individual selfish acts in the interest of the whole community. This ideology supported both ethical egoism, the idea that people ought to act to promote their own self-interests, as well as utilitarianism, according to which the production of the majority's happiness is the measure of morality. Such a foundation also allowed individuals, assumed to be autonomous moral agents, to justify any government they felt to represent a social contract. Thus, all of these early modern moral theories developed an individualist cast that legitimated maximal state neutrality toward individual goals and actions.

In *Moral Boundaries*, Joan Tronto (1993) exposes a gender dimension of the modern liberal separation of ethics and politics. The rationalization of the objective, impartial point of view (Smith, Hume, Kant) joins with the material and ideological encircling of life into private and public spheres to function as a boundary that marks and excludes women from power. Enlightenment thought had to find a way to base ethics on individual rationality as a self-contained area, since it eschewed the earlier notion that ethics was structured into the natural, divine order of things. But by the end of the development of liberal ethics, individual rationality has come to be associated with the public world of men rather than the private world of the family (and women), thus problematizing women as subjects of ethics at all.

At the beginning of the liberal ethical paradigm, in the seventeenth and eighteenth centuries in the Scottish moral sense school, however, passion, not reason, is the foundation of ethics. So how does the paradigm come to reverse itself on this point? Adam Smith, Francis Hutcheson, and

David Hume all tried to develop contextual theories of ethics in which a particular moral passion ("benevolence" for Hutcheson; "sympathy" for Hume; "propriety" for Smith) was at the base of a moral judgment based on the context yet reflective. Moral passions, though, seem like a plausible foundation for moral judgments in situations where people are closely acquainted with others, such as with family relatives, friends, or neighbors. But how is one to assess moral responsibilities to those from which one is socially distant, for example to strangers to whom one may feel no sympathy? Just as the ancients developed more universal and less polis-based ethical ideals as trade and empires encompassed more diverse peoples, so the development of European capitalism and imperialism forced ethical theorists to think about nation-states dealing with diverse citizenry and peoples, e.g., Europeans relating to Native Americans, Africans, and Asians.

Just starting to confront this problem, Hutcheson appealed to education as a means to extend feelings across distance, while Hume developed the idea that nation-states had to create the "artificial virtue" of justice as a corrective for the bias of sympathy. He and Smith developed the "ideal observer" or "impartial spectator" theory of the "moral point of view" in which sympathy would be based on an impartial, detached, universalistic, and knowledgeable perspective. Kant continued this trend of detaching moral judgments from particular feelings and contexts by making reason the foundation for ethics through the categorical imperative as a mode of rationally universalizing and decontextualizing one's moral judgments.

Tronto implies there is a functional reason for this elevation of reason over passion: the division between the right (justice, reason) and the good (values, feelings) allowed those who disagreed strongly about religion, forms of government, family ethics, and structure and national cultural values to be able to work together, to accept principles of free trade and the economic interdependence brought about by national and international markets. Tronto argues that at the same time that feelings became less central for ethics, they also became more associated with women, who were also being increasingly associated with the private sphere. But as capitalist production separated production for use in the family (increasingly defined as exclusively women's work, and devalued) from production for exchange (the entrepreneurial province of men even though women were many of the initial wage earners) it also exaggerated the public/private split between formal justice (a male domain) and family and personal values (a female, hence less important, even less human, domain). In this way it reconstructed a patriarchal order based on a natural, divine order that had lost its legitimacy with the development of individualism and the social contract theory of public justice. Ethical insights based on the social relations involved in women's caring labor in the household were consequently devalued as well.

This genealogical sketch of the politics/ethics split casts doubt on some feminist strategies to preserve the dichotomy but reverse the valuation or definition of each of the terms. Some of these feminist attempts to critique the deleterious effect of the public/private split on women have used the strategy of "reversing the discourse," that is, of revaluing the side of the binary hitherto devalued as feminine. For example, Carol Gilligan's feminine ethics of care or private ethics (Gilligan, 1982), which she contrasts with the masculine ethics associated with politics and the public ethics of justice, has been taken by those as disparate as Nell Noddings (1984) and Sarah Hoagland (1988) to imply that we should reject a masculine ethic of justice in favor of some reconstructed ethic of care that revalues women, or more precisely in Hoagland's case, remoralizes lesbians (Amazon caring). Others have not rejected justice so much as demanded that caring based on mothering needs to be added to justice to get a more balanced ethics (Ruddick, 1989; Held, 1993; Willett, 1995). Susan Moller Okin (1989), on the other hand, has insisted on extending the concepts of the public ethics of justice into the private terrain of the family. But the problem with all these strategies is that they still tend to privilege one side of the binary or the other, thus perpetuating the force of the binary.

A different critical revaluation strategy is used by others, such as Audre Lorde (1984), Maria Lugones (1987), and Marilyn Friedman (1993), who turn to many kinds of personal relations, for example friendship or love, to inform some of their ethical and political thinking. These authors have in common a more general challenge to what has been suppressed by modern liberalism, one shared by other critics as well, for example Merchant, who critiques modern Western male thinkers who associate women with nature in order to conquer both (Merchant, 1980); Anzaldua (1987), who brings out commonalities in the colonial and precolonial situations of those, "la raza" with lesbian experience; Baier, who urges feminists to turn back to aspects of Hume rejected by contemporary liberalism (Baier, 1995); and Willett (1995) who compares mothering with slave moralities in the U.S. Meanwhile important French feminist theorists urge a critical turn to the body for ethical and political insights (Irigaray, 1993; Diprose, 1994).

All of these critical revaluations and reverse discourses together suggest a refiguring of multilayered modern liberal conceptions of gender and the other binary categories by which it has been understood, such as nature/culture, reason/emotion, and mind/body, as well as the hitherto binary social categories with which it intersects, such as race, ethnicity, sexuality, and age. Diana Meyers suggests in *Subjection and Subjectivity* (1994) that these refigurations free the imagination from what otherwise would have distorted moral judgment, allow the construction of novel social forms and are, therefore, part of "dissident speech." According to Meyers, dissident speech is emancipatory only insofar as it facilitates the recognition and satisfaction of the needs of members of sociopolitically excluded groups, is polyvocal, and does not homogenize such groups. At the same time, such speech must be integrated into a comprehensive struggle for a massive social, political, and economic reordering.

Increasingly, feminist revaluation discourses, which do function as dissident speech, are quite polyvocal and growing more so. However, we hold that as yet none of these attempts to bridge the gap between ethics and politics have been completely successful, including Tronto's own efforts at developing a public policy of care to substitute, or at the least supplement, a policy based on rights or entitlements (cf. Ferguson, 1996). Perhaps this is because, in a patriarchal capitalist system, the public/private split cannot be eradicated due to the need of both conservative and radical elements to defend turf now held in the state or in civil society that requires such a division. In such a case, this "moral boundary," in Tronto's terms, acts as a structural limit beyond which the political concepts of state, law, government, equality, democracy, and justice cannot be reconstituted without a feminist democratic socialist revolution.

Whatever the reasons for the persistence of the public/private, politics/ethics split, it is clear that feminist discourses rethinking politics and rethinking ethics, including the articles in this collection, still tend to reproduce this split by the nature of their focus and entry point to the issues. One camp (those reacting to and correcting liberal political discourses) is engaged in rethinking politics, while another camp (those reacting to the limitations of mainstream ethical theory) is engaged in rethinking and producing oppositional feminist values. Each camp can be critiqued by those in the other camp for not having completely answered the central ethico-political question of feminism: *What is wrong with our current state, government, economy from a feminist perspective, and what ethical and political alternative values, visions, and strategies should feminists stand for and engage in?*

Consider the "Politico" camp—Iris Young (1990), Susan Moller Okin (1989), Seyla Benhabib (1992), Chantal Mouffe (1993), Anna Yeatman (1994), Wendy Brown (1995), and Bonnie Honig (1993). These thinkers are preoccupied with deconstructing liberal political theory, either by extending the modern liberal concept of justice into the terrain of the household and the family (Okin), by rejecting its emphasis on distribution to insist on a process-oriented conception that emphasizes participatory democratic process to include hitherto marginalized groups (Young), or by advocating a radical pluralist democracy that challenges liberal ideals of citizenship and the state (Yeatman, Benhabib, Mouffe, and Brown). Others (Honig, 1993; Bickford, 1996) focus on the agonism of difference and the politics of speech and listening evaded by modern liberal discourse. Nancy Fraser's latest work incorporates these other efforts in a comprehensive political theory that includes attention to particular concrete struggles for sociopolitical and economic equality (Fraser, 1997). In spite of their critiques of the existing liberal political discourses of justice, democracy, and equality, however, all are strangely silent on what kind of ethical values and political strategies feminists who accept their critiques of the existing political discourses and power structures should be pursuing. Thus, there is what we can call a *Theory/Practice Gap* in their work.

The "Ethico" feminist authors (that is, those who attempt to address the central feminist ethico-political question of how to live from the side of challenging traditional ethical discourses) include Gilligan (1982), Noddings (1984), Hoagland (1988), Ruddick (1989), Held (1993), Willett (1995), Lorde (1984), Kittay and Meyers (1987), Friedman (1993), Weiss and Friedman (1995), and earlier writing by some authors in this collection, such as Lugones (1987), Bartky (1990), Addelson (1991, 1994), and Ferguson (1995). The emphasis in this writing, aside from the critiques of mainstream ethical theory, is on "remoralizing" women (Hoagland's phrase) by creating alternative ethical visions and political practices for lesbian and feminist oppositional communities. Sometimes such remoralizing is done by pointing to the neglected yet already existing ethical practices of women, such as caring and mothering, which can be used to revalue a feminist ethical sense of self (Gilligan, Noddings, Ruddick). Others reject such a strategy of valorizing present practices by moving to reconstitute them as part of oppositional communities, feminist practices, and alternative ways of life, in order to "prefigure," that is to model, a communitarian feminist vision of class, race, gender, and sexual equality and democracy (Hoagland, Lorde, Lugones, Friedman, Addelson, Ferguson). But the feminist, alternative, communitarian ethical vision by itself does not really confront the problem of justice for others not involved in one's communities. Confronting justice on this level requires taking on the state and political economic power structures as suggested by the Politico camp. *How then can we begin to build a feminist ethico-political discourse and set of political and ethical practices that bridge the gap better than we have done in the past?*

Although the individual authors in *Daring to Be Good* cannot be read as answering this concern, we would argue that the collection as a whole provides an indication of how to proceed. The organization of the collection does not separate ethics from politics, nor do the individual authors bracket off the epistemological, metaphysical, and psychological presuppositions of their theorizing. We hope that this augurs a forthcoming trend to integrate such issues as a means to overcome artificial separations. We have also structured the essays into sections that are designed to remind us to interrogate such divisions. Parts 1 and 2, "Moral Psychology" and "The Ethics and Politics of Knowledge," contain papers that take up general gaps in feminist theorizing about the psyche (Hall, Dwyer, Bartky) and the politics of knowledge production and its ethical implications (Whitt, Davion, Heberle). They also suggest how to frame particular moral issues that go beyond the separations, such as how to confront everyday violence condoned by our allies (Bar On), or how to go about being a responsible traitor (Heldke).

The authors in Part 3, "Identities and Communities," clearly represent the Ethico approach to feminist ethico-politics as we have conceptualized it above. But they begin to overlap the work of the Politico approach in a way that suggests a way to reframe the binary Politico/Ethico division. These papers suggest that not only must we refuse to abstract out ethical questions from those of our ongoing practices situated in oppositional communities (Addelson and Watson-Verran), but we need to understand the multiplicities, overlaps, and conflicts in the many communities women inhabit (Flax, Lugones). Thus, they agree that we need to continue to question the boundaries that separate others from the "we" who count as morally relevant members of our communities. For example, Cuomo and Gruen ask, What about animals? Similar questions can be asked of the Politicos who tend to limit their critiques of the state to those living within its borders rather than those "non-citizens" around the world who are affected by its policies.

When it comes to Part 4, "Policy and Its Issues," the authors more explicitly find ways to bridge the gap between a Politico discourse and an Ethico discourse. Their discussions of concrete policy issues that divide feminists, such as reproductive technology and pornography (Farquhar), prostitution (Ferguson), hormonal contraceptives (Begus), and policies pertaining to drug addiction (Campbell), are characterized both by critiques of the patriarchal capitalist state as power structure and by concern with the ethical conflicts between feminists and our allies as to how to challenge this situation in political positions taken and strategies proposed.

All of the essays in *Daring to Be Good* insist in various ways that not only is the personal ethical but also political, requiring a situated ethics approach to our critiques of public policy. They also show that the psychological and the epistemological involve ethical and political concerns that must be interrogated. So understood, *Daring to Be Good* is about an everyday kind of politics whose importance began to be realized with the New Left in the sixties. This politicization of the personal was central to the development of Western feminism, since before this political development, the modern liberal separation of ethics from politics made it impossible to conceive of "women's personal issues" as political.

Sandra Bartky's essay on the disciplines that produce femininity as well as resistance to it explicitly deals with the personal as political, and bridges the gap between merely describing feminine psychology and critiquing it. Susan Dwyer challenges the descriptive/prescriptive division between moral psychology and ethics in another way by her discussion of moral consciousness as embodied, and argues that women's moral judgments about abortion are based on the phenomenological experience of women's bodies.

We have mentioned above how the articles in the "Public Policy" section by Farquhar, Begus, Ferguson, and Campbell attempt to bridge the ethical/political, private/public gap in various ways, one of which involves problematizing the legitimacy of states (and supra-state bodies like the UN) that is assumed in most public policy. As a result these essays necessarily have to struggle with feminist values and with guidelines for interactions among feminists (who do not necessarily agree with each other) as well as among feminists and nonfeminists in the arena of legislative politics writ large. All four emphasize the importance of the empowerment of women through public policy. Such a principle leads Farquhar and Campbell to argue against conservative moralization and Ferguson and Begus to argue for a transitional morality that contextualizes analysis and solutions but does not preclude an ideal for the future.

Laurie Whitt's essay, which is also about public policy because it interrogates the Human Genome Diversity Project, comes to the question of values and guidelines from a different direction due to its focus on the prevalent practices of the natural sciences. She challenges the scientific distinction between "pure" and "applied" research in order to insist on a normative critique. Whitt represents indigenous critics who stand to be disproportionately affected by the theft and patenting of genetic material, and demands that projects such as the human genome project be put in the political arena for public debate, since no such pure/applied line can be drawn. This essay and others in the anthology stress feminist ethical questions about responsible ways to do the business of knowledge (Heldke); about how honesty contributes to knowledge (Davion); and about how theorizing must be humble enough to understand its need to be connected to practice (Addelson-Verran, Heberle).

The significance of theorizing humbly is emphasized in a different way by Flax and Lugones in their focus on the exclusion of marginalized others and the ignorance or limits that it generates. Yet again, our concrete locations as knowing subjects are emphasized by Bartky's and Dwyer's emphasis on a concretized phenomenological analysis of the structures of meanings. For Bartky they reveal the construction of subjectivity, hence the possibility of agency. Hall and Dwyer raise the questions of what is necessary for agency in general, and whether there is a way we can learn to reflect morally on our experience that will give us a new approach to feminist politics. Bar On asks, Can moral agency exist under extreme conditions? And Cuomo and Gruen raise the question, How can one begin to extend a moral consciousness to include new areas of responsibility such as animals and other living things? These questions of moral psychology are a particularly fruitful field for interrogating the relation between ethics and politics.

Some feminist theorists seem to reject the possibility of a feminist ethics that is other than a moralizing voice. For example, Alice Echols advocates that we "dare to be bad" to counter what she takes to be radical feminist prudery in the feminist sex debate (Echols, 1989). And Judith Butler seems to question the possibility of moral agency when she insists on the primary of the "question of the political construction and regulation of the subject itself," since "subjects are constituted through exclusion, that is, through the creation of a domain of de-authorized subjects, pre-subjects, figures of abjection, populations erased from view" (Butler, 1992: 13). But we need not take these claims at face value: Echols clearly is espousing a pluralist feminist ethics as opposed to a radical feminist one, and Butler is rejecting identity ethico-politics, not necessarily moral agency. While Echols and Butler may stand on different sides of the identity politics question than do most of our authors, all sides insist that ethics be joined with politics. Thus, if Echols and company can "dare to be bad," other feminists like those in this collection can *Dare to Be Good*, albeit with the caution necessary to that strategy, given the justified moral suspicions of the desire to be good (girls!) (Frye, 1991).

References

Addelson, Kathryn Pyne. 1991. *Impure Thoughts: Essays on Philosophy, Feminism and Ethics*. Philadelphia: Temple University Press.

———. 1994. *Moral Passages: Toward Collectivist Moral Theory*. New York: Routledge.

Anzaldua, Gloria. 1987. *Borderlands/La Frontera*. San Francisco: Spinsters/Aunt Lute.

Baier, Annette C. 1995. *Moral Prejudices: Essays on Ethics.* Cambridge: Harvard University Press.

Bartky, Sandra Lee. 1990. *Femininity as Domination: Studies in the Phenomenology of Oppression.* New York: Routledge.

Benhabib, Seyla. 1992. *Situating the Self: Gender, Community and Postmodernism in Contemporary Ethics.* New York: Routledge.

Bickford, Susan. 1996. *The Dissonance of Democracy: Listening, Conflict, and Citizenship.* Ithaca, N.Y.: Cornell University Press.

Brown, Wendy. 1995. *States of Injury: Power and Freedom in Later Modernity.* Princeton, N.J.: Princeton University Press.

Butler, Judith. 1992. "Contingent Foundations: Feminism and the Question of 'Postmodernism.'" In Judith Butler and Joan W. Scott, eds. *Feminists Theorize the Political.* New York: Routledge: 3–21.

Card, Claudia, ed. 1991. *Feminist Ethics.* Lawrence: University of Kansas Press.

———. 1996. *The Unnatural Lottery: Character and Moral Luck.* Philadelphia: Temple University Press.

Diprose, Rosalyn. 1994. *The Bodies of Women: Ethics, Embodiment, and Sexual Difference.* London: Routledge.

Echols, Alice. 1989. *Daring to Be Bad: Radical Feminism in America, 1967–1975.* Minneapolis: University of Minnesota Press.

Ferguson, Ann. 1995. "Feminist Communities and Moral Revolution." In Penny Weiss and Marilyn Friedman, eds. *Feminism and Community.* Philadelphia: Temple University Press: 367–97.

———. 1996. Review of Joan Tronto, *Moral Boundaries.* In *Radical Philosophy Review of Books* 13: 18–26.

Fraser, Nancy. 1997. *Justice Interruptus: Critical Reflections on the 'Post-Socialist' Condition.* New York: Routledge.

Friedman, Marilyn. 1993. *Who Are Friends For? Feminist Perspectives on Personal Relationships and Moral Theory.* Ithaca, N.Y.: Cornell University Press.

Frye, Marilyn. 1991. "A Response to *Lesbian Ethics*: Why Ethics?" In Claudia Card, ed. *Feminist Ethics.* Lawrence: University of Kansas Press.

Gilligan, Carol. 1982. *In a Different Voice.* Cambridge: Harvard University Press.

Held, Virginia. 1993. *Feminist Morality.* Chicago: University of Chicago Press.

Hoagland, Sarah. 1988. *Lesbian Ethics.* Palo Alto, Calif.: Institute of Lesbian Ethics.

Honig, Bonnie. 1993. *Political Theory and the Displacement of Politics.* Ithaca, N.Y.: Cornell University Press.

Irigaray, Luce. 1993. *The Ethics of Sexual Difference.* Ithaca, N.Y.: Cornell University Press.

Jaggar, Alison. 1994. "Introduction." In Jaggar, ed. *Living With Contradictions.* Boulder, Colo.: Westview: 1–12.

Kittay, Eva Feder and Diana Meyers, eds. 1987. *Women and Moral Theory.* Totowa, N.J.: Rowman and Littlefield.

Larmore, Charles E. 1987. *Patterns of Moral Complexity.* Cambridge: Cambridge University Press.

Lorde, Audre. 1984. *Sister Outsider.* Trumansburg, N.Y.: The Crossing Press.

Lugones, Maria. 1987. "Playfulness, 'World'-Traveling and Loving Perception." *Hypatia* 2: 3–19.

MacIntyre, Alasdair. 1981. *After Virtue.* Notre Dame, Ind.: University of Notre Dame Press.

Merchant, Carolyn, 1980. *The Death of Nature: Women, Ecology and the Scientific Revolution.* San Francisco: Harper and Row.

Meyers, Diana Tietjens. 1994. *Subjection and Subjugation: Psychoanalytic Feminism and Moral Philosophy*. New York: Routledge.

Mouffe, Chantal. 1993. *The Return of the Political*. London: Verso.

Noddings, Neil. 1984. *Caring: A Feminine Approach to Ethics and Moral Education*. Berkeley: University of California.

Okin, Susan Moller. 1989. *Justice, Gender and the Family*. New York: Basic Books.

Poole, Ross. 1991. *Morality and Modernity*. London: Routledge.

Ruddick, Sara. 1989. *Maternal Thinking: Towards a Politics of Peace*. New York: Ballantine.

Tronto, Joan. 1993. *Moral Boundaries: A Political Argument for an Ethics of Care*. New York: Routledge.

Weiss, Penny and Marilyn Friedman, eds. 1995. *Feminism and Community*. Philadelphia: Temple University.

Willett, Cynthia. 1995. *Maternal Ethics and Other Slave Moralities*. New York: Routledge.

Yeatman, Anna. 1994. *Postmodern Revisionings of the Political*. New York: Routledge.

Young, Iris. 1990. *Justice and the Politics of Difference*. Princeton, N.J.: Princeton University Press.

ONE

Moral Psychology

Politics, Ethics, and the "Uses of the Erotic"

Why Feminist Theorists Need to Think about the Psyche

Cheryl Hall

The task of developing new theories of ethics and politics has engaged contemporary feminist thinkers for some time now. It is in many ways a unified task, for faced with the unacceptable choice between thinking about ways to be powerful yet dominating, and thinking about ways to be virtuous yet powerless, feminist theorists have followed feminist activists in searching for ways to integrate ethics and politics. Since presumably the ability to act both ethically and politically is neither inherent nor currently well developed, one might expect accounts of the personal development and transformation required for such agency to be a primary focus of feminist ethical-political theories. Yet less attention is paid to this issue than ought to be, and even those theories that have addressed it are not as persuasive as they might be. I will argue in this essay that the problem stems, in part, from insufficient attention to what might be called theories of the psyche.[1]

Considering the substantial body of feminist writing on the general subject of the self, or identity, or subjectivity, one might initially be skeptical of this argument. Yet discussions of the self and subjectivity do not necessarily include what I mean by "theories of the psyche." The term "psyche" originally meant soul or spirit, the "breath of life," but in more contemporary usage it generally refers to the mind or mental processes and activities. By theories of the psyche, then, I mean theories of the possible organizations and operations of mental processes and activities, and the ways in which such organizations may affect human being and action in the world.[2] Now, it is surely a generalization, but I think it is still fair to say that what most feminist work on the self and subjectivity—including explicitly psychological and psychoanalytic as well as ethical and political work—is concerned to explore are the problematic presumptions (of abstraction, independence, coherence, etc.) of masculinist theories of the self and/or the sources and development of particular kinds of (gendered/raced/classed, etc.) persons. That is to say, most of this writing is focused on formulating alternative theories of human connectedness, identity, and identity formation. These subjects overlap with but are still different from what I contend needs more of our attention: the potential interactions and functioning of major faculties of the human mind. The existing feminist work on the self thus does not obviate the concern I raise here.

My argument is that feminist ethical-political theories, even more than theories that do not integrate ethics and politics, require theories of the psyche to be effective. In order to demonstrate this point, this essay will provide an example of what feminist arguments look like *without* a theory of the psyche. For the purposes of this illustration, I have chosen to discuss the relatively compact body of feminist writing on eros and power. Because it is explicitly focused on the issue of personal and political agency, but arguably hampered in important ways by an underdeveloped conception of the psyche, this literature is a good example of both what feminist theories of ethics and politics might contribute and what they still lack. My discussion of this literature begins with a brief synopsis of the general argument about eros (or a closely related concept) that has been advanced in different ways by approximately nine authors (Brock 1991; Dimen 1989; Goodison 1983; Hartsock 1983; Heyward 1984, 1989; Jaggar 1989; Lorde 1984; Schott 1988; and Trask 1988). In the second section, I explore what I take to be the literature's primary weakness, and link it to the absence of a more developed theory of the psyche. In the third section, I suggest that feminist theorists might find some inspiration in the attention that Plato, who also writes about eros, paid to the psyche. I conclude the essay with some thoughts on why metaphors of the psyche may prove useful, and what feminist theories of the psyche might require.

"Uses of the Erotic":
Contemporary Feminists on Eros and Power

One of the features that most prominently characterizes male-stream ethical and political philosophies is an intense focus on the human capacity of reason, and a concurrent hope that ethics and politics can be made as "rational" (and unemotional) as possible. Feminist ethical-political thinking, of course, often challenges this ideal of a reason purified of emotion. One example of such a challenge is the general argument for an "ethics of care." Arguments on behalf of "eros" are another example. Feminist work on eros has been inspired primarily by Audre Lorde's brief but influential essay, "Uses of the Erotic: The Erotic as Power." By eros or "the erotic," Lorde does not mean exclusively sexual desire but rather deeply felt love, desire, and passion of all kinds. In some of her many references to the erotic, she speaks of it as "the *yes* within ourselves, our deepest cravings," the "capacity for joy," and "those physical, emotional, and psychic expressions of what is deepest and strongest and richest within each of us" (1984, 56–57). Such an unconventional definition is quite deliberate, for Lorde contends that it is precisely because "we are taught to separate the erotic demand from most vital areas of our lives other than sex" that eros remains a largely untapped resource (55). It is the point of her essay to suggest how a broader understanding and experience of eros can be profoundly useful to us.

The heart of Lorde's argument can be summarized in one phrase: "our erotic knowledge empowers us" (57). This claim actually consists of two parts. The first step is the contention that eros provides knowledge. Specifically, the point is that the erotic, if we are attuned to it, provides us with knowledge of what we need and want in the world, of what gives us joy. It also provides us with knowledge of what matters to us, of what gives our lives richness and meaning—that is, knowledge of our values. Building on this point, the second contention is that such knowledge provides power. In Lorde's words,

> Once we begin to feel deeply all the aspects of our lives, we begin to demand from ourselves and from our life-pursuits that they feel in accordance with that joy which we know ourselves to be capable of. Our erotic knowledge empowers us, becomes a lens through which we scrutinize all aspects of our existence, forcing us to evaluate those aspects honestly in terms of their relative meaning within our lives. And this is a grave responsibility, projected within each of us, not to settle for the convenient, the shoddy, the conventionally expected, nor the merely safe. (57)

Knowledge of what gives our lives joy and meaning is empowering, then, because it establishes a standard that we can use to evaluate our endeavors. It thus helps *guide* us in making good choices in our lives, choices that will be in accordance with our values. Beyond this, knowledge of what gives our lives joy and meaning is empowering because it *inspires* us to live more meaningfully. It is not easy, Lorde admits, to live up to the responsibility not to "settle," to "demand the most from ourselves, from our lives, from our work" (54)—but, she argues, the erotic experience of satisfaction when we do reminds us that the effort is worthwhile. The more in touch we are both with what we value and with the satisfaction that living up to it brings, the greater our ability and our motivation to "demand the most" will be. And because it helps people take positive action in their lives, such ability and motivation is a kind of power.

The final point in this argument is that this kind of power is especially important for those who are oppressed, those who do not start out in charge of their own lives and who have certainly been expected to settle. Anyone in this situation must *fight* for a more meaningful and joyful existence, and yet many in this situation end up passive out of alienation and hopelessness. Lorde argues that eros counters the apathy and resignation of the oppressed, for "as we begin to recognize our deepest feelings, we begin to give up, of necessity, being satisfied with suffering and self-negation, and with the numbness which so often seems like their only alternative in our society" (58). In this way, eros enables people to fight back and to "pursue genuine change within our world" (59). For Lorde, this is the most important use of the erotic.

Other feminists who write about eros would agree. Many of their arguments follow the same general outlines as Lorde's, understanding eros in similarly broad ways and making similar claims about its ability to impart knowledge and power. While space does not permit a full account of these arguments, a brief look at Carter Heyward and Haunani-Kay Trask's extensive work on eros can complete this discussion. Where Lorde argues that eros provides knowledge about values, both Trask and Heyward tend to see eros as almost an ethic in itself, a specific set of values about the right way to live. Trask speaks of what she calls the feminist eros, "a deep sense for a qualitatively better mode of being and living" drawn from the experience of relational caretaking (1988, 61). Summarizing the content of this vision of how to live better, she says the feminist eros "unleashes a desire—for creative expression, especially in the areas of sexuality and work; for balance among needs, particularly those of autonomy and nurturance; for sharing and interdependence without bondage" (94). For Heyward, a feminist theologian, eros is divine, the movement of God in the world. She believes that

God can be found wherever there is a commitment to justice and "right relation"; hence, "the erotic is the divine spirit's yearning, through our bodyselves, toward mutually empowering relation" (1989, 99).

Moving from the issue of the knowledge or ethical wisdom gained from eros to that of the power it provides, one can find in Trask and Heyward explicit formulations of what is only implicit in Lorde: that erotic power is a nonviolent, nonoppressive kind of power. The title of Trask's book, *Eros and Power: The Promise of Feminist Theory*, conveys her argument that the project of feminist theory has been to bring together love and power, which have largely been seen as separate in the Western tradition. According to Trask, "In the feminist vision, Eros is both love *and* power"—and power is "the courage of self-assertion, the struggle for an alternative, and the strength to live one's passion" (1988, 93, 152). Heyward contrasts eros with "sadomasochism," by which she does not mean only or even especially sexual sadomasochism, but rather the impulse toward and acceptance of "power-over" and "power-under" in all kinds of circumstances (1989, 105). She turns to eros precisely because she believes it offers an alternative model of "being-in-relation" that is *mutually* empowering.

The general feminist argument about eros is thus clearly an argument that connects ethics and politics, for it attempts to identify the source of an ethical form of power, that is, a form of power that can liberate those who have been oppressed without oppressing others in turn. It is also clearly an argument that hopes to investigate the personal sources of ethical-political agency; indeed, this is its primary purpose. In both of these ways, this argument differs from traditional masculinist theories. The argument also differs sharply from masculinist arguments in one more way: in attempting to advance both ethics and politics, these theories turn primarily to eros rather than to reason.[3]

Abuses of the Erotic, or, Where This Argument Falls Short

I believe there is significant promise in the feminist literature on eros and power. To begin with, it articulates and calls attention to a human quality that is often overlooked, even by other feminists, whose discussions of desire tend to focus more on sexual desire. Moreover, it takes on the valuable project of reconceiving both eros and power, and persuasively links passion and desire to personal/political action. In so doing, it addresses the need to account for agency and the personal transformation necessary for social change that I argued for in the beginning of this essay. Yet the feminist literature on eros is also plagued by important problems. The primary problem, in my view, has to do with the assumption that access to the erotic will necessarily lead to ethical choices. Recall Lorde's argument that we should respect "the yes within ourselves, our deepest cravings" and embrace "those physical, emotional, and psychic expressions of what is deepest and strongest and richest within each of us." The question is: What happens if we desire something that isn't good for us, or for others? What if our deepest cravings are for murder? What if hate, or envy, or shame is what's "strongest" within each of us? In these cases, one might doubt that it would be best to embrace the erotic, or at least to use it as a guide for action. But surprisingly, these kinds of possibilities are not raised much in the feminist literature on eros. The prevailing assumption is that our deepest feelings, passions, and desires are for the best.

Part of the problem here might quickly be identified as stemming from essentialist assumptions about human (or women's) nature. This point is perhaps best illustrated by the fact that many of the authors do make an argument that eros tends to get "distorted" or "perverted" in patriarchal society. In this way, they mean to explain such things as sexual violence and the abuse of treating people as objects.[4] But what the language of distortion and perversion in fact reveals is presumption that there is an original, pure, good eros—which is in turn an expression of an original, pure, good self. In other words, deep down, we care about the right things, because deep down, we are good-natured people. Since the difficulties of conclusively proving anything about "human nature" are notorious, this is a profoundly problematic assumption. The argument would stand on stronger ground if it allowed for the widest range of human possibility, assuming instead that our passions and desires, whether inherent, or socially constructed, or some complex combination of the two, may be either beneficial or destructive to the greater well-being of both ourselves and others.

From this perspective, however, it becomes clear that there is another problem with the feminist literature on eros and power. For if even our deepest passions and desires may be either beneficial or destructive, then we need to learn how to deal with either possibility. We need to learn how to interpret our emotions, how to make judgments about which passions and desires to act on and which to attempt to transform, and how to transform those desires we would like to change. But how are such things done? How do people learn to do them? Lorde, Trask, and Heyward offer little discussion of these issues. They describe some desires as "distorted," but by and large they seem to imply that, once identified as such, the need to change such desires will be self-evident and the ability forthcoming. Lorde, for example, speaks briefly of "the fear that we cannot grow beyond whatever distortions we may find within ourselves" (58). She acknowledges this fear, but considers it unnecessary, for she believes that "once recognized, those [desires] which do not enhance our future lose their power and can be altered" (57). Yet she does not clarify how we are to recognize a "distorted" desire when we see one, let alone how simple recognition can lead to emotional growth.

My argument is that we need theories of the psyche in order to address all of these questions. Of course a theory of the psyche is not in itself sufficient to answer the first question of what constitutes (in Lorde's terms) a distorted desire, or (as I would put it) the question of how our various passions and desires may affect our greater well-being and that of others. That is an ethical question and requires an ethical theory for a response. But surely one part of addressing this question involves analyzing the beneficial or destructive impact of our passions on our own mental health, and to do this one also needs a theory of the psyche. Moreover, to analyze what needs to be done to change destructive passions and desires, and to propose a method (or methods) for achieving such transformations, requires a theory of the psyche as well. Recall that I defined a theory of the psyche as a theory of the possible organizations and operations of mental processes and activities, and the ways in which such organizations may affect human being and action in the world. As an argument about the human capacity for passion and desire, and the role that this capacity might play in inspiring action, the feminist argument about eros does provide a partial theory of the psyche. But the argument includes little exploration of what eros looks like from the "inside": how it relates to other capacities we have, in particular the capacities to reason and to will, and what it means to "work with" passion and desire. As a consequence, the picture it gives of eros is, ironically, rather static. What is offered is a vision of an ideal (eros), rather than a realistic vision of how passion and desire can *move* us in different possible ways. In other words, without a theory of the psyche, the feminist writing on eros is unable to provide an effective account of personal transformation and the sources of ethical-political agency.

Eros and the Chariot:
A Classical Political Theory of the Psyche

At this point, a counter-example may be helpful. What does an argument about eros look like when it does *not* lack a theory of the psyche? I want to suggest that Plato's dialogues on eros can provide a valuable illustration in this area.[5] I hasten to add that this is not to suggest that feminists should adopt Plato's specific arguments about eros or the psyche, let alone his larger political and metaphysical perspectives. Despite the radically unconventional argument for women's "equality" in Book V of the *Republic*, from any number of feminist perspectives there are problems with Platonic thought. I do suggest, however, that feminist theorists might usefully turn to Plato's dialogues for an example of how a theory of the psyche can contribute to thinking about ethics and politics.

Even from his starkly different historical and cultural context, Plato has some concerns that are remarkably similar to those of contemporary feminists. Disputing Sophist attempts to detach politics from ethics, many of his dialogues assert the integral unity of the two. Plato also explicitly links personal and political transformation, and in thinking about how personal transformation occurs, he too turns to eros. That he does so is not immediately evident in the *Republic*, for here it often seems that desire is blamed for most of what can go wrong in human life. But while it is true that the *Republic* presents *epithymia* (perhaps best translated as "appetite") as for the most part a destructive force, in Plato's thought *epithymia* is ultimately distinguished from eros, which is defined in the *Symposium* and the *Phaedrus* as the desire for the good. That eros plays a pivotal role in the attainment of the good life is developed more fully in these dialogues, where it becomes clear that the desire for the good in a sense brings the divine in reach of humanity. As the character Diotima explains, the demon Eros "is the mediator who spans the chasm which divides [the gods and men], and therefore by him the universe is bound together" (202e). Thus, Plato too sees eros as a form of power; one might even say that he too argues for the "uses of the erotic" in guiding and inspiring people to act well, to achieve their highest potential, to reach "across the chasm" to the gods.

Unlike the contemporary feminist argument about eros and power, however, Plato's argument is supported by a complex picture of the psyche (usually translated as "soul"). The model of the psyche set out in the *Republic*, with its tripartite division between reason, spirit, and appetite, is perhaps best known, although often oversimplified. The complexity of the model emerges in later books of the *Republic*, where it becomes apparent that each part of the psyche in fact has its own desire. This more detailed model is further elaborated in the *Symposium* and, especially, the *Phaedrus*. In the *Phaedrus*, the psyche is described using the image of a chariot. The human "chariot" is comprised of a charioteer and two winged horses, one noble and obedient, the other ignoble and insolent, whose mismatch explains why the chariot is so difficult to manage (246b). Using this image, the dialogue provides an extended narrative of the struggle that ensues within the psyche upon beholding a beautiful person. It is a struggle, for the most part, to rein in the brutish horse, who would like to "leap" on the beloved, although it is also a struggle to prevent the charioteer from fearfully pulling back entirely (254a–e). Again, a common, oversimplified interpretation of this image is that the three members of the team correspond to the same parts of the psyche identified in the *Republic,* and that the ideal outcome of the struggle is thus for reason (the charioteer) to control desire (the brutish horse). Yet careful readings show that the interactions between the members of the chariot team are actually far more complicated; for example, in the struggle, "it is the bad horse who adopts persuasive language and the methods of reason, while the charioteer maintains control by sheer strength and wordless violence" (Ferrari 1987, 186). This apparent reversal suggests that the purpose of the metaphor is less to illustrate a simple distinction between (and proper ordering of) reason and desire than to illustrate a complicated distinction between (and proper ordering of) those forms of reason and desire that aim for the overall good of the person (the charioteer) and those forms of reason and desire that aim for partial and potentially detrimental satisfactions (the brutish horse).

As should be apparent from even this brief discussion, Plato's images of the psyche allow him to illustrate how he believes various capacities and tendencies within a person may interact with each other in different possible ways, some "better" than others. As a consequence, his argument on behalf of the power of eros is not vulnerable to the criticism that he has simply assumed that eros will lead people to make ethical choices. On the contrary, grounded in a fully developed theory of the psyche, the theory not only acknowledges the possibility of destructive desires but provides an analysis of what transforming such desires might require. Plato's dialogues delineate difficult processes of intellectual, emotional, and physical growth that can result in the *achievement* of cultivating not only good desires but good thoughts and good actions, that is, the "best" parts of ourselves. Moreover, because of this attention to processes of growth, Plato's picture of eros is not static; rather, his dialogues help illustrate how eros can work to *move* people toward "the good." In these ways, Plato's theory of the psyche contributes to his thinking about ethics and politics.

Conclusion

Let me repeat once more that I do not think feminists ought to take up Plato's image of the chariot for our own use. In important respects already noted, it is not a helpful vision for us. But my point is that we need our own images of the psyche, in order to make our own arguments about personal and political transformation. Now, one might still ask: Why advocate images or metaphors as part of a theory of the psyche? Aren't metaphors by definition fictions of language, fictions that moreover carry the risk of essentializing and/or universalizing a particular theory of the psyche? I think metaphors do indeed pose these dangers. But I do not believe we can avoid using them when attempting to represent intangible things. Because the psyche is not something that can be characterized in literal terms, thinking about its structure and processes requires an image (or images) of some kind. Moreover, such images are especially necessary for theories of the psyche to help people think on an everyday level about how to change their thoughts, wishes, and behaviors. That is to say, a picture of what it means to work with desire requires some kind of "picture" of the psyche. Models of the psyche—and perhaps even the "psyche" itself—may well be fictions, then, but perhaps they can be useful fictions. For this reason, I argue we should embrace them self-consciously as constructions, using care in our choice of metaphors.

My purpose has been to argue that feminist thinking about ethics and politics would benefit from theories of the psyche. The plural in this formulation is important: there is no need to argue that only one theory of the psyche can be "correct," and much reason to believe that more than one model may be helpful. Theorists may wish to emphasize different capacities and qualities, or suggest different possible interactions between these capacities. Nevertheless, it seems clear that attention to such primary human faculties as perception, cognition, emotion, and will would be important in any feminist vision of the psyche. I think it is particularly important for feminist models of the psyche to address both reason and emotion; indeed the real key, I would argue, is to figure out how these two qualities can work together, and may even be interwoven in more complex ways than we have so far been able to imagine. In this sense, the task is to put together the traditional masculinist focus on reason with the contemporary feminist focus on eros (or care) as a foundation for ethics and politics.

Notes

1. With some reservations, I have chosen to use the term "psyche" instead of "soul" to describe what I think needs to be theorized. "Soul" is a powerful, resonant word, and for me it conveys a sense of that somewhat mysterious entity, the mind/"moving spirit" of a person, better than psyche does. Nevertheless, I am persuaded that the language of souls has many disadvantages, chief among them its spiritual, metaphysical, and idealist overtones. Since I have no wish to conjure an image of some immaterial and essentialist entity independent of institutions, practices, and even bodies, I have opted not to use this language. I thank Ann Ferguson for encouraging me to think more carefully about terminology.

2. I use the more cumbersome term "theory of the psyche" rather than "psychology" in order to emphasize that I am not calling for a "*science* of the nature, functioning, and development of the human mind (formerly, of the soul), including the faculties of reason, emotion, perception, communication, etc." (as "psychology" is defined in the *New Shorter Oxford English Dictionary*).

3. It is important to note that most of these authors claim to advocate an integration of reason and eros. But although they argue against the common understanding of eros as "irrational," most do not actually provide any models of the relationship of reason and desire, and many appear to hold that eros is more important than reason in guiding our actions. Consider Lorde's message when she writes in "Poetry is Not a Luxury" that "The white fathers told us: I think, therefore I am. The Black mother within each of us—the poet—whispers in our dreams: I feel, therefore I can be free" (1984, 37). A significant exception to this general rule may be found in the work of Jaggar and Schott.

4. Lorde argues that "looking away" from our experience of the erotic gives rise to "that distortion which results in pornography and obscenity—the abuse of feeling" (59). Heyward claims that "rape is an act of violence, indeed of sexual perversion, as are all acts of violence." She goes on to define perverted as "turned completely around from itself" (1984, 131).

5. Turning to a canonical masculinist thinker for the primary positive example in a feminist essay is clearly an ironic and potentially problematic move. But the development of feminist theory is best served, I strongly believe, when we take advantage of all the resources available to us and thereby avoid having to reinvent wheels. On the specific topic of eros, I would argue that Plato's dialogues provide a model that is both helpful and hard to find elsewhere.

References

Brock, Rita Nakashima. 1991. *Journeys by Heart: A Christology of Erotic Power*. New York: Crossroad Publishing Co.

Canto, Monique. 1986. "The Politics of Women's Bodies: Reflections on Plato." In *The Female Body in Western Culture: Contemporary Perspectives*, ed. Susan Rubin Suleiman. Cambridge: Harvard University Press.

Dimen, Muriel. 1989. "Power, Sexuality, and Intimacy." In *Gender/Body/Knowledge: Feminist Reconstructions of Being and Knowing*, ed. Alison Jaggar and Susan Bordo. New Brunswick: Rutgers University Press.

Ferguson, Kathy. 1993. *The Man Question: Visions of Subjectivity in Feminist Theory*. Berkeley: University of California Press.

Ferrari, Giovanni R. 1987. *Listening to the Cicadas: A Study of Plato's "Phaedrus."* Cambridge: Cambridge University Press.

Fox Keller, Evelyn. 1985. "Love and Sex in Plato's Epistemology." In *Reflections on Gender and Science*. New Haven: Yale University Press.

Ginzberg, Ruth. 1992. "Audre Lorde's (Nonessentialist) Lesbian Eros." *Hypatia* 7(4)(Fall 1992): 73–90.

Goodison, Lucy. 1983. "Really Being in Love Means Wanting to Live in a Different World." In *Sex and Love: New Thoughts on Old Contradictions*, eds. Sue Cartledge and Joanna Ryan. London: The Women's Press.

Hartsock, Nancy C. M. 1983. *Money, Sex, and Power: Toward a Feminist Historical Materialism*. New York and London: Longman Press.

Heyward, Carter. 1984. *Our Passion for Justice: Images of Power, Sexuality, and Liberation*. New York: Pilgrim Press.

———. 1989. *Touching Our Strength: The Erotic as Power and the Love of God*. San Francisco: Harper and Row.

Hyland, Drew A. 1968. "Eros, *Epithymia*, and *Philia* in Plato." *Phronesis: A Journal for Ancient Philosophy* 13: 32–46.

Jaggar, Alison. 1989. "Love and Knowledge: Emotion in Feminist Epistemology." In *Gender/Body/Knowledge*, ed. Jaggar and Bordo. New Brunswick: Rutgers University Press.

Lorde, Audre. 1984. *Sister Outsider*. Trumansburg, New York: The Crossing Press.

Nussbaum, Martha C. 1986. *The Fragility of Goodness: Luck and Ethics in Greek Tragedy and Philosophy*. Cambridge: Cambridge University Press.

Okin, Susan Moller. 1979. *Women in Western Political Thought*. Princeton: Princeton University Press.

O'Neill, Eileen. 1989. "(Re)presentations of Eros: Exploring Female Sexual Agency." In *Gender/Body/Knowledge*, ed. Jaggar and Bordo. New Brunswick: Rutgers University Press.

Plato. 1953. *Symposium*. In *The Dialogues of Plato*. Vol. 1, 4th Ed. Trans. Benjamin Jowett, ed. D. J. Allan and H. E. Dale. Oxford: Clarendon Press.

———. 1953. *Phaedrus*. In *The Dialogues of Plato*. Vol. 3, 4th Ed. Trans. Benjamin Jowett, ed. D. J. Allan and H. E. Dale. Oxford: Clarendon Press.

———. 1992. *Republic*. Trans. G. M. A. Grube, revised by C. D. C. Reeve. Indianapolis: Hackett Press.

Rorty, Amelie Oksenberg, ed. 1980. *Explaining Emotions*. Berkeley: University of California Press.

Saxonhouse, Arlene. 1976. "The Philosopher and the Female in the Political Thought of Plato." *Political Theory* 4(2): 195–212.

———. 1984. "Eros and the Female in Greek Political Thought: An Interpretation of Plato's *Symposium*." *Political Theory* 12(1): 5–27.

Schott, Robin May. 1988. *Cognition and Eros: A Critique of the Kantian Paradigm*. Boston: Beacon Press.

Solomon, Robert. 1993. *The Passions: Emotions and the Meaning of Life*. Indianapolis: Hackett Press.

Spelman, Elizabeth V. 1988. *Inessential Woman: Problems of Exclusion in Feminist Thought*. Boston: Beacon Press.

Trask, Haunani-Kay. 1988. *Eros and Power: The Promise of Feminist Theory*. Philadelphia: University of Pennsylvania Press.

2

Skin Deep

Femininity as a Disciplinary Regime

Sandra Lee Bartky

The Questions

The editors of this anthology have put a number of questions to its contributors. In what follows, I shall consider two of these questions in particular: First, what is the relation between ethics, politics, and the body? And second, how does the body relate to an ethico-political psychology? I shall approach these and related questions not in the mode of abstract theorizing but through a fleshed-out example of the production of the personal, of what Merleau-Ponty would have called "the body-self" in the midst of the political. This production, as I hope to show, is at once a crucial aspect of public life as we know it and, at the same time, of personal life, i.e., of individual psychology. The body to which I refer throughout is the ideal feminine body of advanced industrial society.

But first, some preliminary observations: the split between public and private spheres is, as we know, quite recent, one of the many consequences of industrialization, urbanization and the rise of capitalism. Kant, as an early theorist of this period, appears to have believed that a purely private morality was possible, though perhaps more difficult to achieve, regardless of the character of the public sphere from which the moral subject is to emerge. I prefer to follow the Greeks, who believed in the inextricability of ethics and politics. While the two are analytically distinct, they intermingle and intermesh in daily life as we live it. In a society that is corrupt, people will learn all the wrong things, argued Aristotle; they will achieve neither virtue nor happiness. Here is the feminist expression of this insight: no personal solutions! The feminist notion of "the political" encompasses more than what is ordinarily understood by this term. The "political" includes "the social" and "the cultural." Part of what, from the first, has been meant by the Second Wave slogan "the personal is political" is that social and cultural meanings, practices, and institutions are sites wherein power is exercised and subjectivities are engendered. So what is involved in the production of a "properly" feminine subject?

Suffering to Be Beautiful

My topic is not the female, but the feminine body and the feminist critique of the cultural norms that teach us what it is to achieve and to maintain such a body. *The Oxford English Dictionary* defines "femininity" as "the quality or assemblage of qualities pertaining to the female sex" (OED, 982). Yet, one can be a member of the female sex and fail or refuse to be feminine; conversely, one may be a biological male and a drag queen. "One is not born a woman, but, rather becomes one," said Simone de Beauvoir (de Beauvoir, 1973, 301) having in mind the "properly" feminine woman. Femininity is a set of qualities of character and behavioral dispositions as well as a compelling aesthetic of embodiment. It is "a mode of enacting and re-enacting received gender norms which surface as so many styles of the flesh" (Butler, 1985, 11).

There is a question, first of all, of what it is to inhabit a feminine body, in particular a body that exhibits the "styles of the flesh" that now hold sway. Phenomenological philosophy has tried to rehabilitate embodied experience in spite of its almost total neglect in the work of its founder, Edmund Husserl. However, to the degree that phenomenologies of embodiment have taken male embodiment covertly as emblematic of embodiment per se, they have merely recapitulated the male bias that marks the Western philosophical tradition as a whole. This can be remedied by setting aside "normal" phenomenology, i.e., the search for the a priori, necessary structures of any embodied consciousness whatsoever, in favor of an analysis of the structures of meaning embedded in the experience of a historically, culturally, and sexually specific subject. A phenomenology so altered can also be described as a contribution to an "ethico-political feminist psychology."

Iris Young's classic "Throwing Like a Girl: A Phenomenology of Feminine Body Comportment, Motility and Spatiality" finds that a space seems to surround women in imagination: this manifests itself both in a reluctance to reach, stretch, and extend the body to meet resistances of matter in motion—as in sports or in the performance of certain physical tasks—and in a typically constricted posture and general style of movement. A woman's space is not a field in which her bodily intentionality can be freely realized but an enclosure in which she feels herself positioned and by which she is confined (Young, 1990). Rereading this earlier work, Young has herself found that this piece takes as paradigmatic white, middle-class experience. Still, the piece has value because not only does it indeed describe the spatiality and comportment of many women but it also lays out some of the norms of properly feminine motility that, unsurprisingly, reflect values of the dominant social groups, whether they elicit conformity or not. Early women's movement pieces that circulated as pamphlets in the early seventies (e.g., Meredith Tax, "Woman and Her Mind"; Dana Densmore, "On the Temptation to Be a Beautiful Object"), gave rise to other phenomenologically oriented studies of sexual objectification and sexual self-objectification (Bartky, 1990).

The properly feminine body exhibits a specific repertoire of gesture, posture, and movement. This body must learn to display its charms, but discreetly. The properly feminine woman must never allow herself to sprawl into the available space. She must avoid the looseness in body comportment that is the mark of the "loose" woman. At least in the West, a woman must learn to be guided physically by a man in a way that normally goes unnoticed. Males in couples may literally steer a woman everywhere she goes: down the street, into elevators, through doorways, around the dance floor. The man's movement "is not necessarily heavy and pushy or physical in an ugly way; it is light and gentle but firm in the way of the most confident equestrians with the best trained horses" (Henley, 1977, 149). In regard to its size and its various parts, the properly feminine body must remain within the appropriate parameters and it must display itself, again within the proper parameters, as an ornamented surface.

I shall argue in what follows that the imposition of normative femininity upon the female body requires training, that the modes of training are cultural phenomena properly described as "disciplinary practices," and that the discipline they represent is disempowering to the woman so disciplined. I follow Michel Foucault in defining discipline as a "system of micropower that is essentially non-egalitarian and asymmetrical" (Foucault, 1979, 222). Disciplines of the body in general fragment and partition the body's time, its space, and its movements; in this case, they drill the recruit to the disciplinary regime of femininity in the proper techniques necessary to maintain the current norms of feminine embodiment. Later, I shall examine as well the profound ambiguity that femininity has for women: its seductiveness as well as the pain it causes and its hold on our very identities.

Consider, for example, dieting as a disciplinary practice of femininity. The current body of fashion is taut, small-breasted, and narrow-hipped; its slimness borders on emaciation; it is a silhouette that seems more like that of an adolescent boy or a newly pubescent girl than a mature woman. It seems that the more women appear in what was formerly masculine public space, the less space our bodies are to occupy. Since most women do not look like adolescent boys, they must diet. National studies have shown that the majority of American women are on a diet *all the time*. Girls as young as nine and ten are now beginning to diet (as many as 40 percent, according to the National Heart, Lung and Blood Institute, cited in *USA Today* [August 12, 1996].Virtually every major women's magazine has a dieting or exercise regimen (or both) in every issue.Women greatly outnumber men in groups such as Weight Watchers and Overeaters Anonymous—in the case of the latter, by well over 90 percent (Millman, 1980). Fat can now be eliminated surgically, by liposuction; women, not surprisingly, avail themselves of liposuction in far greater numbers than men. Women typically perceive their bodies as too large, but sometimes, as in the case of breasts, as not large enough, hence the frequency of surgical breast augmentation, since become a national scandal.

Dieting disciplines the body's hungers: appetite must be monitored at all times and governed by an iron will. Since the innocent need of the organism for food will not be foregone, one's body becomes the enemy, an alien being bent on thwarting the disciplinary project. Anorexia nervosa and bulimia, now approaching epidemic proportions, are to the women of today what hysteria was to women in the nineteenth century: the crystallization in a pathological mode of a widespread cultural obsession (Bordo, 1993).Women who fall into the dreaded category of the "overweight" are often seen as morally deficient individuals who lack self-discipline and suffer from weakness of will. What is regarded as the inability to control one's appetite for food has taken on the moral stigma formerly reserved for those who could not control their appetite for sex: the "overeater" as libertine, unable to resist the "sinfully delicious" (Bordo, 1993). Columnists for upscale magazines like *Vogue* find, not only in the "overweight" but in all those who refuse the disciplinary program, no moral deficit, rather a mild psychological disturbance.Women who refuse to shave their legs or to get regular manicures are exhibiting a deficiency of self-esteem, which accounts for their refusal to care properly for their bodies.

Here is a second example, the disciplinary practices that have to do with skin care. A woman's skin must be soft, supple, hairless, and smooth; ideally, it should betray no sign of wear, experience, age, or deep thought. Hair must be removed not only from the face—with tweezers, hot wax, foul-smelling depilatories, or, for a more permanent result, by painful and expensive electrolysis—but from large surfaces of the body as well, from legs and now, with the new high-leg bathing suits and leotards, from much of the pubic area. The development of what one "beauty expert" calls "good skin-care habits" requires not only attention to health, the avoidance of strong facial expressions, and the performance of facial exercises, but the regular use of skin-care preparations, many to be applied oftener than once a day: cleansing lotions (ordinary soap and water "upsets the skin's acid and alkaline balance"), wash-off cleansers (milder than cleansing lotions), astringents, toners, makeup removers, night creams, day creams, nourishing creams, eye creams, moisturizers, skin balancers, body lotions, hand creams, lip pomades, suntan lotions, sun screens, facial masks. Black women may wish to use "fade creams" to "even skin tone." Skin-care preparations are applied to the skin according to precise rules: eye cream is dabbed on gently in movements toward, never away from the nose; cleansing cream is applied in outward directions only, straight across the forehead, the upper lip, and the chin, never up but straight down the nose and up and out on the cheeks. If this regimen, dermabrasion, and chemical peeling fail to disguise the effects of aging, as sooner or later they must, there is always the scalpel, i.e., the face lift.

The ordinary circumstances of life as well as a wide variety of activities cause a crisis in skin care and require a stepping up of the regimen as well as an additional laying on of preparations. Skin-care discipline requires a specialized knowledge: a woman must know what to apply if she has been skiing, taking medication, doing vigorous exercise, boating, swimming in chlorinated pools; if she has been exposed to pollution, heated rooms, cold, sun, harsh weather, the pressurized cabins on airplanes, saunas or steam rooms, fatigue or stress. Like a schoolchild or prisoner, the woman mastering good skin-care habits is put on a timetable: Georgette Klinger requires that a shorter or longer period of attention be paid to the complexion *at least four times a day* (Klinger and Rowes, 1978).

I offer dieting and skin care merely as examples of the disciplinary practices of femininity; the whole story would take too long to tell, and so I pass over in silence such things as manicure, pedicure, hair care, and exercise. The language of "beauty experts" recognizes quite explicitly the disciplinary character of their project ("There are no ugly women," said Helena Rubinstein, "only lazy ones"). Now the imposition of discipline is not always disempowering. One thinks, for example, of the discipline involved in mastering Zen meditation. Arguably, the discipline I had imposed upon me and that I imposed upon myself in graduate school was empowering:

my degree allowed me (entering the academic job market at a propitious time) to find challenging and, in time, secure employment at a decent wage (indeed, at a wage far above what most women in the workforce earn). But I will argue that, on balance, the disciplinary practices that produce normative embodied femininity are indeed disempowering to women.

Item: The disciplines of femininity are an enormous drain on women's time and women's money. I assume that women could put their time to better use (vocational training, perhaps, or political agitation). In a world so marked by misery and hunger, the billions spent on cosmetics could be put to better use as well.

Item: Women submit to this discipline in large measure because we have been persuaded that our bodies are defective. A variety of cultural discourses and practices have brought it about that we inhabit what I have called elsewhere an "inferiorized" body (Bartky, 1990). "Inferiorization" has both objective and subjective moments. The objective moment has complex determinants, but represents, at the most obvious level, the happy marriage of patriarchy to profit. A "fashion-beauty complex," as much an articulation of patriarchal capitalism as the "military-industrial complex," presides over the forms in which the sexual objectification and self-objectification of women will manifest themselves. Overtly, the fashion-beauty complex glorifies the female body; more important is its covert aim, which is to depreciate this body. A host of discourses and social practices construct the female body as a flawed body that needs to be made over, hence the popularity in magazines and TV of the "makeover." The media images of perfect female beauty that bombard us daily leave no doubt in the minds of most women that we fail to measure up; we submit to these disciplines against the background of a pervasive sense of bodily deficiency, perhaps even of shame. It is, I venture, the very pervasiveness of this sense of bodily deficiency—like the pervasiveness of a sense of sin—that accounts for women's widespread obsession with the body and the often ritualistic character of our daily compliance. ("I can't go out without putting on my face.")

Item: The disciplines of femininity feed racism and class oppression. The beauty ideal toward which beauty discipline is directed is still largely white and northern European in character; ideal beauty is normally the beauty of the women of those social groups in the "developed" world that have social, economic, and cultural primacy. Hence the popularity of hair-straighteners and "fade-creams" among African-American women, eye-slant removing operations for Asian women, and "nose-jobs," now a virtual rite of passage for many adolescent Jewish girls. The market for blue contact lenses is growing in Bangkok, Nairobi, and Mexico City. Many poor women lack the time and resources to provide themselves with even the minimum of what such a regimen requires, e.g., a decent diet or membership in a health club. Here is an additional source of shame for poor women, who must bear what our society regards as the more general shame of poverty.

Item: Alienation. I am defective not just for others but for myself: I inhabit this body, yet I live at a distance from it as its judge, its monitor, its commandant. I speak of fragmentation: a typically male connoisseur, formed complexly by a host of discourses resides within the consciousness of most women. We stand perpetually before his gaze, subject to his evaluation. There is some truth to the claim that "women dress for other women." Who but someone engaged in a project similar to my own can appreciate the panache with which I bring it off? Insofar as women live within the constraints of compulsory heterosexuality, they know for whom this game is played: they know that a pretty young woman is likelier than a plain one to become a flight attendant or to get the requisite amount of attention in the singles' bar. This interiorized witness that is, after all, *myself*, has put me under surveillance. It is disempowering to be perpetually under surveillance, as even the British royal family has discovered.

Item: The witnesses for whom the feminine body is constructed as spectacle are external as well as internal: we are under surveillance from without as well as from within. Hence, competition among the judged for the judges' approbation; hence the beauty contest, the street hassling, hence the male students on my campus who lounge on benches in the spring and call out to passing women, with appropriate catcalls and sounds meant to suggest kissing: "Hey, baby, you're a nine," or, very loudly, "Hey, get a load of this one, not even a two." The sense of entitlement that allows these young men to set themselves up—successfully, to judge by the embarassment of women who must run this gauntlet—is simply a local expression of the male entitlement they enjoy generally. It is our superiors who judge us; indeed, the power to judge is part of what it is to occupy a superior position in the first place.

Item: Consider now what meanings are inscribed in the ideally feminine body. Women's typical restraint in posture and movement is understood to be a language of subordination when it is enacted by men in male status hierarchies (Henley, 1977). The current ideal body type lacks flesh and substance; it takes up little space. Is this perhaps a response to anxiety generated by the increasing visibility of women in public space? (Consider the volume and mean-spiritedness of the invective heaped upon Hillary Rodham Clinton.) This is also a body in whose very contours the image of immaturity has been inscribed. The requirement of a smooth and hairless skin underscores the theme of inexperience, feeding the suspicion that this infantilized body mirrors what one might call, with only a little exaggeration, the effort at a continuing social infantilization of women.

Item: The disciplinary project of femininity is a set-up: it requires such radical and extensive measures of bodily transformation that virtually every woman who gives herself to it is destined to fail. Diets are notorious failures: normal aging processes cannot be disguised forever; the face-lift, painful and expensive, must be regularly repeated. Since every woman is under a virtual obligation "to make the most of what she has," failure may become still another occasion for shame.

Item: Think finally of the situation of those women who, through luck as well as assiduous attention to proper discipline, have become famous beauties. To succeed in the provision of a beautiful or sexy body gains a woman attention, admiration, even money, but little real respect and rarely any social power. Further, this envied status must contend with an entire cultural tradition that has traditionally elevated mind over body, spirit over flesh, hence masculinity over femininity. Even women admired most for their bodies complain routinely of their situation in ways that reveal an implicit understanding that there is something demeaning in the kind of attention they receive. Marilyn Monroe and Elizabeth Taylor wanted passionately to become accomplished actresses, that is to say, *artists* and not just "sex objects."

I do not believe that the critique I have offered concerns matters that are trivial, though this is how it will appear to many; certainly, there are matters more pressing than the question of whether or not we should choose to follow Georgette Klinger's regimen for baby-soft skin. At stake here is what Judith Butler has called the "performance" of gender, indeed the performance which *is* gender and the skills and techniques that are required by a successful performance (Butler, 1990, 1994). While femininity exceeds the norms of embodiment, the idea of the feminine comes more and more to be identified with women's sexuality and appearance, and less, as in the past, with women's maternity. As some of us come more and more to escape the domination of fathers, husbands, and clergymen, the norms of ideal feminine appearance and the disciplines we impose on ourselves come to represent submission to new forms of domination. Furthermore, the requirement that we "look like women" is perhaps the most visible way in which we are marked by gender. This compulsive and compulsory marking serves the identificatory purposes of a system of caste privilege. Using the term "sex" where we would now use "gender," Marilyn Frye expresses this nicely: "Constant sex-identification both defines and maintains the caste boundary without which there could not be a dominance-subordination structure" (Frye, 1983). But our story is only halfway told.

Siren Songs of the Feminine

An obvious question now presents itself: If the culture of beauty is as oppressive as my analysis would suggest, why is it that so many women appear to have capitulated to it? Indeed why do so many women appear to embrace it with enthusiasm? The production of femininity is more perplexing and multivalent than the analysis so far has shown. The ethico-political psychology of feminine embodiment in the venues I have been examining is tangled and ambivalent. But what is it then that holds us so tightly in the grip of a set of oppressive cultural norms?

First, the obvious: it is hard to get and then to keep a job, even a poorly paying job, unless one presents oneself as a woman who has submitted, to some degree, to the disciplinary practices of femininity. Some firms, e.g., law firms and brokerage firms, enforce a very rigid dress and appearance code; here is discipline if ever there was discipline. Not only jobs are on the line; unless she belongs to a radical political subculture (and these have mostly vanished) a woman who has (arguably) the misfortune to be heterosexual will find it difficult to signal her availability and interest except through a conventionally feminine self-presentation. The stakes here are high; unless a woman can sell herself successfully in the heterosexual meat market, she risks the loss of male sexual attention, sexual release, and emotional intimacy that, for better or worse, she is seeking. While feminist theory might prefer to ignore them, these needs in heterosexual women can be *imperious*.

Think now of the pleasures of normative femininity. Once again, we draw upon the resources of an ethico-political feminist psychology. The disciplines have multiple meanings, both social and personal. So, for example, while high-heeled shoes are, to my mind, the modern equivalent of footbinding, the occasion of getting one's first pair is an important rite of passage into adulthood. Memories (often poignant), longing, and the pleasures of female bonding cling to the disciplines. Many body rituals and the camaraderie that surrounds them are important occasions for feeling solidarity with other women. Unless new forms of female solidarity appear, women will be loathe to abandon the forms they know.

Femininity is also importantly an aesthetic; men and women alike cling to what they take to be beautiful, especially in the absence of an alternative. What alternative aesthetic of the body do feminists propose to put in place of the one that now holds sway? This is one reason (there are others) why the image of the feminist for so many comes to be associated with that of the "bull dyke." If feminists, enemies of glamour, do not want to be women, i.e., to look and act like proper women, then it follows that they must want to look and act like men.

What pleasure there is in drawing upon oneself the gaze of admiration or desire! The power of allure changes the odds in the battle of the sexes, albeit temporarily. This may well be the most power a woman will ever exert, at least in her dealings with other adults; no wonder that this moment, the moment in which she attracts or fascinates, is repeated over and over again in the romance novel. In catching the reflection of myself in the admiring glance of the other, I fuse my gaze with his and enjoy myself as he enjoys me. But there are more straightforward narcissistic pleasures at work in the production of femininity, pleasures of a sort that is not permitted men. Constant attention to the body—brushing the hair, anointing oneself with creams and lotions, soaking in a tub of Vitabath—these are surely occasions of auto-eroticism. Like all narcissists, we are fascinated by our image; hence the scopophilia that makes it impossible to pass a mirror without looking (however, the sight of our facial skin in the harsh light above the dental chair may produce scopophobia!) The fashion-beauty complex does the impossible: it addresses our narcissistic needs and at the same time covertly assaults our narcissism, creating a sense of lack that only its products can fill. The pleasures of self-love are balanced by the pain of self-hatred. The pleasures of femininity, like the pleasures of smoking, are purchased at too high a price. The trick here may be to figure out how to get the pleasure without paying the price.

I come lastly to what it is that ties us perhaps most securely to this system: our identities. The norms of feminine body discipline are not imposed upon fully formed subjects; they are importantly implicated in the very construction of our subjectivities. Hence, while femininity may be a performance, here actor and role—while not identical—are highly fused. To have a body felt to be feminine, i.e., a body constructed through the appropriate practices, is crucial in most cases to a woman's sense of herself as female and, since, in the binary system in which we appear to be trapped, every person must be either male or female, to her sense of herself as an existing individual. To possess such a body may also be essential to her sense of herself as a sexually desiring and desirable subject. If my analysis is correct, then any political project which aims to dismantle the machinery that turns a female body into a feminine one may well be apprehended by a woman as something that threatens her at best with desexualization, at worst with outright annihilation.

Postmodernist feminism has taught us, however, that identity is never unitary, i.e., fully self-consistent, and also that identities or aspects of identities are often acquired under protest. Moreover, the "discourses"—the disciplines and practices—within which our identities are constructed are multifarious and often contradictory. So, in learning that we must become "feminine," we also learn (officially) that we are the equals of men, a proposition that appears, to say the least, compromised by many aspects of feminine body display. In this society, we learn too that we are to be responsible agents, that we must cultivate our individuality and that we are, finally, self-determining. Again, the ethical structures contained within these discourses sit uneasily alongside the conformist and ambiguously demeaning "subtext" of the discourse of femininity.

Resistance and Transformation: What Is to Be Done?

In spite of the seductions of femininity, there is, from some, resistance. Perhaps the mass audience for Naomi Wolf's *The Beauty Myth* are potential resisters. Female body-builders are resisters; they impose upon themselves another discipline, one that offends against the aesthetic of femininity. The younger women who work in the financial district of Chicago take off their pumps at the end of the day and wear running shoes on the bus home: in a small way, they too are resisters. Cross-dressers and drag queens are, ambiguously, resisters. Women who take self-defense courses and study martial arts are resisters. Women in radical lesbian communities are resisters. Size is not regarded with disgust; moreover, aging in these communities is sometimes seen to enhance a woman's sexual allure, not to signal its disappearance. Some radical lesbians have adopted modes of self-presentation that are original, expressive, and not imitative either of the more austere garb of many of their sisters or the conventional feminine body display of the conventionally heterosexual. Participants in the "big and beautiful" movements that ask us to revision large bodies as beautiful bodies are also resisters. These resistances, what do they amount to? Are these resisters like termites invisible to the landlord who will one day bring down the house of discipline?

When the women's movement is in a position to go once more on the offensive, it must develop as part of its cultural politics, a new politics of the body, an invention of new "styles of the flesh." I doubt that a genuinely novel politics of the body can come about within a consumerist capitalist society; unless the mode of production within which we transform ourselves is itself radically transformed, a new aesthetic of beauty would become nothing but an opportunity for the development of new disciplinary practices. Hence, more is required than "gender bending" or parodies of conventional gendered presentations of self, valuable though these strategies may be.

Much has been written in this century about revolutionary aesthetics and about cultural revolution generally. Nowadays, the term "cultural revolution" brings to the racist mind a vision of hysterical Chinese teenagers on the rampage. But I believe that we must discover, or perhaps reinvent, as part of a radical political vision, the idea of a radical cultural politics. In the past, the question of a "revolutionary aesthetics" was raised exclusively in relation to works of high or popular art. I am suggesting here that we need a revolutionary aesthetic of the body.

State-sponsored and enforced cultural revolutions normally reflect little more than the tastes of the ruling bureaucracy or of the rulers themselves. (One thinks with distaste of the cultural depredations of a Hitler or Stalin.) What results from this is a stifling of creativity and a generally inferior cultural production. Sometimes the principles of politically correct aesthetics are said to follow from higher-order political principles, e.g., from the iron laws of dialectical materialism, even from feminism. But given the proliferation of feminisms, the current contestation of gender norms, even the contestations of the concepts of sex and gender themselves, the imposition—as an orthodoxy—of any revolutionary feminist aesthetic appears not only unwise but theoretically impossible. This should not be taken as a declaration of the impossibility of freeing the imagination for new ways of revisioning the body.

I have seen this happen in my own time, first in the imaginative unisex inventions of the hippies, later in the Black liberation movement. This movement addressed not only economic and political issues but the low self-esteem that was tied to the inferiorization of Afro-American bodies. "Black is beautiful," they said, and it became beautiful. Dark skin and kinky hair were no longer occasions for shame but marks of pride. The Afro became at once fashionable and revolutionary. Those in the Black community today who wear African dress and jewelry, dreadlocks or corn rows, have kept this tradition alive, but departures from the norm carry a price yet. That new revisioning took hold in the 1960s and 1970s, and informs my analysis and feeds my hopes.

The transformation of bodies and identities that must be part of a cultural politics of the future will require altered modes of sexual desire and a new aesthetic, a new sensibility that can undertake a radical revisioning of the body. This revisioning will extend our conception of physical beauty— in both males and females—far beyond the narrow limits within which it is now confined. This new aesthetic will be more democratic and more inclusive than the exclusionary aesthetic that now holds sway. Self-presentation will encourage fantasy, play, imagination, and experimentation. Since people will be free, they will of course be free to refuse ornamentation on behalf of austerity or utter simplicity. Presentations of self will no longer be constrained by the necessity of announcing one's gender, for the emergence of a revolutionary aesthetic of the body will announce the actual or immanent demise of the gender system. Presentations of self will no longer be constrained by the necessity of broadcasting one's class, because class will be on its way out as well. The radicalization of beauty norms can, I believe, come about only in a radically democratic society; radical democracy as I understand it is incompatible with class society. As this society of the future comes more and more to value diversity, self-presentation will reflect this, both in the affirmation of one's own cultural heritage and, insofar as this is possible and appropriate, in the sharing of racial and cultural markers. It is futile to try to imagine very concretely how the inhabitants of this post-revolutionary society will revision their bodily selves, for they will do this freely, unconstrained by the sophisticated disciplinary regimes that are so inescapably a fixture of the current cultural landscape.

References

Bartky, Sandra. 1990. *Femininity and Domination: Studies in the Phenomenology of Oppression.* New York: Routledge.

Bordo, Susan. 1933. *Unbearable Weight: Feminism, Western Culture and the Body.* Berkeley: University of California Press.

Butler, Judith. 1985. "Embodied Identity in de Beauvoir's *Second Sex.*" Read to Pacific Div. American Philosophical Association, March 22.

———. 1990. *Gender Trouble: Feminism and the Subversion of Identity.* New York: Routledge.

de Beauvoir, Simone. 1973. *The Second Sex.* New York: Bantam.

Foucault, Michel. 1979. *Discipline and Punish.* New York: Vintage.

Frye, Marilyn. 1983. *The Politics of Reality, Essays in Feminist Theory.* Freedom, Calif.: The Crossing Press.

Henley, Nancy. 1977. *Body Politics.* New York: Prentice-Hall.

Klinger, Georgette and Rowes, Nancy. 1978. *Georgette Klinger's Skincare.* New York: William Morrow.

Millman, Marsha. 1980. *Such a Pretty Face: Being Fat in America.* New York: Norton.

Young, Iris Marion. 1990. *Throwing Like a Girl and Other Essays in Feminist Philosophy and Social Theory.* Bloomington: Indiana University Press.

3

Learning from Experience
Moral Phenomenology and Politics

Susan Dwyer

Against the prevailing view that moral thinking is or ought to be politically neutral, many feminists claim that moral argument is not and can not be insulated from broader political and legal considerations. Feminists recognize the inevitable political inflection of moral thinking in at least two ways. First, drawing on a critical reading of the history of philosophy, feminist theorists have argued that fundamental moral categories—for example, moral agency—have been constructed to reflect (as if natural) and to maintain certain asymmetries of social power (Little, 1995). Second, and more concretely, some argue that to approach particular moral problems as a feminist requires bearing in mind the socially and historically specific location of one's theorizing, with an eye to how one's deliberations are likely to affect the actual conditions of women now and in the foreseeable future (Markowitz, 1990). Despite these different emphases, the main point is that feminists do not attempt to purge political considerations from moral thinking. But this gives rise to a problem. History is testament to the fact that when political conditions are hostile to women (as they so often are), the political inflection of moral argument has negative consequences for women. So if feminists do not want to purify moral argument of all political considerations, we face the challenge of providing a *normative* account of how political concerns may enter into moral thinking.[1]

I have two aims in this essay. First, I want to suggest that some resources for meeting the challenge just outlined are available within another branch of feminist thinking about morality, specifically in that work which focuses on moral psychology. There are a variety of views here, but the theme I wish to highlight is the weight feminists more or less explicitly give to the *phenomenology of moral experience*. Moral questions are illumined by a serious examination of moral consciousness, where this consciousness has two important features: (1) it is ineliminably an *embodied* consciousness, and (2) it is a consciousness shaped (though not fully determined) by an agent's political, cultural, legal, and social environment. Now feminists (and others) have provided analyses of the systemic oppression that characterizes such environments. We might, then, expect to be able to formulate a principled account of how the political and the ethical are substantively connected that can serve as the basis for the normative theory feminists need.

My second aim is to show that attention to moral phenomenology provides feminists with a more productive critique of "traditional" ethics than has heretofore been offered.[2] When moral questions are examined from the embodied perspectives of morality's clientele—women and men—it becomes clear that moral life is considerably more fine-grained than it has been taken to be for the purposes of articulating moral rules and principles. It is important to understand that to the extent that feminists have focused on moral consciousness they have not *just* told women's side of the story. Rather, they have employed a methodology and uncovered data that are *generally* relevant to the construction and justification of moral theories. As such, these feminist contributions to moral theory cannot be dismissed by traditional ethicists as marginal.

In developing my argument I will focus on a particular feminist approach to thinking about pregnancy and abortion. I choose this topic only because it best serves my illustrative purposes; the argument could be made on the basis of feminist thinking about other moral issues. My present interest is not in the morality of abortion itself, nor in the justification of particular abortion laws, though no doubt what I say here has implications for these pressing questions.

Moral Intuitions as Data for Moral Theory: The Partiality Problem

Every one of us has moral intuitions, and philosophers have always more or less explicitly relied on these intuitions in constructing moral theories and articulating moral principles. Indeed, one might say the existence of moral intuitions is the very impetus to moral theorizing. Moral intuitions constrain which problems count as moral problems and what count as plausible solutions to them. In my view, our intuitions are pretty much all we have to go on in the initial construction of moral theory. But moral intuitions can seem problematic for number of reasons.

When moral intuitions are taken to be the deliverances of a special quasi-perceptual faculty, as G. E. Moore appeared to believe, we run into nasty metaphysical difficulties having to do with the existence of nonnatural facts (Mackie, 1977). Others have suggested that moral intuitions are mere feelings—perhaps, emotional reactions—and as such carry no epistemic weight. If ethics really does rest on intuitions, then, we must give up on moral cognitivism; that is, on the idea that ethical propositions admit of truth values. Finally, even if intuitions are held to be judgments or, if you will, beliefs, questions readily arise concerning the source and justification of these beliefs. As manifestations of convention or evidence of our social conditioning, it is hard to see how they can play their epistemic role in theory construction. Also, moral theories would be unacceptably conservative since there appears to be little room for moral critique of the status quo. Matters are not improved if we say that moral intuitions are self-evidently true. For it is a fact that sometimes intuitions about cases diverge: my intuition is that action A in circumstances C is permissible, while yours is that A is impermissible in C. We cannot both be right. Again, the attempt to ground ethics in our intuitions appears to rule out any idea that ethical propositions are objective or that ethical disagreement is rationally resolvable. Of course, the friend of moral intuitions is at liberty to bite these bullets, though I do not think she has to. While I cannot argue for it here, the appeal to moral intuitions in the construction of moral theories and in the evaluation of moral principles is defensible (Nelson, 1990, 1991). And in any case, it is the undeniable ubiquity of the appeal to moral intuitions that motivates my present concerns.

Assuming that moral intuitions are judgments, let me outline another sort of difficulty that might be thought to confront the philosopher who takes such intuitions seriously as data for moral theory. This difficulty, which I shall call the problem of partiality, has two dimensions. Consider first an individual agent, Sarah. Her moral intuitions will encompass direct judgments about what she ought to do in a given situation in which she confronts a moral choice; judgments about the rightness or wrongness of action performed by others (or by her in the past); and judgments of praise and blame (Mandelbaum, 1969). Like her nonmoral judgments, Sarah's moral judgments depend upon other beliefs she has. No plausible conception of moral intuitions will hold that these judgments spring *ab initio* from an unsullied faculty of moral cognition. Moreover, in order both to escape

the charge of conservatism and to capture the fact of genuine moral disagreement, moral intuitions must be rationally revisable. So it is best to
think of Sarah's moral intuitions as part of her overall web of beliefs. Thus,
the content of her intuitive (moral) judgments will be affected not only by
fairly abstract considerations, like her views about metaphysical possibility,
say, but also by quite substantive matters, like her political views. (Imagine,
if you will, the ways in which the moral intuitions of the anti-Semite will
be deeply influenced by his views about Jews.)

In the second place, Sarah's intuitions, no matter how insightful she is,
will not exhaust the data base relevant to the construction of an ethical theory, which, after all, is intended for people besides Sarah. *Human beings* are
morality's clientele, and while many human beings inhabit the same or a
similar world to Sarah's, many others do not. So Sarah's set of intuitions will
be partial in another sense; there will likely be a range of issues about which
she simply fails to have moral intuitions. In constructing a theory, the
philosopher will want to take only some of Sarah's intuitions into account.
She will want to discard the moral judgments Sarah makes because she is a
racist, say, and yet the philosopher will not want to limit herself to the
unproblematic intuitions Sarah has.

Now groups of people share intuitions too. And the judgments of a
group—its common moral wisdom—can be biased in the same ways that
those of an individual are. Arguably, when we look at things from the group
perspective, the existence of partiality in both its dimensions is even more
likely. Typically, groups come and are held together in terms of some set of
beliefs their members jointly affirm. In turn, groups are often individuated
in terms of such shared commitments. Among the beliefs that play these
sustaining and individuative roles are the political and cultural beliefs that
circumscribe the normative life of particular communities. Thus the moral
judgments that members of groups are disposed to make will be heavily
influenced by political and cultural factors. It is also important to note that
this influence may not be explicity recognized as bias by the members of
the group in question. Indeed, a certain amount of taken-for-grantedness
must characterize the beliefs that bind a community together, for one of the
epistemic advantages of being a member of a particular group is that one
can rely on others sharing some pretty fundamental commitments. That the
set of moral intuitions of a particular group are likely to be partial in the
second sense—that is, incomplete or impoverished—should be fairly clear.
It is in the very nature of individuating properties to exclude. So, to the
extent that a particular group is characterized in terms of the moral intuitions of its members, we know that those intuitions do not exhaust the
data for moral theory.

When we put these ideas together and apply them to the history of moral philosophy, we can begin to explain the inadequacies of certain moral theories. If it is true that, until relatively recently, moral philosophy has been largely the province of privileged white men; and if it is true that those men appealed to *their* intuitions in constructing theories and testing principles, then those theories and principles are partial in both senses. In short, to the extent that moral philosophers have not considered the intu- itions of all of morality's clientele—and here I am particularly concerned with the intuitions of women—they have (perhaps) misidentified certain problems as moral problems, failed to recognize other issues as morally loaded, and have offered inadequate analyses of and solutions to the moral problems they have countenanced. Male philosophers have relied on their intuitions for centuries, and where they have granted agency to women as well as to men they have made the mistake of thinking that the life of a man is in all morally relevant respects identical to the life of a woman. In other words, there has been no robust recognition of sexual difference in moral theorizing.

This is especially evident in the bulk of philosophical literature on abor- tion. Pregnancy is something only persons with female bodies can experi- ence, yet the bodies that feature in most arguments concerning the permissibility of abortion (albeit implicitly) have been male bodies. For example, in discussing a standard approach to the problem of abortion, which sees it primarily as a conflict between the pregnant woman's right to bodily integrity and the right to life of the fetus, Michael Tooley (1972) argues that a woman's right to bodily integrity might not even justify the removal of the fetus from her uterus (let alone the death of the fetus) because, whereas it might be possible to compensate the woman for the violation of her right, it is impossible to compensate the fetus for the viola- tion of its right to life. Tooley characterizes the right to bodily integrity as the right to rid one's body of "harmful and annoying parasites," (48) pre- supposing that being pregnant is no different from housing a (potentially) harmful and annoying parasite. And while this might be a way of getting men imaginatively to project themselves into the situation of being preg- nant against their will, it is implausible to think that this is how women understand being pregnant, even reluctantly (Diprose, 1994). However, as I have said, our moral intuitions are the primary data for moral theory. So we need a way to identify and articulate partiality (bias and incompleteness), if we are to have empirically adequate moral theories. My suggestion is that one fruitful way of doing this is to examine the relation between moral agency and embodiment.

Morality and Embodiment

Persons are essentially embodied. Or, to put the point slightly differently, a person's body is not merely a container for or an accessory to her "real" self. The container view is not incoherent; our bodies are correctly describable by standard physical predicates. But this physical conception ignores the fact that a person's body is the very locus of her agency. The particular physical features of my body delimit the possibilities for my (physically) negotiating the world—for example, they determine the size and shape of the objects I am able to carry, and whether I can run, or bear and nurture new members of my species. Further, because these features are imbued with considerable cultural significance, having a certain body also circumscribes how I am able socially to negotiate the world. For example, the dimensions of my body are cues to whether I am "fat" or "thin," where such terms are essentially normative. Indeed, there is an entire complement of norms governing the appearance of the "normal" female body (Bartky, 1990).

The relation between agency and embodiment admits of a strong and a weak reading, depending upon how we interpret the notion of embodied subjectivity. In distinguishing these readings, it is helpful to reflect on Elizabeth Grosz's (1993) claim that "the body can be regarded as a kind of *hinge* or threshold: it is placed between a psychic or lived interiority and a more sociopolitical exteriority that produces interiority through the *inscription* of the body's outer surface" (196). The question, then, is whether having a certain body (1) *fully determines* one's subjectivity, or (2) inescapably *affects* one's subjectivity. On the first classical phenomenological view, something is amiss if a person's body becomes present to her consciousness as an object—for example, when she is in severe pain. On the second, weaker reading we need not assume that something has gone wrong when a person explicitly considers her bodily comportment. Indeed, on this view, such considerations are to be expected, since the idea is that a person's body plays a crucial role in her self-concept, or self-understanding. But in either case, and contrary to some philosophers' fanciful thought-experiments about brains in vats, it is clear that a person cannot act, cannot entertain thoughts, cannot have beliefs and desires and so on without the experience of embodiment.

We cannot make sense of the notion of agency *simpliciter* without taking note of embodied subjectivity. So, in particular, we cannot think of *moral* agency, which encompasses both judgment and action, in abstraction from the bodily experience of persons. What a person is able to do is a crucial factor in determining her responsibilities: "Ought implies can." Hence an individual's judgments about what she ought to do in a given situation, about the rightness or wrongness of others' actions, and of praise and blame will depend upon her assessments of what she can do in that situation and what others can do, respectively. Now, as the discussion above suggests, a person's beliefs about what she is able to do are grounded in her physical properties as well as in how those properties are interpreted in her culture. Importantly, if a woman has internalized the set of norms governing the behavior of people with bodies "like hers," her beliefs about what she is able to do will be constrained by these norms. Women are schooled not to take up too much room; "genuine" feminine bodily comportment is tentative. Conforming one's posture and movements to these norms makes one feel physically vulnerable. And this cannot help but affect where one ventures, and also whether one draws attention to oneself, by speaking up and initiating action. Hence, whether a woman recognizes she has options with respect to action is in part determined by the body she has.

The point I wish to emphasize by providing this hasty sketch of the connection between moral agency and embodiment is this. A variety of forces—covert and overt—operate on our grasp of ourselves as embodied creatures, thus making it inevitable that our very moral consciousness is partially shaped by the political and cultural environments in which we are variously embedded.

All this may be granted, but one might ask how focusing on embodiment is going to help us make progress on substantive moral problems. In answer to this, I turn now to a brief discussion of one feminist approach to thinking about pregnancy that takes embodiment seriously. I believe it serves well to illustrate the advantages of pursuing an embodied approach to moral thinking.

The Moral Uniqueness of Pregnancy

Until relatively recently, arguments about the moral permissibility of abortion have taken two main directions. Either they have been premised on claims about the ontological/moral status of the fetus (is the fetus a person?), or they have construed abortion as a problem of competing claims, namely, the claims of the fetus versus the claims of the pregnant woman. There is nothing about these argumentative strategies *per se* that precludes taking women into account or making women the principal subject of concern (Thomson, 1971; Warren, 1973). But, as a matter of fact, there are grounds for dissatisfaction with the way in which proponents of these types of arguments have interpreted the moral relevance of women to the question of abortion. Pregnant women have been elided from the discussion altogether, as when, for example, the moral status of the fetus is assumed to depend solely upon its intrinsic properties (Tooley, 1983). Alternatively, when women are explicitly taken into account, as in the second type of argument, they are often assumed to have precisely the same moral status as fetuses, at least insofar as the same set of abstract rights are accorded to the pregnant woman and to the fetus (Brody, 1975).

The central difficulty with both these approaches is that they each pre-suppose that it is intelligible and appropriate to think of the pregnant woman and the fetus she carries as entirely separate entities. This presupposition is not surprising. Normative ethics is typically concerned with the actions of *individual* agents; *each* person is a unique locus of moral concern; *each* person has her or his own complement of rights and duties; *etc*. The very language philosophers have had at their disposal has circumscribed the ways in which they have been able to approach the question of abortion. The particular inadequacy of traditional approaches to abortion is high-lighted by work in feminist ethics that emphasizes the unique human rela-tion that pregnancy instantiates.

Catriona Mackenzie (1992) has developed a new approach to thinking about pregnancy that provides a useful foundation for thinking about the morality of abortion. Mackenzie argues that pregnancy is morally unique for two related reasons. First, pregnancy is not something that "just hap-pens" to women. Pregnant women are not passive fetal containers: from the moment she learns that she is pregnant, and throughout her pregnancy, a woman faces crucial choices. According to Mackenzie, pregnancy is "an active and social process which places women in a situation of moral responsibility" (147; also Young, 1990). Second, the physical and psychical connections between a woman and the fetus she carries give rise to "a unique bodily perspective" (147). Crucially, a pregnant woman's responsi-bilities are mediated by this unique bodily perspective, making it the case that we cannot adequately discuss the moral issues concerning pregnancy in abstraction from the embodied subjectivity of pregnant women themselves. In particular, if we focus on "pregnant embodiment," we achieve a better understanding of the moral problems to which abortion gives rise: we are able to articulate a plausible account of the moral status of the fetus and provide a clearer picture of how women's autonomy is implicated in preg-nancy. It will be helpful to examine these two features of the moral unique-ness of pregnancy a little more closely.

In saying that pregnancy places women in a position of moral responsibil-ity, Mackenzie, granting that the fetus has some moral standing, distinguishes between what she calls decision responsibility and parental responsibility. Decision responsibility is the responsibility "to make a decision or a series of decisions about your future relationship with the being whose existence you have directly brought about" (140). Given the physical facts of pregnancy, causal responsibility and decision responsibility are inseparable for women. Once a woman discovers she is pregnant, she cannot avoid deciding whether or not to continue that pregnancy. That decision will inevitably involve a wide range of considerations having to do with how a child will impact her life and the lives of others close to her, including already existing children, and whether the woman believes she is able or prepared to provide the necessary care for the fetus and the child it will become. And in light of these considerations, one such decision might be to have *no* future relationship with the fetus because that being will not exist. Parental responsibility is the "commitment to bringing into existence a future child" (141), where this involves doing what is required to ensure the continued existence and flourishing of the fetus, as well as the provision of care and protection for the child it will become. A woman can assume parental responsibility only after she has made a decision not to abort, though it does not follow that she may not relinquish this responsibility upon further reflection. With the distinction between the two aspects of moral responsibility in pregnancy in place, it is clear that maternity is not the *only* morally responsible response to pregnancy.

Focusing on biological and psychological facts, Mackenzie argues that women's experience of pregnancy undermines the proposition that the woman and the fetus are separate entities in any ordinary sense of separate. She writes:

> Phenomenologically, the experience of pregnancy, particularly in the early stages, is unique in the sense that it defies a sharp opposition between self and other, between the inside and the outside of the body. From the perspective of the woman, there *is* no clear-cut boundary between herself and the foetus, between her body boundaries and the body boundaries of the foetus. (148)

As the pregnancy progresses, however, the woman begins to feel the fetus become more and more physically differentiated from her. It still inhabits her body, but it moves "of its own accord." These sensations give rise to the idea that the fetus is becoming a being that *will* be separate from her. As Mackenzie notes, "this gradual physical differentiation . . . is paralleled by and gives rise to a gradual psychic differentiation, in the experience of the woman, between herself and the fetus" (149). And together these changes underpin the woman's emotional attachment to the fetus and her understanding of her responsibilities with respect to the separate being the fetus will become.

A woman's moral identity is fundamentally reshaped by the experience of pregnancy. First, her body undergoes massive changes, the impact of many of which is internal to the woman's consciousness. Her conception of what she is able to do changes. At times, being pregnant feels like a physical obstacle; at other times, being pregnant produces a sense of awe in one's physical capacities. Second, in many cultures, the overt changes to a woman's body wrought by pregnancy affect how the woman is treated, and so in turn affect her self-understanding. Third, when a woman assumes parental responsibility she "take[s] on a particular moral task and ... simultaneously render[s] [her]self vulnerable in a variety of ways, perhaps for a lifetime" (Gatens-Robinson, 1992, 57–58). Being a parent in the moral sense (as opposed to the biological sense) partly consists in having a particular set of responsibilities to particular others. A woman's moral agency is thus partially constructed around her maternity. In patriarchal cultures, this process is often coercive, but it need not be. Indeed, an analysis like Mackenzie's, which emphasizes how the woman experiences pregnancy "from the inside," shows us the ways in which women can engage in a process of *self*-definition during pregnancy.

Mackenzie's analysis of pregnancy not only provides resources for a more accurate assessment of the responsibilities involved in pregnancy, it also underpins a highly plausible account of the moral status of the fetus. Traditional ways of thinking of the latter suggest that the moral permissibility of abortion depends upon whether the fetus is a person: abortion will be permissible just in case the fetus is *not* a person. The idea that personhood exhausts the possible moral standing of a fetus forces women who are considering abortion into a false dilemma. On this construal, there is little theoretical room to recognize both that the fetus has some moral standing and that abortion is morally permissible. When we listen to women who are considering abortion, it becomes clear that few really believe that having an abortion is morally on a par with getting a hair cut (see Gilligan, 1982).[3] So we need a different way to think about the moral status of the fetus.

Mackenzie's account makes clear, firstly, how the fetus's moral standing is a function of *both* its intrinsic properties and its relational properties, and secondly, that this standing changes throughout the course of pregnancy. Most of us believe that the moral status of the fetus changes over time: our feelings about miscarriages in the second or third trimester differ significantly from our feelings about those that occur in the first few weeks of pregnancy; some of us believe that late-term abortions are in some sense morally worse than early-term abortions, though perhaps justifiable. Now to what can we appeal to make sense of these judgments? The fetus's physical properties change dramatically, but so do its relational properties. Susan Sherwin (1991) writes: "There is no absolute value that attaches to fetuses apart from their relational status determined by the context of their particular development" (336). And the context of a fetus's development will always involve the kind of responsibility the pregnant woman has assumed for it. For example, when a woman assumes parental responsibility for a fetus, she takes on particular obligations for its care and nurturance, which give it some claims against her, whether or not the fetus is a person.

Not for Women Only

I have just sketched some of the philosophical advantages of taking the phenomenological experience of pregnancy seriously in our moral thinking about abortion. It is a fair question, however, how a more adequate moral theory is supposed to emerge from a consideration of phenomenology. There are several complex issues here, and I shall try to address them in a way that brings out more clearly the relation I am urging between ethics and phenomenology. First, it might appear that an emphasis on embodied subjectivity will produce only reports about how things are with particular individuals. An ethics that seeks to articulate generalizations (albeit *ceteris paribus* generalizations) would appear to have little use for such idiosyncratic musings. A second and related difficulty is this: if judgments that issue from Sarah's embodied subjectivity are about how things *seem* to her, then it is hard to see how Sarah can ever be mistaken in her moral judgments. (I might be wrong in claiming that there is an oasis up ahead, but I cannot be wrong about it *seeming* to me that there is an oasis up ahead.) Third, even if we can point to commonalities between various women's experiences of pregnancy (or whatever), how can theorists who have not or cannot have these experiences take them into account? After all, my claim is that this line of feminist thinking provides a *productive* critique of "traditional" ethics, so it had better be the case that *any* ethicist can make use of facts about embodied subjectivity.

All of these difficulties are epistemological, and they connect up with some of the standard objections made to the use of moral intuitions in the construction and justification of moral theory that I mentioned in the second section. If we can point to a primary concern, it is this: that the deliverances of moral consciousness are too *subjective* for use in the normative enterprise of ethics. Moral intuitions are personal; they vary interpersonally at a time and intrapersonally across times. Some intuitions strike many of us as flat out mistaken. Moreover, to the extent that some intuitions are formed on the basis of having certain experiences, questions about third-person accessibility to the content of some intuitions arise.

My short response to these worries relies on stressing the fact that our subjectivities, *because they are embodied*, are not radically solipsistic. I argued earlier that a person's self-understanding and her point of view on the world is necessarily mediated by the body she has. A number of perfectly objective (though in many cases objectionable) norms apply to bodies of a certain type—for example, female bodies. So it is not implausible to expect that there will be deep, objectively identifiable commonalities across the subjectivities of female persons in a given culture. I think this is borne out by the kind of recognition that individual women receive in consciousness-raising activities. (It is important to note that other nongendered norms apply to human bodies too, and so it would be a mistake to think that inter-subjectivity is gender-specific. I return to this point below.) I also argued that a person's moral consciousness is not inferentially isolated from the rest of her epistemic set: an agent's moral intuitions are colored by her other nonmoral beliefs; thus they are open to rational revision as she acquires new beliefs. So, again, it is not surprising either that there are moral disagreements between people, or that a person's intuitive moral judgments change over time. The nonconvergence of intuitive judgments poses a severe challenge to the view I am advancing here only if I insist that moral theory be held entirely hostage to moral intuitions. But that is not my point. I claim only that moral intuitions are an invaluable source of data for moral theory.

Notice also that the moral philosopher is not precluded from critically examining the source and content of moral intuitions. This is important, for as I indicated earlier, some persons' intuitions will be deeply informed by morally problematic attitudes like racism. The fact that some people judge slavery to be just is an indication that they have some radically false beliefs elsewhere in their belief set. Similarly, we need not take the deliverances of anyone's experience as sacrosanct. For example, some proponents of so-called man-boy love claim, on the basis of their experience, that there is nothing morally problematic about their practices. But while we must be careful in judging a person's own account of his experiences, nothing prevents us from assessing that account in light of other moral and nonmoral knowledge. Indeed, it seems to me that to insist that we must *always* take first-person reports about desires and experiences at face value is to undermine the very idea that these desires and experiences are the desires and experiences of *rational* agents. One of the hallmarks of rationality is to admit to one's fallibility.

Finally, focusing again on pregnancy and abortion, let me say something about the accessibility problem. Of course, it is a contingent fact that only women give birth and so a contingent fact that some women have moral experiences that men and other women are unable to have. But it does not follow that *only* particular pregnant women are in a position to make or assess arguments concerning the permissibility of abortion; just as it does not follow that *only* the ill can argue about the distribution of health-care resources. To be sure, a pregnant woman is likely to be better epistemically placed than her health-care provider to determine the nonmedical effects of carrying the child to term, and sensible and just health-care planning will take into account the submissions of the chronically ill. But even this knowledge—acquired in virtue of having certain experiences—is not in principle inaccessible to others "experientially deprived"[4] in the relevant senses. One might think otherwise, if one held that the experiential knowledge acquired in pregnancy, say, is of a type that is *incommunicable.* A view like this is bruited by Vrinda Dalmiya and Linda Alcoff (1993) in their discussion of what they call "gender-experiential knowledge." Using the phenomenology of childbirth as an example, they argue that "there are some gender-specific 'subjective facts' that are not accessible to subjects who are not of that gender" (229). And they suggest that such knowledge might be intersubjectively available only if it can be expressed in a "gender-neutral language" (230). Here Dalmiya and Alcoff draw on Thomas Nagel's (1979) claim that the knowledge of what it is like to be a bat will be forever beyond us because "there are facts [about being a bat] that do not consist in the truth of propositions expressed in a human language" (166). But I think we should resist the idea that facts about gender-specific experiences are like facts about bat experiences in needing a special kind of language. I do not deny that there are some human experiences that defy adequate linguistic expression—for example, experiences of severe trauma. But to make the accessibility of a large amount of experientially acquired knowledge depend on the knower and the inquirer being of the same gender is not only philosophically unmotivated, it is dangerous as well. The last thing feminists should welcome is an "argument" that warrants the further privatization and hence invisibility of women's moral experience.

So, to repeat my central claim. Feminist thinking about pregnancy and abortion reveals a perfectly *general* difficulty in existing approaches to reasoning about concrete moral issues—certain sources of epistemically accessible data have been ignored.

Replies to Some Lingering Worries

There are (at least) three worries that might still be thought to attend my discussion. I have focused on a particular aspect of some women's experience—namely, that of pregnancy. But, first, there is a set of familiar objections surrounding the use of expressions like *"women's* experience of X." Such talk seems to assume that all women—or most women, or paradigmatic women—experience X *in the same way*. This assumption is unwarranted, and, more importantly, appears to ignore the relevance of class and race, to name just two other salient features (besides gender) of human experience (hooks, 1984; Spelman, 1988). Second, my focus on something as physical as pregnancy might appear to reiterate a mind/body dualism, some implications of which feminists have shown to be problematic. Does not my focus simply reinforce the stereotype that women—and in particular, women's moral agency—are to be primarily associated with the body? And third, individual women's experiences are the experiences of subordinated individuals, and so we ought to be skeptical of employing them as the foundation (or even the inspiration) of any positive moral or social theory. In emphasizing women's experience we must not simply valorize products of oppression (Allen, 1983; Bar On, 1993).

Fortunately, my argument is not vulnerable to any of these important worries. I do not assume identity between each woman's experience of pregnancy; all I need for my case is that human fetuses grow inside women's bodies. And while I spoke of the moral *uniqueness* of pregnancy, what I meant by this term is not that there is some *one* experience of pregnancy. Rather the term is intended to capture the idea that we distort the moral dimensions of pregnancy, if we continue to think about pregnancy by drawing analogies between pregnancy and other human relationships. With respect to the second worry, I can only emphasize that I am interested in the *methodological* implications for moral theory of taking embodied experience seriously. To speak of embodied experience requires distinguishing between an agent's body and her beliefs, but there is no pernicious dualism lurking here. Indeed, the very notion of embodied experience is predicated on the idea that mind and body are inextricably linked. Ethics is about persons, and I have taken the Strawsonian notion of a person as primitive: persons are the kinds of creatures to which *both* mental and physical predicates apply (Strawson, 1959).[5] Finally, while it is true that women have certain experiences because they are members of a socially subordinate group, it does not follow that feminists should eschew taking those experiences as central to theory. After all, regardless of their source, these are experiences women actually have. My project is to take moral phenomenology into account as data for moral theory, where the point is not to discover how women experience their moral lives in order to argue that that is how they *ought* to experience it (or not). Rather, the hope is to understand some heretofore unexplored areas of human moral life, with the intention of using this understanding to test the empirical adequacy of existing moral theories. And, crucially, a critical examination of the content of women's experiences as oppressed persons will throw into sharp relief some of the ways in which ethics and politics are connected.

Conclusion

Human beings—male and female—are morality's clientele. At the very least, moral theory must resonate with our lived moral experience. In articulating moral principles and in evaluating moral arguments, the moral philosopher must take human moral intuitions seriously as constraints on her enterprise. To the extent that our intuitions are shaped by political factors, politics enters ethical theory at the ground floor. A systematic investigation of the political inflection of our moral experience is essential to reasoning about moral issues. Human moral phenomenology has been largely ignored in the history of ethics. But it has taken a feminist awareness of the elision of women from moral philosophy to bring this matter to the fore.

Acknowledgments

For ongoing discussion about the issues that animate this paper I would like to thank Paul Pietroski. Ann Ferguson and Bat-Ami Bar On provided helpful comments on earlier drafts, for which I am grateful. Finally, thanks to Elizabeth Elbourne for sharing with me her experience of pregnancy.

Notes

1. There are interesting parallels here with work in feminist epistemology. Harding (1991) and Longino (1990)—and "even" Carnap (1950)—express a general suspicion about the possibility and the desirability of excluding contextual assumptions from the practice of science. Once the untenability of the observation/theory distinction and of the atomistic theory of confirmation is revealed, a central question in the philosophy of science becomes how to provide a principled story about when and how context may be taken into account. Speaking of epistemology generally, Antony (1993) puts the problem nicely: "Once we've acknowledged the necessity and legitimacy of partiality, *how do we tell the good bias from the bad bias?*" (189)

2. "Traditional" appears in scare-quotes because I do not believe that the tradition in philosophical ethics is as theoretically homogeneous as some of its critics appear to believe.

3. Warren (1973) infamously claims that those who oppose restrictive abortion laws believe "that abortion is obviously not a morally serious and extremely unfortunate, though sometimes justified act, . . . but rather is closer to being a normally neutral act, like cutting one's hair" (65). I believe that many feminists who have said that abortion is not morally serious have done so for strategic reasons. And while some women report that their own abortion was a morally neutral act, I am inclined to read this as a rationalization, albeit one that is forced on women who wish to avoid thinking they are vile for not wanting to be mothers.

4. I owe this expression to Ann Ferguson.

5. I do not deny that philosophers have made illegitimate use of mind/body dualism; for discussion see Lloyd (1984) and Bordo (1987). But it is worth noting that analytic philosophers are taking the body more seriously these days; see Campbell (1994) and Harré (1991). Ironically, this heightened interest in the body is the result of philosophers' involvement with "cognitive" science; philosophers of mind now need to know some psychology—especially, some developmental psychology—and work in this field makes considerable use of facts about the human body.

References

Allen, Jeffner. 1983. "Motherhood: The Annihilation of Women." In *Mothering: Essays in Feminist Theory*, ed. Joyce Trebilcot. Totowa, NJ: Rowman and Allanheld.

Antony, Louise M. 1993. "Quine as Feminist: The Radical Import of Naturalized Epistemology." In *A Mind of One's Own*, ed. Louise M. Antony and Charlotte Witt. Boulder, CO: Westview Press.

Bar On, Bat-Ami. 1993. "Marginality and Epistemic Privilege." In *Feminist Epistemologies*, ed. Linda Alcoff and Elizabeth Potter. New York: Routledge.

Bartky, Sandra L. 1990. *Femininity and Domination*. New York: Routledge.

Bordo, Susan. 1987. *The Flight to Objectivity: Essays on Cartesianism and Culture*. Albany: State University of New York Press.

Brody, Baruch. 1975. *Abortion and the Sanctity of Human Life*. Cambridge, MA: MIT Press.

Campbell, John. 1994. *Past, Space, and Self*. Cambrige, MA: MIT Press.

Carnap, Rudolph. 1950. "Empiricism, Semantics, and Ontology." *Revue Internationale de Philosophie* 4: 20–40.

Cornell, Drucilla. 1995. *The Imaginary Domain*. New York: Routledge.

Dalmiya, Vrinda and Linda Alcoff. 1993. "Are 'Old Wives Tales' Justified?" In *Feminist Epistemologies*, ed. Linda Alcoff and Elizabeth Potter. New York: Routledge.

Diprose, Rosalyn. 1994. *The Bodies of Women: Ethics, Embodiment, and Sexual Difference*. New York: Routledge.

Gatens-Robinson, Eugenie. 1992. A Defense of Women's Choice: Abortion and the Ethics of Care. *Southern Journal of Philosophy* 30: 39–66.

Gilligan, Carol. 1982. *In a Different Voice*. Cambridge, MA: Harvard University Press.

Grosz, Elizabeth. 1993. "Bodies and Knowledges: Feminism and the Crisis of Reason." In *Feminist Epistemologies*, ed. Linda Alcoff and Elizabeth Potter. New York: Routledge.

Harding, Sandra. 1991. *Whose Science? Whose Knowledge? Thinking From Women's Lives*. Ithaca: Cornell University Press.

Harré, Rom. 1991. *Physical Being*. Oxford: Blackwell.

hooks, bell. 1984. *Yearning: Race, Gender, and Cultural Politics*. Boston: South End Press.

Little, Margaret Olivia. 1995. "Seeing and Caring: The Role of Affect in Feminist Moral Epistemology." *Hypatia* 10(3): 117–137.

Lloyd, Genevieve. 1984. *The Man of Reason: "Male" and "Female" in Western Philosophy*. Minneapolis: University of Minnesota Press.

Longino, Helen E. 1990. *Science as Social Knowledge*. Princeton: Princeton University Press.

Mackenzie, Catriona. 1992. "Abortion and Embodiment." *Australasian Journal of Philosophy* 70: 136–155.

Mackie, J. L. 1977. *Ethics: Inventing Right and Wrong*. Harmondsworth: Penguin.

Mandelbaum, Maurice. 1969. *The Phenomenology of Moral Experience*. Baltimore and London: The Johns Hopkins Press.

Markowitz, Sally. 1990. "Abortion and Feminism." *Social Theory and Practice* 16: 1–17.

Moore, G. E. 1903. *Principia Ethica*. Cambridge: Cambridge University Press.

Nagel, Thomas. 1979. "What Is It Like to Be a Bat?" In *Mortal Questions*. Cambridge: Cambridge University Press.

Nelson, Mark T. 1990. "Intuitionism and Conservatism." *Metaphilosophy* 21: 282–293.

———. 1991. "Intuitionism and Subjectivism." *Metaphilosophy* 22: 115–121.

Sherwin, Susan. 1991. "Abortion Through a Feminist Ethics Lens." *Dialogue* 30: 327–342.

Spelman, Elizabeth V. 1988. *Inessential Woman*. Boston: Beacon Press.

Strawson, P. F. 1959. *Individuals*. London: Methuen.

Thomson, Judith Jarvis. 1971. "In Defense of Abortion." *Philosophy and Public Affairs* 1(1): 47–66.

———. 1990. *The Realm of Rights*. Cambridge, MA: Harvard University Press.

Tooley, Michael. 1972. "Abortion and Infanticide." *Philosophy and Public Affairs* 2: 37–65.

———. 1983. *Abortion and Infanticide*. Oxford: Oxford University Press.

Warren, Mary Ann. 1973. "On the Moral and Legal Status of Abortion." *The Monist* 57: 43–61.

Young, Iris Marion. 1990. "Pregnant Embodiment." In *Throwing Like A Girl and Other Essays in Feminist Philosophy and Social Theory*. Bloomington and Indianapolis: Indiana University Press.

4

Everyday Violence and Ethico-Political Crisis

Bat-Ami Bar On

As Frantz Fanon noted in *The Wretched of the Earth* in 1961 and Hans Magnus Enzensberger and John Keane have rearticulated recently in *Civil Wars* and *Reflections on Violence* respectively, violence, and especially everyday violence, brings about a complex crisis of conscience. What I want to do here is look at just one of the aspects of this crisis, specifically, the ethico-political impoverishment that it can (and perhaps even tends to) reveal, if not generate, in people. I think that this ethico-political impoverishment points at a "fragility of virtue" under extreme conditions. This "fragility of virtue" complicates feminist Hegelian-like conceptions of violence as inducing the kind of deep psychological transformations that in Marxist discourses have been taken to yield a liberatory-oriented agency.

Everyday violence is common rather than rare. It is the violence that is intertwined with, and therefore configures, people's everyday lives of public or private work, sustenance, recreation, and intimate relations. In the case of a large number of women, rape and battering are everyday violence. For Turks in today's Germany, everyday violence is a function of skinheads' neo-Nazi attacks. In Rwanda and Afghanistan, everyday violence is post-colonially spawned by the conflicts of current warlords.

Exploring the place of violence in the everyday life of the African-American community in the urban ghetto, where all sorts of violence have become too usual, Manning Marable says in a humanist-Marxist voice:

> People resort to violence in their relations with each other when they devalue the humanity and dignity of those individuals with whom they are in conflict. Disagreements are inevitable within all societies. But when people are routinely shot for less than ten dollars, or a young black man in Detroit can be murdered on a city bus for no reason, a very disturbing level of human alienation and social decay has been reached. (p. 21)

The two examples that I am going to use, of the kind of "devaluation" of the "humanity and dignity" of others that Manning sees in the African-American ghetto situation, are from Israel and Palestine. Here too, even if differently, one can also speak of a "disturbing level of human alienation and social decay." Both of my examples are, however, of women's conduct rather than that of men.

My first example is of a phone call between Edna Azaria, a Jewish-Israeli whose husband was knifed to death by a Palestinian man, and Ytzchak Rabin, then Israel's prime minister. Their conversation was reported in *Al Hamishmar*, a local newspaper, to be as follows:

EDNA AZARIA: Mr. Prime Minister, I am the wife of Natan Azaria. If you do not explode the murderer's house, I will do so personally. Don't tell me stories. You must explode it. And don't tell me about the Supreme Court. Otherwise you will not be our prime minister. And if you do not explode the murderer's house, I will send someone to do that. You have to know this.

YTZCHAK RABIN: I understand you. But, I cannot according to the law. Even I, as the prime minister, must act according to the law. . . . The procedure is that the area's military commander has to recommend the explosion of the house.

EDNA AZARIA: Then tell him to recommend it. Now. He has to do it now. (p. 1)

My second example is of a conversation that David Grossman, a leftist and pro-peace Jewish-Israeli journalist, had at a kindergarten in Dahisha, a Palestinian refugee camp in the West Bank. He reports it in *The Yellow Wind*, beginning with the voice of one of the kindergarten teachers.

> "I have obligations here at the camp . . . due to my parents and my own suffering."

"And because of these obligations you will not even try to get any measure of happiness for yourself?"

"I cannot. I do not want any."

"What if Arafat will be able to arrange for a political solution?"

"Understand: We are against Arafat because Arafat wants peace. We want a violent solution. What was taken by violence will be returned by violence. Only this way."

"And the children," I ask.

"The children here know everything," she says and her friend, the other teacher, nods in agreement, "the children are sometimes a fourth generation at the camp."

"Sometime ago," says the friend, "I was asked by the military governor if I taught the children negative things about Israel and the Jews."

"And what did you say?"

"I said that I did not but his soldiers did."

"What do soldiers do?" I ask a four year old girl.

"Searches and beatings."

"Who are the Jews?"

"The military."

"Are there other Jews?"

"No."

Suddenly a little boy pretends to shoot me.

"Why do you shoot me?"

He hides behind the teacher and laughs. He is two years old.

"Who do you want to shoot?" the teachers ask, proud of the child.

"The Jews."

"And so another generation is being raised to hate? Maybe you could try a different way?" I say to the teachers.

"There is no other way," they say. (pp. 19–20)

Edna Azaria and the Dahisha kindergarten teachers speak from unlike social locations. While not a member of the Ashkenazi hegemonic group within Jewish-Israeli society, Edna Azaria is, nonetheless, a Jewish-Israeli and, thus, shares in the privileges of the Jewish-Israeli conquest of the Palestinians. The Dahisha kindergarten teachers, on the other hand, are from the most economically depressed Palestinian group—refugee-camps dwellers—and, consequently, their experience is that of a seldom and barely mitigated, prolonged historical oppression that is due to Jewish-Israeli conquest. Still, there are striking similarities between Edna Azaria and the Dahisha kindergarten teachers.

First, they speak from their pain; Edna Azaria speaks from the immediate pain of the loss of her murdered husband, while the Dahisha kindergarten teachers speak from the pain of a present life under Jewish-Israeli occupation and from the pain of their people and families past. And second, they speak a will to revenge that is not mixed with or limited by other feelings, dispositions, or principles. The purity of their will to revenge exhibits itself in a lack of any consideration for their others; Edna Azaria, seeking the destruction of Palestinian homes, does not try to understand what about Palestinian life might have motivated the attack on her husband and does not concern herself with the Palestinian lives that would be affected by the violence she wants unleashed, while the Dahisha kindergarten teachers see all Jewish-Israelis in the same light and do not concern themselves with the Jewish-Israeli lives that would be affected by the violence *they* want to unleash. It also manifests itself in an apathy to alternative modes of settlement. Edna Azaria has no use for the law, not even the so often anti-Palestinian-biased military procedural justice, as a channel for her needs; while the Dahisha kindergarten teachers have no use for the extremely slow and so often very disappointing political negotiations led by Arafat as a channel for their needs.

There is a third axis of resemblance between Edna Azaria and the Dahisha kindergarten teachers. I believe that it is a function of their gender and its construction in their societies which, generally speaking, places violence in men's hands. As a result, though Edna Azaria and the Dahisha kindergarten teachers can speak their pain and will to revenge, they have to turn to others to act on their will to revenge; Edna Azaria demands action from the male Israeli prime minister and military, while the Dahisha kindergarten teachers guide the boy children in their care toward the action they seek.

Because of the totalizing force that the will to revenge exerts on Edna Azaria and the Dahisha kindergarten teachers, I would describe them as ethico-politically impoverished. Their ethico-political poverty, just like ethico-political richness, is acquired. Grady Scott Davis's discussion of war and morality in *Warcraft and the Fragility of Virtue* can help explain some of this.

Davis, who supplements Martha Nussbaum's work in *The Fragility of Goodness*, notes that virtues (which he defines in quite standard Aristotelian terms, as habituated dispositions that enable a certain activity to be chosen and pursued well), are fragile. Davis describes this fragility, stating that

> [it] is not an unfortunate happenstance but an essential aspect of what it means to be a virtue. . . . There is no rest in the past achievements of

virtue. . . . Virtue, if it is to flourish, must be practiced, not merely possessed. Like any other skill or art, it will weaken and eventually vanish if not regularly employed. The most common enemies of virtue are indifference, self-indulgence, and despair, which persuade someone that something need not be done, or not just now, or can't possibly be accomplished . . . and thus might as well be dispensed with. (p. 85)

According to Davis, war is the laboratory in which the fragility of virtue is tested because, like a plague "with its constant and unanticipated variations on horror, [war] breads despair, self-indulgence, and indifference to the way" (p. 87) one shapes one's life. Davis seems to indirectly suggest a weakness of the will behind the changes of character that war breeds. But Johnathan Shay dispels the idea of such a weakness in his *Achilles in Vietnam*, pointing out that the undoing of character in war is a result of the experience of trauma under certain social conditions and within a certain culture.

Edna Azaria and the Dahisha kindergarten teachers have been living with a protracted war between Jewish-Israelis and Palestinians. Even if she is on the unjust side and they on the just side of this war, they all live under its inescapable, tremendous stresses. And, none of them seems to have come through the stresses of this war unscathed. Though women, and hence the most typical of civilians, rather than combatants, their character, like the character of combat veterans, has been undone by the war.

To have a character undone by the trauma of war or other violence results, on Shay's account, in a loss of the ability to want or think into the future, a deep disbelief in the possibility of conducting a passionate struggle that is not a life-and-death struggle, and in a profound distrust of people and the power of words. For Shay, what this means is that the character of the traumatized is inclined to be undemocratic, since, when understood in a civic-political context, it is a character that lacks "the cognitive and social capacities that enable a group of people" (p. 181) (or the virtues that are needed) to engage in democratic processes.

Shay's description of the violently undone character stands in stark contrast to Hegelian-based expectations from such an undoing. According to Hegel's *Phenomenology of Mind*, a life-and-death struggle is essential for a mutual recognition of selfhood and personhood. This, Hegel claims, is impossible without facing and making another face the risk of annihilation, which is the source of a renewed and more complicated affirmation of life in community. Thus, Hegel states, [two self-consciousnesses] prove themselves and each other through a life-and-death struggle. They must enter into this struggle, for they must bring their certainty of themselves, the certainty of being for-themselves, to the level of objective truth, and make this a fact both in the case of the other and in their own case as well. . . . The individual, who has not staked his life, may no doubt, be recognized as a Person; but he has not attained the truth of this recognition as an independent self-consciousness. (pp. 232–233)

What Hegel asserted in 1807, Jean Paul Sartre reasserted in his preface to Fanon's *Wretched of the Earth*, writing about the violent anticolonial struggle:

Make no mistake about it: by this mad fury, by this bitterness of spleen, by their ever present desire to kill us, by the permanent tensing of muscles which are afraid to relax, they have become men: men *because* of the settler, who wants to make beasts of burden of them—because of him and against him. (p. 17)

In a somewhat different way, feminists have also been reproducing the Hegelian expectation from the trauma of violence. In her *Women and the War Story*, Miriam Cooke, for example, describes Arab women's writing about war in the postmodern/postcolonial period as "repeating in stereo the daily experience of violence that has become ordinary," and, at the same time, assigning women's "own meanings to what they have felt and done," (p. 41) thereby telling the "daily experience" in ways that undermine existing male paradigms and "constructing a memory that is responsible to the future." (p. 43) Like Cooke, Simona Sharoni too calls attention to the transformative power of women's experience of war, telling in *Gender and the Israeli-Palestinian Conflict* about women whose encounter with death and injury resulted in a critical consciousness and resistance to what they conceived as man-made war and social order.

In the conclusion to her book Sharoni says:

Some may argue that the voices, perspectives, and struggles of the Palestinian and Israeli-Jewish women highlighted in this book are not representative of the majority of Jewish women in Israel or Palestinian women in the West Bank and the Gaza Strip. Yet, it is precisely these women's experiences that highlight dimensions of the Israeli-Palestinian conflict that often remain unaddressed. Taking these experiences seriously has a transformative potential in that it makes contestable the often taken-for-granted assumptions behind the dominant interpretations of the Israeli-Palestinian conflict, which render gender invisible. (p. 151)

The voices, perspectives, and struggles that Sharoni does not highlight are those of Edna Azaria and the Dahisha kindergarten teachers and the many women who like them have been ethico-politically impoverished by violence. I, obviously, think that they have to be taken as seriously as the women that Sharoni wants to make exemplary. This is not because they are *not* exemplary. To the contrary. I think that they, as well as the women whose stories move Cooke to her nuanced rethinking of war, are inspirational. What I feel wary about is Sharoni's and Cooke's willful inattention to the fragility of women's virtue and its violent undoing. It is this willful inattention, I believe, that frees these writers to prematurely generalize women's position more abstractly as promising a revolutionary ethico-political perspective.

For Marx, the proletariat offered the hope of an ethico-political revolution. Marx describes the rise of the proletariat in *The Communist Manifesto*, and according to him, the life conditions of the proletariat justified its selection as the class that makes the radical transformation of capitalism possible.

> In the conditions of the proletariat, those of old society at large are already virtually swamped.... [The proletariat] have nothing of their own to secure and fortify.... The proletariat movement is the self-conscious, independent movement of the immense majority, in the interest of the immense majority. (pp. 494–495)

Marx's expectations from the proletariat depend on his expectations for capitalism to develop in such a way that inter-state as well as intra-state differences would be homogenized and that two classes, the oppressive exploiting capitalists and the oppressed and exploited proletariats, would emerge globally. But, capitalist development has been different for different nation-states, and especially so for the core and peripheral nation-states of the capitalist world-system. Additionally, race, ethnicity, nationality, and religion, as well as gender, sexuality, age, and also disability, have been reformulated and reasserted rather than subsumed under class.

Capitalism, not developing as Marx expected, has frustrated Marxist expectations for the proletariat. This is not to say that class has not been a mobilizing identity. But, the mobilization has not been consistently, opposi-tionally progressive. As Stanley Aronowitz points out in *The Politics of Iden-tity: Class, Culture, Social Movements*, the consequence of this is that,

> [w]hat is in question is [the working class's] position with respect to social transformation. When they do not act as part of the opposition . . . their status becomes ambiguous. All of which raises the question of what is "left" in the current conjuncture. (p. 270)

The Aronowitz question needs, I believe, to be asked as poignantly about the position of women with respect to social transformation, given that taken as a group women are, empirically, an ambiguous lot when it comes to ethico-politics. Like men's virtues, women's virtues are fragile and tested by violence. More often than not, they seem to be violently undone. This is not insignificant, and what is needed is not just a turn to women's resistance to violence for inspiration but also a better understanding of the gendered nature of the fragility of women's virtue and its violent undoing.

References

Al Hamishmar. 1993. 03 March. Tel-Aviv.

Aronowitz, Stanley. 1992. *The Politics of Identity: Class, Culture, Social Movements.* New York: Routledge.

Cooke, Miriam. 1996. *Women and the War Story.* Berkeley, CA: University of California Press.

Davis, Scott Grady. 1992. *Warcraft and the Fragility of Virtue: An Essay in Aristotelian Ethics.* Moscow, Id.: University of Idaho Press.

Enzenberger, Hans Magnus. 1996. *Civil Wars: From L.A. to Bosnia.* New York: The New Press.

Fanon, Frantz. 1968. *The Wretched of the Earth.* Translated from the 1961 French edition by Constance Farrington. New York: Grove Press.

Grossman, David. 1988. *The Yellow Wind.* Translated from the Hebrew. New York: Farrar, Strauss, and Giroux.

Hegel, G. W. F. 1967. *The Phenomenology of Mind.* Translated from the 1807 original in 1910 by J. B. Baillie. New York: Harper and Row.

Keane, John. 1996. *Reflections on Violence.* London: Verso.

Marable, Manning. 1992. *The Crisis of Color and Democracy: Essays on Race, Class and Power.* Monroe, ME: Common Courage.

Marx, Karl. 1976. "Manifesto of the Communist Party." In *Karl Marx/Frederick Engels Collected Works: Volume 6: Marx and Engels 1845–1848.* New York: International Publishers.

Nussbaum, Martha C. 1986. *The Fragility of Goodness: Luck and Ethics in Greek Tragedy and Phi-losophy.* Cambridge: Cambridge University Press.

Sharoni, Simona. 1995. *Gender and the Israeli-Palestinian Conflict: The Politics of Women's Resis-tance.* Syracuse: Syracuse University Press.

Shay, Jonathan. 1994. *Achilles in Vietnam: Combat Trauma and the Undoing of Character.* New York: Simon and Schuster.

Two

The Ethics and Politics of Knowledge

Conceptualizing Truth in Teaching and Learning
Implications of Truth Seeking for Feminist Practice

Becky Ropers-Huilman

Politics and ethics exist in dynamic tension within educational settings. This tension can be simultaneously exciting and painful, supporting regularity and comfort, dissonance and fear. Because we are all stakeholders in educational processes, we have an interest in determining what should be valued in educational communities and whose understandings should be placed at their core. Thus, one of the important questions involved in making ethical and political educational choices, I suggest, concerns debates over what types of knowledge, hence truths, are worth knowing.

Feminist academics have played a crucial role in higher education's heightened attention to the nature of truth. Analyses of feminist teaching practices suggest an expansion of teachers' and students' roles, as well as an expansion of the knowledges and truths with which they engage. Several scholars suggest that power within classrooms needs to be critically analyzed and understood as it may affect and be affected by truth, knowledge, and, subsequently, educational experiences (Ellsworth, 1989; Orner, 1992; Ropers-Huilman, 1996). Others assert that feminist education should be context-specific, creating truths from and about participants' life experiences and encouraging them to incorporate their own experiential knowledge into learning (Lewis, 1990). Still others believe that feminist education supports action on the part of its participants, encouraging those involved to mobilize the knowledge they understand from their classroom experiences to make a difference in their lives outside formal classrooms (Bennett, 1991; Gore, 1993; Lather, 1991). It seems, then, that knowledge in feminist higher education takes on multiple forms and may open up a wide range of possibilities for use in feminist movement.

In this essay, I consider the implications of multiple perspectives of truth for developing feminist politics and ethics. With Adriana Hernandez (Eichhorn et al., 1992), I believe that it is necessary to constantly examine how feminism is taking shape in educational practice because of the close relationships feminist education purports to have with politics and experiences outside educational environments. I use feminist education as the centerpiece of this work to argue that understanding *how* feminists learn, teach, and utilize truth is as important to feminist politics and ethics as is understanding *what* is considered to be valuable truth. Here, I provide an analysis of "truth-seeking" in feminist education and consider the implications truth definitions may have for feminist politics. I argue that there are multiple definitions of truth and suggest that conceptualizing truth claims and processes of truth-seeking as tools or strategic devices, rather than only as facts or as constructed beliefs, provides participants with useful opportunities for developing feminist agendas.

I begin my argument by situating feminist and poststructural discussions within a long history of those who have struggled in various ways to understand and define truth. I then explore several ways that the concept of truth has been understood in relation to teaching and learning, and how those concepts can be both useful and harmful in feminist work. Finally, I conclude by proposing that the consideration and questioning of claims to truth in teaching and learning environments be an important part of developing feminist ethico-political agendas.

Situating Truth in Education

Pondering the status and roles of truth has been and continues to be a regular event in the works of philosophers and educators. Over the years, truth has been conceptualized as leading to enlightened citizens; as being generated within given contexts; or as subconsciously affecting persons and actions (Foucault, 1992, orig. 1984; Lechte, 1994). Educational scholars have focused on truth as being linked to students' own experiences and their interactions with social conditions (Dewey, 1990, orig. 1900; Palmer, 1993, orig. 1983). Further, some focusing on truth and knowledge as they are understood in higher education has urged that we return to understanding truths as facts (Bloom, 1987) or that we seek to understand how our methods of working with and understanding truth affect subsequent teaching and learning practices (Barber, 1992; Damrosch, 1995). Below I explore feminist and poststructural critiques of truth and consider how the premises they suggest may be useful in crafting teaching and learning practices.

Feminist Critiques of Truth

Feminist involvement in education arose in part from an increasing awareness that the truths receiving attention in academic environments were partial, incomplete, and biased (Gore, 1993; Howe, 1977; Luke and Gore, 1992; Robinson, 1973). As Marilyn Boxer (1985) describes, "The most significant contribution of the new feminism of the 1960s and 1970s to the education of women lay in its perception that sexism in the curriculum . . . made 'coeducation' a myth" (p. 6). Feminist education, as a result, attempted to disrupt traditional understandings of knowledge by breaking down error, rebuilding knowledge, and transforming teaching and learning in higher education classrooms.

Some feminist scholars also suggest that knowledge can never be "objective" because those who conceive and present it do so in their own specific historical and cultural contexts (Boxer, 1985). As Vivian Makosky and Michele Paludi (1990) express, "The reality is that beliefs and values are such an integral part of the self that they are indistinguishable from absolute truth or fact" (p. 3). It is extremely difficult, if not impossible, to break a "truth" or "fact" away from the context in which it was produced and expressed. Following this line of thought, the belief that objectivity in academic knowledge was unattainable (and, for some, undesirable) led to an education that sought other sources and means for creating increasingly tentative and locally defined knowledge.

One outcome of the breakdown of objectivity in truth-seeking as a primary goal in feminist higher education is the acceptance and validation of personal and experiential sources of knowledge and understanding. Literature on feminist classrooms suggests that teachers refrain from demanding that students defer to preconstructed, objective truths and knowledge bases (Bennett, 1991; Fagan, 1991). Instead, "the construction of the feminist classroom engages rather than dismisses students' experiences as a fundamental aspect of teaching and learning" (Giroux, 1989, p. 7). Teachers' and learners' experiences are seen as valuable, invested knowledge to be discussed and validated as a form of truth within feminist education.

Poststructural Critiques of Truth

Poststructuralism suggests that there are multiple ways of interpreting experience and defining truth. Rather than questioning, "Is this true?" poststructural scholars ask questions like, "What is the present field of possible experiences?" (Foucault, 1988a, orig. 1984, p. 95). "Why, in fact, are we [in Western society] attached to truth? Why the truth rather than lies? Why the truth instead of myth? Why the truth rather than illusion?" (Foucault, 1988b, orig. 1984, p. 107). Knowledge and truths in poststructuralism are viewed as always partial and political; power relations are, while not synonymous with knowledge, "directly implied" by it (Gore, 1993). Jane Flax (1993) describes the postmodern approach relating knowledge to power as not focusing "on reason, method, and the relationships between subject and object. They treat truth as an effect of multiple and various discursive practices including the circulation of power" (p. 48). And Michel Foucault (1988b, orig. 1984) reminds us, "Truth is no doubt a form of power" (p. 107). Conceptualizing truth as inscribed *on* or ascribed *to* given entities or events, rather than objectively described *about* them, is also a central concept in poststructural thought.

Truth as we currently understand it, and as we will construct it in the future, is and will always be flexible and partial (Ross, 1988; Weedon, 1987), as well as constantly shaped by the historical and societal contexts in which we are situated (Lather, 1991). Truth, and the meanings related to truth, are shifting and determined always by social, historical, and political forces that are, in a specific situation, acting upon it. As Judith Hoover and Leigh Anne Howard (1995) say, "Postmodern argumentation rejects essentialist truths in the same way it rejects universal formalism. . . . Instead, they seek hidden sources of power in the discourses through which truths are generated. Postmodern philosophy urges us not toward order but toward multiplicity or even randomness" (p. 971). Since multiplicity and randomness are not qualities fervently revered in many higher education contexts, poststructural conceptualizations of truth suggest new ways of teaching and learning, as well as new ways of thinking about the politics involved in feminist education.

Truth in Teaching and Learning

I believe that interpretations of truth and knowledge must be connected to teaching and learning practice. Indeed, one's understandings of truth are expressed through one's practices whether purposefully or accidentally. In other words, the beliefs about truth that are embraced in higher education greatly influence the interactions and outcomes we are able to enact. In this section, then, I suggest several interpretations of truth and potential implications for the enactment of those interpretations in feminist education. In each subsection, I consider a teaching and learning practice that might support that particular view of truth and then discuss how each view could be both useful and harmful in political contexts in which we live and work.

Truth as Fact

Those who believe in truth as fact suggest that while we might not have figured them all out yet, there are indeed truths that are "out there" waiting to be discovered. Much of higher education has been centered on this view of truth, emphasizing that research is the discovery of truth, while teaching is the dissemination of truth. In this view, truth is seen as a commodity, goal, or possession.

Teaching and learning in this context is likely what educational participants have engaged in and come to expect in the majority of their formal educational experiences. A fill-in-the-blank type of exam conveys that there is only one right answer that is acceptable in the context of that classroom. Students who continually question, "Will this be on the exam?" represent one learning aspect in the interpretation of truth as fact. They see their learning as continually directed from the outside, hoping to gain facts, truths, and knowledge from outside sources. Their hope is that they will leave the class *possessing* more information than when they first entered.

Defining truth as fact can be beneficial for developing a feminist politics. For example, if collected statistics demonstrate a systemic mistreatment of a certain group of people—perhaps related to employment or compensation, language use or conversational strategies—those statistics may be useful for those trying to define the parameters of a political agenda and the areas in which their efforts could be most effectively focused. Additionally, that factual knowledge could provide feminists with information around which they could build informed political stances, locating points of resistance and similarities between and among group members and positions or approaches.

In one example from my research on feminist teaching, Chris told of the ways in which her teaching practices reflect her view of truth as factual,[1]

> I lecture a fair amount. . . . I see my role as someone who is giving out information and knowledge and ways of thinking. And it's [the students']

role to be learning that material.... I have this role of lecturer dispensing ideas and their role is to take those and be processing that information and learning it.

Chris, in this case, felt that as a feminist teacher, it was important for her to ensure that students learned key concepts and facts about the subject area. She felt it useful to engage in practices that reflected that belief.

Understanding truth as fact is certainly not novel. While many feminists have often moved to seek other interpretations of truth, others lament the loss of a time when the usefulness of this approach was more widely accepted. For example, Daphne Patai (1994) argues that feminist education should continue its tenuous and difficult struggle toward this factual type of truth. In her words:

> Feminism, today, as it conflates politics and education and effaces any distinction between political agendas and the protocols of research, is in danger of suppressing ... any calm, reflective stance that sees some strengths in the efforts ... to set biases aside and ... regard research as a valuable and satisfying endeavor not in need of quite so much postmodernist angst. By its refusal to recognize the distinct boundaries that do and ... should demarcate the realms of politics and education, and politics and scholarship, feminism threatens to entirely delegitimize any research effort not hopelessly mired in collective ideological conformity or in individualistic self-reflexive shenanigans.... To refuse to draw a distinction here is like saying: As we can never be sure that we are being entirely truthful, we might as well lie all the time. (p. 62)

With these words, Patai encourages those involved in feminist education and research to continue holding factual truth as the primary goal of their efforts, purporting that the opposite of telling the truth is lying, and that since we would not hope to be in search of lies, we must hold fast to our search for factual truth.[2]

Peter McLaren and Colin Lankshear (1993) suggest a less firm definition of truth and knowledge, and yet nevertheless believe that truth conceptualized as stable knowledge or fact may have potential for emancipatory agendas both in education and elsewhere. They further suggest that by conceptualizing truth and its expression as always embedded and developed within social and historical parameters, educators risk neglecting factors that perhaps may not be seen as primary or relevant in current analyses. Current truth constructions can make invisible previous interpretations.

Therefore, conceptualizing truths as context-bound and unchangeable once established can prove to be both inclusive and useful.

Understanding truth as fact, though, can also easily be misleading or detrimental to developing feminist practice. If accepted uncritically, truths take on only the meanings that those constructing the truths intend them to take. Other interpretations are silenced, and the reasons for collecting and focusing on those truths, as opposed to others, are obscured. To demonstrate the silencing of others' interpretations when only one view of truth is embraced, another teacher told me about a strategy that she uses to amplify the ways in which teachers can privilege their truths over those of their students. As Andrea described:

> I made a joke [in class] about how oftentimes, in a class, a professor asks a question and they want a specific answer. . . . One day, I actually said [to students], "I have decided what I think the answers are and so I want you to just be calling them out and if it's not exactly right, I'll be fitting it to what exactly I want to put on the board." . . . I would make a joke and . . . say [their answers were] "exactly right" . . . then I'd write mine on the board.

Understanding truth as immutable, "correct" fact also mitigates against certain types of questioning that cannot find a place, or would not "make sense," within the norms or structures of that truth (Lance & May, 1995). If truth is understood only as fact, as somehow "free" from its current contextual and historical development or usage, then other interpretations or truths developed in other contexts or from other standpoints may not be accepted as valid truth or knowledge. Even if understood as facts, truths are motivated by something and come from somewhere for some purpose. If used exclusively, conceptualizing truth as factual mitigates against multiple interpretations and options for teaching and learning.

Truth as Constructed Belief

Those who conceptualize truth as constructed belief understand truth and knowledge to be used and constructed through people's interactions with the world around them. As Patti Lather (1991) claims, "Facts are not given but constructed by the questions we ask of events" (p. 105). In other words, people's beliefs *are* their truths and are more or less compelling for others depending on the similarity of questions and conclusions those others are considering. Mark Lance and Todd May (1995) espouse the belief that "The formation of concepts and the formation of theoretical hypotheses go hand in hand. . . . Thus one cannot have a single concept without many, nor observation without presuppositions as to the nature of the system being observed" (p. 980). Reality is based, on this view, on what people have come to understand from their experiences and how they approach knowing about the world from a multifaceted standpoint.

A teaching practice that may support a view of truth as constructed belief is a requirement to synthesize reading and experience about a given topic and, based on understandings from both sources, to present tentative philosophies or approaches woven together from various strands of thought. Additionally, though, students may be asked to examine how their current contexts, and those of other class participants, have influenced the possible truth constructions that were available for use, interrogation, and adoption. Students' critical questioning of a concept, doubting and testing the relevance of presented truths as related to their own experiences, represents a learning position taken by many who view truth as constructed belief. These practices encourage persons to allow multiple and varied texts and perspectives to influence their belief systems and truths with the understanding that what will emerge as truth will be unique in each person's circumstance, depending on contextual factors. They also support the possibility of a fluctuating and changing truth.

Defining truth in this way may be quite beneficial for developing feminist politics. For example, there is great potential in this approach to bring into discussion multiple views of reality and experiences for a more expansive analysis of what those perspectives could mean for processes and products of knowing. Additionally, instead of insisting on agreement of what is and is not valid truth, those holding this view of truth allow for a wide variety of interpretations and tentative conclusions of the multiple texts brought to classrooms. They further interrogate their own constructions and positions with the hope that they can understand others' constructions as well. For example, Andrea talked with me about how white students' knowledge constructions are influenced by their experiences of being white and how understanding whiteness could help them better relate to those from other racial positions. In her words:

> I talk [in class] about how whiteness is so normalized that we don't think
> about it. And we do gender because it's . . . a way that we can interact in
> the world, but white isn't. So there's a sense that if you're a white person
> you've kind of been normalized in such a way that you don't think about
> it. So I ask them to talk to their neighbor about what it might mean to be
> the norm. . . . What I try and do is talk about whiteness in a way that

allows them entry into their own constructions . . . and allows them a way to think about people of color.

When considering the multiple perspectives encouraged in a view of truth as constructed, J. Daniel Schubert (1995) suggests that those participating in academic education can reconstruct segments of society through the examination and construction of beliefs that undermine traditional truth forms. He states that "Constructing versions of social reality is what we [academics] do. We must break with both official and common conceptions of reality. . . . At the same time that we are defetishizing social limits by transgressing them, we are reconstructing society in other ways" (p. 1013). Understanding truth as constructed belief suggests teachers' and students' abilities to become part of each other's experiences and, through that participation, to change each other's truths.

This approach to truth is not without its criticisms. It can be problematic in developing feminist politics because power relations continue to affect belief constructions. In other words, the beliefs or truths of some will be considered as more useful than the truths of others. Further, power relations in classrooms can never be fully known or understood (Ellsworth, 1989). Even with this view of truth, I agree with Michael Apple (1993) that: "What counts [in education] as legitimate knowledge is the result of complex power relations and struggles among identifiable class, race, gender, and religious groups. Thus *education and power* are terms of an indissoluble couplet" (p. 196). Adopting this belief to finally be "rid of" power in education will be a futile gesture. I cannot foresee a time when those enacting feminist politics will not hold a stake, and a related desire for power, in educational processes and knowledge constructions.

Truth as Tool

Those who believe truth is best understood as a tool recognize that truth can take on many different forms, be constructed through many different processes, and be used in many ways for many purposes. They assert that one's use of truth is best aligned with one's current political stances and educational purposes. They do not restrict themselves by rejecting factual or constructed truths, but rather embrace them both, examining their potential uses and possibilities. When truth and truth-seeking processes are seen as tools, the question, "What is most useful?" becomes primary.

Poststructuralism is a philosophy that has been criticized for its lack of practicality—its failure to be of use to "real" problems (Nicholson, 1995). I argue in this section that poststructuralism can be a very powerful and useful tool in the construction of feminist political movement, especially in relation to conceptualizing truth in potentially influential higher education environments. Feminist poststructuralism urges us to consider truth as a tool available for use by those who have created, interpreted, or supported that truth. Poststructuralism analyzes relations of truth and knowledge to power and suggests that, "Everyone might be better off if we acknowledge we are all operating on the terrain of power and not truth or objectivity. What counts as 'better knowledge' depends in part on its utility for particular political ends" (Flax, 1993, p. 12).

Teaching and learning practices that espouse poststructural approaches to knowing and truth encourage participants to critically examine their own positions and those of others in the process of creating and engaging with knowledge claims. Further, these practices allow for analytical questions to come from a variety of standpoints and "positions." For this reason, it is difficult to circumscribe poststructural teaching or poststructural learning, as poststructuralism encourages all participants to engage within their educational experiences in ways that circumvent and expand traditional roles of teacher and student. Vicki expressed her struggles in reconceptualizing what changed roles of students and teachers might mean for truth and knowledge usage, saying,

> I am constantly struggling [in my teaching, and] I locate that struggle mostly in how to get over the course of a semester the best possible balance between how much I give of what I know and think versus how much I give free reign to the students to determine what it is that they talk about, what it is they're interested in. That is the hardest thing for me.

The difficulties of dealing with truth as a tool do not end with a negotiation between students' and teachers' knowledge. For those who value truth as fact, any attempt to illustrate how truths are used for certain purposes draws criticism about the lack of objectivity and, therefore, the lack of applicability. For those who value truth merely as constructed belief, power relations are negated and the potential for political action is diminished. In both cases, the truth-tool is rendered less effective. For this reason, proposing that truth can and should be used as a tool in feminist education is, in some contexts, a difficult proposition to suggest.

Acknowledging those difficulties, yet embracing the possibilities for action from poststructural standpoints, conceptualizing truth as a tool can become especially helpful. A class exercise that encourages members to question common understandings of truth would be one where multiple questions from different paradigms were generated by class members. Those questions might then be discussed with the intent to explore as many responses as possible, not to ultimately define the "correct" or agreed upon one, but to consider multiple possibilities for and implications of these questions. Both factual-type responses as well as responses drawing from participants' previous experiences would be considered and valued as important and relevant to other participants' learning.[3] All questions and truths posed would be examined for how they were being and could be used. Additionally, classroom participants would consider the various facets of the contexts in which certain questions were able to be generated.

Viewing truth as a tool, often through feminist poststructural lenses, is an approach that I argue has potential to be most useful for developing feminist political movement. One of its most valuable lessons is that which concerns transgression of common academic practice through the very acknowledgment that truth and power are implicated by each other. As J. Daniel Schubert claims: "If transgression generally is the act of going beyond or exceeding a limitation, then transgressive academic practice is important politically. It exposes the relations between truth and power" (p. 1005). And Jane Flax (1993) suggests: "In our culture we must produce truth. There can be no exercise of power without its concomitant production of truth. Legitimate power requires grounding in and justification by a set of rational rules" (p. 41).

Conceptualizing power and knowledge as inextricably related is useful in analyzing and deconstructing the arguments of those hoping to do harm to developing feminist agendas. This approach also allows those interested in understanding and advancing feminist politics to hold as tentative and shifting words and actions expressed in the name of feminism. In other words, conceptualizing truth as a tool allows feminists to reflect on their own educational practice to ensure that the questions and answers they are posing reflect their current political commitments and purposes. Rather than asserting timeless truths that support feminist goals, conceptualizing truth as a tentative and power-linked tool allows feminist agendas to shift in relation to the contexts in which they find certain truths are most needed or useful.

There are, of course, quandaries that arise from this approach, most of which seem to be generated from within the two preceding frameworks. As Daphne Patai (1994) seems to question in her work, if we recognize and insist that power and politics are embedded in both localized and generalized truth, aren't we "in fact" lying or at least stretching truth beyond its "normal" parameters? I suggest that there are reasons to act, in certain contexts, as if truth can be held as indisputable. There are reasons to act, in certain contexts, as if truth is no more than constructed beliefs. There are reasons for, and explanations of, multiple other concepts of truth as well, all of which can serve purposes within feminist politics. I suggest that we do not have a definitive answer; we have not found, nor should we be seeking, *one* truth.

Meaning in Truth: Truth in Meaning

Learning and teaching others how to think about the assumptions informing knowledge and truth claims in education should remain a focal point of exploration and contestation as educators struggle to develop feminist political agendas with their students. First, in efforts to be more inclusive and benefit from differences among educational participants and in educational literature, it is useful to explore multiple definitions of and approaches to truth as they relate to those affected by feminist movement. People and politics shift depending on power relationships. Defining truth as a tool whose many interpretations can be used to support feminist work breaks free from the chains of defining truth in only one way and, in doing so, shuts off all other opportunities to be informed by and inform claims to truth and the power that accompanies those claims.

Further, constantly considering assumptions that inform truth allows those concerned with ethics and their relationships to politics to remember that truths are not "innocent" nor are they applied without a purpose. As Jane Flax (1993) suggests:

> Postmodernism calls into question the belief (or hope) that there is some form of innocent knowledge available. . . . By innocent knowledge I mean the discovery of some sort of truth that can tell us how to act in the world in ways that benefit or are for the (at least ultimate) good of all. Those whose actions are grounded in or informed by such truth will also have *their* innocence guaranteed. They can do only good, not harm, to others. They act as the servant of something higher and outside (or more than) themselves, their own desires, and the effects of their particular histories or social locations. (p. 133)

Undoubtedly, conceptualizing truth as a tool poses a challenge for feminist communities as they develop and contest feminist political agendas and viewpoints. It is not easy to think of truth from standpoints other than the ones that have informed one's own education and experience. It is even more difficult to decide when strengths from one perspective outweigh potential weaknesses. Conceptualizations of truth in feminist education are not clear; yet they are indeed political. Beliefs about truth affect both teaching and learning practices in higher education and, consequently, evolving understanding of politics from feminist standpoints. Feminist education is feminist politics.

Notes

1. My research on feminist teaching consisted of twenty-two in-depth, open-ended interviews with feminist teachers at a large, midwestern university. Additionally, I observed six classrooms from one to two times, and acted as a participant observer in two classes for an entire semester. For more information on this research, see Ropers-Huilman (1996).

2. Poststructural literature has focused on the tendency of Western thought to set up dichotomous relationships between similar and related concepts (Lather, 1991; Orner, 1992). In this case, Patai's assumptions that the opposite of truth-seeking or truth-telling must be lie-seeking or lying demonstrates this tendency. My question is: Are there no other options than telling a factual truth or purposefully telling a lie? In this paper, I try to sketch possibilities for options that Patai seemingly does not see as feasible.

3. For a more descriptive analysis of poststructural implications for educational practice, see Ropers-Huilman (1996).

References

Apple, Michael W. 1993. "Between Moral Regulation and Democracy: The Cultural Contradictions of the Texts." In *Critical Literacy: Politics, Praxis, and the Postmodern*, ed. Colin Lankshear and Peter L. McLaren. Albany, NY: State University of New York.

Barber, Benjamin R. 1992. *An Aristocracy of Everyone: The Politics of Education and the Future of America*. New York: Oxford University.

Bennett, Roberta S. 1991. "Empowerment-Work Over Time: Can There Be a Feminist Pedagogy in the Sport Sciences?" *Journal of Physical Education, Recreation, and Dance* 62: 52–67, 75.

Bloom, Allan. 1987. *The Closing of the American Mind*. New York: Simon and Schuster.

Boxer, Marilyn J. 1985. "Women's Studies, Feminist Goals, and the Science of Women." In *In the Company of Educated Women: A History of Women and Higher Education in America*, ed. Barbara M. Solomon. New Haven: Yale University.

Damrosch, David. 1995. *We Scholars: Changing the Culture of the University*. Cambridge, MA: Harvard University.

Dewey, John. 1990; orig. 1900. *The School and Society*. Chicago: University of Chicago.

Eichhorn, Jill, Sara Farris, Karen Hayes, Adriana Hernandez, Susan C. Jarratt, Karen Power-Stubb, & Marian M. Sciachitano. 1992. "A Symposium of Feminist Experiences in the Composition Classroom." *College Composition and Communication* 43 (3): 297–322.

Ellsworth, Elizabeth. 1989. "Why Doesn't This Feel Empowering? Working Through the Repressive Myths of Critical Pedagogy." *Harvard Educational Review* 59 (3): 297–324.

Fagan, G. Honor. 1991. "Local Struggles: Women in the Home and Critical Feminist Pedagogy in Ireland." *Journal of Education* 173 (1): 65–75.

Flax, Jane. 1993. *Disputed Subjects: Essays on Psychoanalysis, Politics and Philosophy*. New York: Routledge.

Foucault, Michel. 1992; orig. 1984. "What Is Enlightenment?" In *Postmodernism: A Reader*, ed. Patricia Waugh. New York: Routledge, Chapman and Hall.

———. 1988a; orig. 1984. "The Art of Telling the Truth." In *Michel Foucault: Politics, Philosophy and Culture: Interviews and Other Writings 1977–1984*, ed. Leonard D. Kritzman. New York: Routledge.

———. 1988b; orig. 1984. "On Power." In *Michel Foucault: Politics, Philosophy and Culture: Interviews and Other Writings 1977–1984*, ed. Leonard D. Kritzman. New York: Routledge.

Giroux, Henry. 1993. "Literacy and the Politics of Difference." In *Critical Literacy: Politics, Praxis, and the Postmodern*, ed. Colin Lankshear and Peter L. McLaren. Albany, NY: State University of New York.

Giroux, Jeanne Brady. 1989. "Feminist Theory as Pedagogical Practice." *Contemporary Education* 61 (1): 6–10.

Gore, Jennifer. 1993. *The Struggle for Pedagogies: Critical and Feminist Discourses as Regimes of Truth*. New York: Routledge.

Hoover, Judith D. and Leigh Anne Howard. 1995. "The Political Correctness Controversy Revisited: Retreat From Argumentation and Reaffirmation of Critical Dialogue." *American Behavioral Scientist* 38 (7): 963–975.

Howe, Florence. 1977. *Seven Years Later: Women's Studies Programs in 1976: A Report of the National Advisory Council on Women's Educational Programs*. New York: State University of New York.

Lance, Mark and Todd May. 1995. "Beyond Foundationalism and Its Opposites: Toward a Reasoned Ethics for Progressive Action." *American Behavioral Scientist* 38 (7): 976–989.

Lather, Patti. 1991. *Getting Smart: Feminist Research and Pedagogy with/in the Postmodern*. New York: Routledge.

Lechte, John. 1994. *Fifty Key Contemporary Thinkers: From Structuralism to Postmodernity*. New York: Routledge.

Lewis, Magda. 1990. "Interrupting Patriarchy: Politics, Resistance and Transformation in the Feminist Classroom." *Harvard Educational Review* 60 (4): 467–488.

Luke, Carmen and Jennifer Gore. 1992. "Introduction." In *Feminisms and Critical Pedagogy*. New York: Routledge.

Makosky, Vivian P. and Michelle A. Paludi. 1990. "Feminism and Women's Studies in the Academy." In *Foundations for a Feminist Restructuring of the Academic Disciplines*, ed. Michelle A. Paludi and Gail A. Steuernagel. New York: Haworth.

McLaren, Peter L. and Colin Lankshear. 1993. "Critical Literacy and the Postmodern Turn." In *Critical Literacy: Politics, Praxis, and the Postmodern*, ed. Colin Lankshear and Peter L. McLaren. Albany, NY: State University of New York.

Nicholson, Carol. 1995. "Postmodern Feminisms." In *Education and the Postmodern Condition*, ed. Michael Peters. Westport, CT: Bergin & Garvey.

Orner, Mimi. 1992. "Interrupting the Calls for Student Voice in 'Liberatory' Education: A Feminist Poststructuralist Perspective." In *Feminisms and Critical Pedagogy*, ed. Carmen Luke and Jennifer Gore. New York: Routledge.

Palmer, Parker J. 1993; orig. 1983. *To Know As We Are Known: Education as a Spiritual Journey*. New York: HarperCollins.

Patai, Daphne. 1994. "Response: When Method Becomes Power." In *Power and Method: Political Activism and Educational Research*, ed. Andrew Gitlin. New York: Routledge.

Pels, Dick. 1995. "The Politics of Critical Description: Recovering the Normative Complexity of Foucault's Pouvoir/Savoir." *American Behavioral Scientist* 38 (7): 1018–1041.

Robinson, Lora H. 1973. *Women's Studies: Courses and Programs for Higher Education.* Washington, DC: American Association for Higher Education.

Ropers-Huilman, Becky. (1996) *Feminist Teaching in Theory and Practice: Situating Power and Knowledge in Post-Structural Classrooms*: New York: Teachers College.

Ross, Andrew. 1988. "Introduction." In *Universal Abandon: The Politics of Postmodernism.* Minneapolis: University of Minnesota.

Schubert, J. Daniel. 1995. "From a Politics of Transgression Toward an Ethics of Reflexivity: Foucault, Bourdieu, and Academic Practice." *American Behavioral Scientist* 38 (7): 1003–1017.

Weedon, Chris. 1987. *Feminist Practice and Poststructuralist Theory.* Oxford: Basil Blackwell.

6

Resisting Value-Bifurcation
Indigenist Critiques of the Human Genome Diversity Project

Laurie Ann Whitt

Dedication

This essay is dedicated to a Guaymi Indian woman whose name is being kept secret. If she is still alive, she will be 31 this year. Diagnosed with leukemia in 1991, she sought treatment in a hospital in Panama City. While there, samples of her blood were drawn and her cell line was "immortalized" and stored in the U.S. without her knowledge or consent. Two American scientists, listing themselves as "inventors" of her cell line, applied for a patent in 1993 and placed it on sale at the American Type Culture Center for $136. They did so on behalf of the Centers for Disease Control, because of the cell line's commercial promise, and since the government encourages scientists to patent anything of interest. According to one of them, "I think that most people wouldn't understand all the details of all the laboratory work that was being done and I don't think anyone ever really felt it was necessary. . . . So in terms of specifically notifying the Guaymi that a patent application was being put forth, I don't think that was done. But again, mainly because I don't think anyone ever felt it was really necessary" (Kaplan in WMF 1994).

"We Are Scientists, Not Politicians"

This essay focuses on indigenist critiques of the Human Genome Diversity Project, and on how they illustrate and resist the presence, force, and consequences of value-bifurcation in Western culture. Three concepts are central to my discussion: value-neutrality, value-bifurcation, and indigenist science criticism. Value-neutrality is a familiar, widely acknowledged thesis about the practice and ideology of Western science, especially in its positivist and neo-positivist formations. At its simplest, it is the claim (or assumption) that science is value-free, unburdened by "external" ethical and political values. As even the most ardent defenders of value-neutrality grant that political and moral values enter into the uses of science, the thesis rests on a distinction between pure and applied science (or science and technology) whose tenuous nature is increasingly admitted. Given the relations between Western science and industry, the role of industry in academe, and the constraints on research reliant on government or corporate funding, it is difficult if not impossible "to separate a passive, disinterested 'science' from a transformative, engaged 'technology'" (Proctor 1991, 3–4).

Value-neutrality is buttressed by the long-standing Western philosophic practice of value-bifurcation, which sharply distinguishes ethics from politics. Politics, it is said, "is social and collective, while ethics only pertains to the behavior of individuals" (Grosz 1989, xvii). The bifurcated nature of the distinction is crucial: "there is a logical juncture where ethics finds its limits and politics begins" (Winner 1991, 379–80). In practice, it deflects normative criticism away from the political. As J. Berlan notes regarding biopatents, "Because we do not confront these questions politically, we turn to ethics" (1989, 26). Talk of how politics and power enter into the origins and development of science is effectively silenced. The result is an apolitical ethics of science in which issues of power in ethics are ignored, or channeled into very narrowly envisioned accounts of informed consent and the violation of individual autonomy. In some cases, it has also produced an amoral politics of science, and more discussion of science "policy" than of the politics of science.

The conjunction of value-neutrality and value-bifurcation facilitates dismissal of radical critiques of Western science; it mutes charges of material oppression and conceptual domination by shielding science from direct involvement in moral and political debate. When ethics and politics are moved out of the space of knowledge production, and a depoliticized ethics is reserved for assessing knowledge use, the cultural politics of science becomes so much ideological fluff. Political values are reduced to ideological biases, and Western science is held to be neither ideological nor particular (i.e., "Western"). Ethical values become subjective biases, and objectivity and universality are extended as desiderata and preconditions of any science. Neither of these are merely "academic" developments. They are of strategic, pragmatic benefit to the Western knowledge system, enabling it (especially science) to ignore the dynamics of power that mediate relations between Western and non-Western cultures.

The history of the encounter of Western science and indigenous peoples has been devastating, and it is being updated, reproduced, daily. The current partnership between the biosciences and the $45 billion biotechnology industry, for example, directly impacts and often targets indigenous peoples (Kloppenburg 1990). Indigenous opposition to these developments is growing, forceful, and effective. The demands of activism and practice are driving theory, which is as it should be. What they indicate is an already vital indigenist theoretical perspective that analyzes the political role of science with special attention to how it impacts indigenous peoples.

Justice cannot be adequately addressed in the abstract; "the actual forces that undermine it, as well as those that support it" (Sherwin 1992, 55) must be examined, if justice is to be secured. Indigenism insists that the power structures and dynamics that facilitate and maintain the oppression of indigenous peoples be exposed. Indigenist critiques of science do not rely on the myopic ethics produced by the conjunction of value-neutrality and value-bifurcation; it is not enough to assert merely that a particular practice is morally wrong and ought not continue. The relations of power responsible for it, which are themselves morally reprehensible, must be challenged if the practice is to be effectively countered. Indigenism conjoins contextualized critique of the oppression of indigenous peoples with concrete proposals for realizing justice, and with recognition of the existence, effectiveness, and potential of indigenous agency.

To resist value-bifurcation and secure both a politically enriched ethics and an ethically informed politics, every critique must consider "which questions get asked and which are ignored . . . whose interests are affected by the decisions that have been made and who has the power to control the agenda" (Sherwin 1992, 4). Indigenists (whether indigenous or non-indigenous) also address how a specific practice, project, or institution impacts indigenous peoples, cultures, and lands. To morally evaluate specific initiatives of biotechnoscience involves establishing moral criteria to determine whether and how such initiatives should be undertaken; it also involves making political judgements (Sherwin 1992, 51). These judgments are made whether one supports or attacks the initiative, and irrespective of one's role in it. To assert, as one proponent of the Diversity Project has, that "we are scientists, not politicians" (Feldman in Gutin 1994, 75) is self-deceptive. So

too is the failure to be "sceptical . . . about the very notion of informed consent as a tool for negotiating bodily practices in situations where unequal
power relations are present" (Lock 1994, 605). The political role of science
and the ways in which it has supported and participated in the complex
systems of practices that constitute the oppression of indigenous peoples
figure prominently in indigenist critiques of contemporary biotechnoscience initiatives.

"Not a Question of Whether . . . But of How"

Since 1988, the Human Genome Organization (HUGO) has been engaged
in a massive ($3 billion) effort to map and sequence the human genome,
known as the Human Genome Project (HGP). Since the HGP does not
consider population-level variation, population geneticists proposed a collateral study, the Human Genome Diversity Project (HGDP). At an esti-
mated cost of $25 million, the HGDP is being developed under the
auspices of HUGO, which formally adopted it in January 1994. The debate
over the HGDP vividly illustrates the conjunction of the pure/applied science distinction, the thesis of value-neutrality, and the practice of value-
bifurcation. How they work together to deflect substantive ethical and
political critiques of science, and how such critiques may yet be effectively
and forcefully made, is especially apparent in the debate between the Project's proponents and its indigenist opponents. This issue is also one of great
ethical and political urgency. Indigenist critics have had considerable success in delaying the Project, but recent developments such as the NSF's call
for research proposals (NSF 1996) indicate the struggle's immediacy.

On the eve of the Columbus Quincentenary, several leading geneticists
proposed the HGDP in an article in *Genomics* entitled "Call for a Worldwide Survey of Human Genetic Diversity: A Vanishing Opportunity for the
Human Genome Project." The stated goal, at least initially, was to collect,
analyze, and preserve for future study DNA from diverse populations in
order to understand human variation, to learn more about human origins,
evolution, and ancient migration patterns. "Isolated" human populations
were of most interest, and those specifically mentioned were all indigenous.
The effort to discern the microphylogeny of human populations before
population "contact" (taken to have begun in 1492), has been criticized on
conceptual and methodological grounds. Anthropologists, archaeologists,
and linguists gathered to draw up an initial list of the 722 populations "most
worthy of genetic study" by having their cell lines immortalized. "This is
just 50 people trying to represent the world," one said (Weiss in Roberts
1992, 1301). The gate to this study is "closing rapidly" because these "Isolates

of Historic Interest" (Roberts 1993, 675) are "vanishing," "rapidly disappearing," and "in danger of dying out or being assimilated" (Roberts 1991,
1992). The visual images accompanying the articles are telling. An anonymous individual from the Arawete tribe is captioned as a "vanishing
resource," and a sidebar entitled "A Few of the Chosen" includes images of
Yanomami and Chukchi people, with the caption "They made the list"
(Roberts 1991, 1992). Indigenous peoples have dubbed it the "vampire project" (Dodson 1993).

A main venue for much of the controversy has been Native-L.[1] The
depth and force of indigenous opposition to the Project apparently took
many by surprise. "I don't think it [initially] crossed anyone's mind that [the
HDGP] would be controversial," one supporter notes (Kahn 1994, 720).
Such surprise stems from a failure to contextualize the HGDP, to situate it
in the broader cultural politics in which practices of Western science—
especially those impacting indigenous peoples—are, and have historically
been, steeped. Indigenist critiques are attentive to this. Historically
informed and politically aware, they are filled with the hard lessons learned
from prior encounters with Western science and acutely conscious of social
and power relations. Okanagan activist Jeanette Armstrong (1995), for
example, precedes her discussion of the HGDP by reviewing how indigenous genetic resources have been exploited in the name of pharmaceutical
science. Debra Harry (1994) and Aroha Mead (1996) also situate it in the
cultural politics governing the interaction of Western science and indigenous peoples, as do many other indigenist critics.

By contrast, Project proponents tend to proceed as though it were possible to abstract, isolate, and immunize the Project from history and politics.
The hand-washing comment of the frustrated geneticist that "We are scientists not politicians" is typical, and has been met with the trenchant response
"As if opening the veins of indigenous peoples of the world might not constitute a significantly political act" (Marks 1995a, 72). The pure/applied science distinction is invoked, ethical issues are reserved for the latter,
management of them is handed over to a special ethics committee, and
political issues are largely (if not very successfully) displaced. The New
Zealand Health Research Council, for instance, recently organized a con-
ference with the promising title "Whose Genes Are They Anyway?" Yet the
"Consensus Report" asserts: "The spirit of science is independent of commercial, political and religious interests. The application of knowledge
derived from science should be for human good and open for public
scrutiny" (Centre for Genome News 1995). And in an article assessing the
ethical implications of the Diversity Project we find: "Knowledge in and of
itself is not immoral; however the potential for adverse effects from the

acquisition and utilization of this knowledge has contributed to this moral dilemma" (McPherson 1995, 42).

The skirting of moral issues and political realities is striking in the Project's FAQ, which states that if sampling is too long delayed, some human (that is, indigenous) groups may disappear as discrete populations "usually through urbanization or other forces leading to the loss of their language or the other characteristics that identify them as a separate group" (FAQ 1996). This convenient, politically numb dismissal of the many ways in which oppression historically has impacted, and continues still to impact, the survival and well-being of indigenous peoples is the rule rather than the exception in the writings of Project proponents. "Nowhere in the HGDP literature," Aroha Mead asserts, "have I ever sighted acknowledgement of the extent and effects of the first wave of colonization. . . . [H]ave they even thought about political distinctions or, in pursuit of a 'pure scientific goal,' are they ignoring the social, political, economic cultural realities?" (Mead 1995). The assumption of inevitability is also in full play in these documents. Despite massive, emphatic, and reiterated objections from the major indigenous organizations at the international, national, and local levels, the Project relentlessly rolls on, now with the assistance of the National Academy of Sciences. Henry Greely, at a heated meeting in Guatemala, admitted to indigenist critics that the West and Western science had done terrible things to indigenous peoples, but ". . . that our project was different—that we were trying to do things right. . . . I encouraged them to become involved in order to help us insure that the Project did not harm their interests" (Greely 1993).

The official goal of the Project is to collect and analyze DNA samples from diverse populations and "to develop databases and resources that could be used to investigate new questions in the future." Why should this be done? The central justification is that of "pure science"—it will advance knowledge: "already there are indications of the wealth of information harbored in the DNA of aboriginal peoples" (Roberts 1991, 1617). Advancing knowledge is regarded as inherently good, a significant benefit and a reason the HGDP morally ought to be pursued. There is also an appeal to "possible biomedical applications" (NRC 1996), and not just increased knowledge about genetic diseases. The samples may "help lead to identification of genetic factors in some human diseases and eventually to ways to treat or prevent those diseases" (FAQ 1996).

Yet this application argument has been muted in the actual debate. There are reasons for this. If medical applications were a goal, they would need data they have no plans to collect, including "phenotypes or life-history data to accompany the genetic material they plan to warehouse" (Marks 1995a, 72).

As one critic observes, the HGDP's mandate is simply "to collect, database and maintain genetic samples and data, not to develop medical applications" (Harry 1994, 13). This appeal also sits uneasily with the oft-repeated disavowal of the likelihood of commercial applications and the attendant question of who will profit: "the proposed HGDP is not and will not be a commercial venture. It is thought the chance that this research will lead to the development of commercially valuable products is very remote" (Cavalli-Sforza and Greely 1995).

Whatever medical applications do result are likely to benefit those who can afford expensive pharmaceuticals and genetic therapy tests. That is very unlikely to be the primarily indigenous populations providing the samples. The appeal also fails to address the role of environmental conditions in the health of indigenous communities, conveniently skirting thereby issues of social justice and of political, cultural, and economic oppression. Moreover, this appeal can be used coercively to secure the participation of subjects based on the false hope of medical miracles: "The enticement of potential medical benefits is an empty promise which will be used to gain access to communities for the collection of samples" (Harry 1994, 14).

Such justifications travel a one-way moral assessment street. The potential good that may come from the Project in knowledge gained is seen as adequate reason for pursuing it, while potential harm is inadequate reason for abandonment. It is not that potential good is held to outweigh potential harm, but that potential harms are never allowed to tell against the conduct of the research itself. The pure vs. applied science distinction is thus invoked very selectively. It serves as a protective normative buffer against arguments opposed to the HGDP; a negative moral evaluation of the uses or results of scientific knowledge does not reflect back on, or impede, the acquisition of that knowledge. While in supporting arguments, the distinction serves as a facilitating normative transducer; a positive moral evaluation of the uses or results of scientific knowledge is to count as reason for acquiring that knowledge.

Potential harms are to be managed and minimized by an ethics committee, chaired by law professor Henry Greely. Ethics is reduced to applied ethics and the ethical (and political) considerations involved in producing the knowledge in the first place are sidestepped. How likely is it that applied ethics will offer substantive value criticism of initiatives like the HGDP? As Sue Sherwin notes, "the apparatus of technical theory is invoked to defend or, at most, modestly reform existing practices." Such ethics committees are "chiefly occupied with establishing an ethical rationale for existing practices within the field" (1992, 87).

What is achieved by distinguishing pure from applied science, by relegating ethical concerns to the latter, and avoiding the role of politics altogether? The terms of the debate are effectively defined: the issue becomes not *whether* but *how* something will proceed; "there is no question that the project should continue. That is, ethical issues arise not in decisions about *creating* this knowledge, but only in its *use*." Stemerding and Jelsma (1996) characterize this as producing a "compensatory ethics" that seeks to control the implications of scientific and technological developments only through compensatory measures that should prevent undesirable effects of new knowledge and technologies (346–47).

Ethics becomes a "supplementary activity" (348), concerned only with the implications of specific projects for society. By restricting ethics to knowledge-application, and creating an ethics committee, concerns about the HGDP can be rhetorically managed, and research will proceed apace. Political issues can be ignored or displaced, reduced to policy and regulatory concerns such as patenting and informed consent. The real issues of power are avoided.

The recent development of a Materials Transfer Agreement and a Database Access Agreement in response to indigenous concerns about commercial exploitation is a case in point. Value issues become compensatory ethics; they are reserved for the space of knowledge application, and not allowed to impact that of knowledge production. The thirty-three-page report of an early ethics workshop is revealing. Only questions regarding how the Project should proceed are discussed. Significant misgivings are raised about its conduct, but no one raises the question of *whether* or *why* it should proceed.

Who benefits if the HGDP is funded? Most plainly and immediately, the population geneticists who would be involved. According to one, by 1984 new molecular tools became available that transformed their field. Since the populations they most wanted to study were "disappearing," they decided to collect and preserve DNA samples from indigenous peoples immediately. However, funding was a problem; they usually had to ask anthropologists to collect samples. "[We] have been frustrated by the difficulty of getting grants for this kind of work" (Kidd in Gutin 1994, 72). Funding will be less of a problem with the HGDP underway. The Project is also often portrayed as involving a mere change of scale: "the work doesn't constitute anything fundamentally new. . . . [It] is merely a way to organize" (Gutin 1994, 72) the collecting of samples that has been going on for years. The significance of the fact that it will be "a large-scale, publicly visible, and highly funded 'Project'" (Marks 1995a, 72) that not only permits but encourages them to do so is downplayed.

Indigenists repeatedly argue that the priorities and interests the HGDP represents are not those of indigenous people. Responding to a UNESCO paper on the Project that distinguishes (and regrets the "confusion of") social ideologies with scientific goals, Maori activist Aroha Mead stresses that "science is only of use if it improves the quality of life and society. Without that, it serves no useful purpose to humanity, only a purpose for a minority exclusive group of western professionals, possibly at the expense of the unity and survival of indigenous communities struggling to remain intact" (1996, 49).

Debra Harry invokes the 1964 Helsinki Declaration, which states that "in research on man, the well-being of the subject takes precedence over science and society" (in Butler 1995, 373), to argue for a halt to the HGDP on the grounds that indigenous people will not only not benefit from it, but may experience increased discrimination as a result. This is not an idle worry, given the history of Western science when it comes to the study of human differences and the ease of accessing such a database. Moreover, for many indigenous peoples basic health care, and survival itself, are central concerns; genetic research "is not a priority. . . . They've come to take our blood and tissues for their interests, not for ours" (Harry in Butler 1995, 373). If indigenous interests were the concern, priorities would be different, and the money would be spent otherwise. As José Acosta points out: "We are not opposed to sharing with humanity. What we oppose is being exploited when our poverty is not resolved" (in WMF, 14).

What response is made to such objections? A typical comment is that "all scientific research uses money which could be used instead for social expenditures," but that it would be "unfair" to single out any particular project as "to blame for relative distribution of resources" (Vicedo 1992, 259). Accepting the current allocation of resources, presumably, is less "unfair," or less disturbingly so. To the question, "Couldn't that money be better spent?" the response is "perhaps, but there is no reason to believe that it would be . . . that those funds, if not spent on the HGDP, would be better spent on relieving poverty. More likely they would be spent on another scientific project" (FAQ).

Besides, "$5 million a year would not go far toward solving those problems, even in North America" (FAQ). Such comments plainly testify to the effects of the Western commitment to value-neutrality and value-bifurcation. There is a huge shrug of denial in them, a refusal to acknowledge, and assume responsibility for re-ordering, the moral and political priorities that shape scientific knowledge production. What are the implications of the observation that $5 million a year wouldn't make enough of a difference anyway? Perhaps that no proposal to address serious, systemic social problems should be taken seriously unless there is enough funding (how much is that?) to make a difference? Or that $5 million could be cut from existing social programs since it does "not go far toward solving those problems"?

In response to indigenous opposition, supporters have modified their arguments and rhetoric. The emphasis and wording of the Project's goals have been altered. Not only will it increase knowledge in valuable ways, it will do so in one particular way. The HGDP "seeks to understand the diversity and unity of the entire human species" or "family." Without it science will largely define "the" human genome, with its historical and medical implications, as that carried by a small number of individuals of European ancestry. At a time when we are "increasingly concerned with preserving information about the diversity of the many species with which we share the Earth surely we cannot ignore the diversity of our own" (FAQ).

Bodmer describes it as a "cultural obligation of the Human Genome Project" (Roberts 1991, 1615). Ken Weiss, head of the North American Diversity Project, echoes his point: "If we don't go ahead with this . . . when the Human Genome Project is done, a Navajo, say, will look at those results and ask, 'Why did they bother? How well does that represent *me*?'" (Gutin 1994, 72). The HGDP, then, will solve racism. Not surprisingly, UNESCO's International Bioethics Committee regards this as the "most debatable" claim made by its proponents, arguing that "the prejudice that gives rise to racist and eugenic attitudes tends to pervert scientific results to its own ends" (Butler 1995, 373). Moreover, the HGDP is avowedly focused on population-based difference, and one of its objectives is the locating of "those relatively few genetic markers which are concentrated in specific ethnic groups due to random mutation or the interaction of biological and cultural adaptations in specific ecological niches" (Lock 1994, 604).

Given the nature and scope of the possible abuses, such concerns need to be taken seriously and faced directly, though that involves situating the Project on a continuum of scientific research from which it would like to distance itself. All the pure motives, faultless intentions, and previous good works of all the scientists involved will not alter the fact that such work is embedded in cultural politics, that it bears a considerable historical burden and lends itself to appropriation and abuse by individuals, organizations, and governments.

This characterization of the HGDP as a solution to racism is coupled with reassurances that, despite reports, it is "not an effort to collect samples from isolated populations in danger of disappearing [but] intends to take a representative sample of all human populations. . . . No group is necessarily excluded" (FAQ). All that can be said about such reassurances is that they are painfully transparent instances of rhetorical spin. Granted that Project scientists have never "excluded" any particular group, it is nonetheless true that indigenous peoples were, and are, the focus and scientific "interest" of the Project. It was precisely the HGP's failure to include such groups that motivated the HGDP in the first place. Yet its vigorous, forceful rejection by indigenous peoples not only jeopardized the possibility of locating "cooperative" populations to sample, it badly damaged the Project's public image, and thereby the likelihood of funding.

This response is a rhetorical two-step. Retreat into vague, inoffensive generalities about the "whole human family" and hope no one notices that indigenous peoples are 99 percent of the diversity sought. Emphasize talk of unity in a Project that will study difference, and hope that people will forget the sorry history of Western science's obsession with racial, class, and gender differences. What this does is to further shield the Project from moral and political critique. The indigenous status, and precarious state, of many desired subject populations is cloaked, and the term "human groups" is substituted for "indigenous peoples." Project supporters stress the openness and public nature of their planning, but this rhetoric hides and manipulates. It also adds to the offensiveness of the charge that indigenous peoples have misunderstood and overreacted to the HGDP. Even the International Bioethics Commission report notes that opposition is "based upon more than misunderstandings . . . or antiscience attitudes, but 'is a clash of philosophy and cultural insight'" (Butler 1995, 373).

Indigenist critics emphasize this last important point, but Project supporters make little response. Aroha Mead observes that "many in the HGDP have the mistaken view that the reason for indigenous opposition . . . . rests in lack of understanding of the Project's aspirations, and confusion over minor details" (Mead 1996, 49). The critiques are directed to something quite fundamental—to the clash of knowledge and value systems that lies at the heart of this controversy. While Mead's discussion is framed in Maori beliefs, it resonates with the basic commitments of other indigenous peoples. The concept of the human gene on which the HGDP relies is at odds with the indigenous understanding of what a human gene is, of what and who it represents, of what and for whom its purpose is determined, and of who the "owner or guardian" of human genes is. For the Maori people, and many others, the human gene is genealogy. In Maori "a gene" is translated as *iratangata*—"life spirit of mortals." More commonly *whakapapa*, "genealogy" is used; it is the basis for Maori connecting with themselves and others. Since a gene, or genome, is imbued with a life spirit that has been handed down by the ancestors and is passed on to future generations, it is not and cannot be the property of individuals. It is part of the heritage of families, communities, tribes, and entire indigenous nations. Mead stresses,

> the indigenous and western scientific philosophies differ on (this) fundamental point. . . . [It] is the difference in understanding of the origin of humanity, the responsibility of individuals, and the safety of future generations which sits so firmly at the core of indigenous opposition to the HGDP. . . . [T]his type of research proposes to interfere in a highly sacred domain of indigenous history, survival and commitment to future generations. (Mead 1996, 49)

The only response made to this is that no one will force any population to participate. If a particular group's understanding of the natural world conflicts with that embraced by the HGDP, it can refuse to give consent. Presumably, if it does consent then the Project is not responsible for any unfortunate impacts on that group's belief system. This myopic view of moral responsibility ignores how unequal relations of power compromise the (Western) practice of informed consent and further scientific aspirations at the expense of indigenous peoples: given the isolation of many of the populations involved, their nonliteracy and lack of acquaintance with a cosmology grounded in molecular biology, obtaining informed consent will be a contrived exercise, which, aside from human rights issues, may have some unforeseen results (Lock 1994, 605).

It may also have undesirable but foreseen results that organizers, in response to indigenist concerns about biopiracy (commercial exploitation of genetic materials), attempt to address. Intellectual property rights, one notes, have provoked some "misunderstanding": the Project was viewed as similar to plant prospecting trips, which had enriched the genetic stock available to Western seed or pharmaceutical companies, and ultimately their profits, without providing any benefit to the people who had nurtured and domesticated those plants (Greely 1993).

It is precisely this connection that indigenists emphasize. The HGDP is seen as lying within a continuum of previous and ongoing practices of cultural imperialism, in which the resources (spiritual, material, genetic) of indigenous peoples have been seized and commercially exploited. Organizers insist the HGDP is not a commercial enterprise, that it seeks knowledge rather than profit (although it has not agreed to refuse corporate funding). However, some admit the possibility of commercialization and regard their current position on patenting as "part of the answer (to 'biocolonization'), not part of the problem" (Greely 1996, 87). They propose that patenting be allowed only with prior informed consent. There are various problems with this.

1. The very concept of patenting genes clashes fundamentally with indigenous knowledge and value systems, as we have already seen in the case of the Maori.

2. The proposal still forces an intellectual property regime on indigenous peoples. Intellectual property rights are a Western legal concept developed to facilitate private ownership of intangible resources and to protect individual technological and industrial inventions. Indigenists argue that they are inappropriate instruments to impose on indigenous peoples' communitarian cultural and legal systems.

3. This proposal will not prevent biopiracy. Genome scientists have declared the patent system the "'mechanism of excellence' for commercializing the results of the Human Genome Project" (Butler 1995, 376). Given current biopatent trends, and the potential for corporate biotechnology funding, patenting will likely occur. Researchers associated with the HGDP may agree not to patent indigenous genetic material, but others are not similarly bound.

4. There are serious problems with prior informed consent documents. One is a lesson from history and treaty-making that suggests that legitimate, all-encompassing informed consent documents would not serve to protect indigenous peoples: "This was exactly what did not happen in many First Nations/Wasichu treaty relationships, ultimately resulting in the theft of inherent rights . . . because it was beyond comprehension what might be important in the future" (Dill 1995).

The proposal also imposes a Western model of individualized consent on indigenous peoples. How exactly does one secure the informed prior consent of entire indigenous populations, or of the communities that make them up? Who will determine whether, and on what basis, a certain number of individuals must consent, or only a single "leader"? Who within a given community is authorized to give consent for research that implicates everyone? Is it a tribal governing committee—with no mandate for ethical decisions? Or a spiritual leader? For Native North American peoples, it has been proposed that "an officially recognized tribal government" (FAQ) be the decision-making body. Anyone familiar with current controversies in Indian Country, and the struggle between progressives and traditionals over issues such as gambling casinos and nuclear waste repositories, will recognize in this a horribly divisive scenario. As Mead (1995) states: "the HGDP and other similar-type activities can serve to divide, and cause irreparable damage, to the ability of indigenous communities to trust each other, let alone to trust others."

The divisiveness will only be compounded if government officials of the nation-state in which the indigenous nation is located are given a role in deciding who has the authority to give "consent," to speak for the people. Given the historical relationships between many nation-states and indigenous peoples (say, Iraq and the Kurds, or Guatemala and the Mayans) this could be disastrous; this difficulty is only exacerbated by the Project's regional organization.

5. Communication difficulties will undercut the basis for informed consent. There is a massive tangle of Western institutions, beliefs, and values built into human genetic research—specific collection practices, libraries of cell collections, instruments such as Materials Transfer and Database Access Agreements, intellectual property law, royalties, etc. How will the Project be explained? Anthropologists are touted as essential, but their own interests may figure in important ways. Will their research grants and careers be tied to success in sampling? How extensive and explicit will the information conveyed be? Finally, what of previous and current sampling? In some cases there has been no informed consent at all, much less that obtained in the manner outlined in the proposal. Will the Project allow access to this data?

"Every Question That Is Political Is Also Moral"

Indigenist science critics are contesting the legacy of value-neutrality and value-bifurcation: the deflection of normative criticism away from the production of scientific knowledge; its restriction to dilemmas of knowledge application; and the attendant displacement of reflection on how relations of power factor practically and morally into both. They do so in order to reveal and resist the implications of such practices for indigenous peoples, cultures, and resources. They openly, repeatedly undermine the effort of HGDP proponents to abstract, isolate, and immunize the Project from history. In its early incarnation, "the Project labels threatened peoples 'Isolates of Historical Interest' or 'IHIs' . . . not peoples who have been abused and violated to the point of extinction; not peoples who are in desperate need of respect and support to survive in their integrity; but 'Isolates of Historical Interest'" (Dodson 1993).

In its most recent incarnation, the Project adopts a rhetoric of justification that attempts to obscure even the fact that those who will be sampled are predominantly indigenous. Ethics becomes a supplementary, or compensatory, activity, tacked on to the uses of science and focused exclusively on developing measures to mitigate undesirable effects.

Indigenist critiques of the Diversity Project not only reveal the conjoined operation of value-neutrality and value-bifurcation in contemporary biotechnoscience, they directly challenge it. Politics (the "social and collective") does not begin where ethics ("the behavior of individuals") ends. Ethics never finds its "limits." According to Joabquisho (1996): "Every question that is political is also moral. Every question. And you have to answer it morally." And issues of power in ethics, particularly in the ethics of science, are rarely if ever absent. They continue to be played out vividly and resolutely in the ongoing struggle over the Human Genome Diversity Project.

Note
1. "Native-L" is a listserve newslist dealing with indigenous issues. The listserve coordinator is Gary S. Trujillo. His e-mail address is: gst@gnosys.svle.ma.us.

Acknowledgment
I am grateful to the Humanities Research Centre of the Australian National University for the support provided by a Visiting Fellowship that assisted in the completion of this essay.

References
Armstrong, Jeannette. 1995. "Global Trade Targets Indigenous Gene Lines." *National Catholic Reporter*, 27 January: 11–12.

Beckwith, Jon. 1993. "A Historical View of Social Responsibility in Genetics." *BioScience*, 43(5): 327–33.

Berlan, Jean-Pierre. 1989. "The Commodification of Life." *Monthly Review*, December: 24–30.

Burrows, Beth. 1994. "Life, Liberty and the Pursuit of Patents." *The Boycott Quarterly*, 2(1): 32–35.

Butler, Declan. 1994. "Geneticists Find Consensus on Patents." *Nature* 373, No. 6513: 370.

———. 1995. "Genetic Diversity Proposal Fails to Impress International Ethics Panel." *Nature* 377: 373.

Cavalli-Sforza, L. Luca and H. T. Greely. 1995. In a posting to Native-L (16 July). [List serve.] To access, see footnote 1.

———, A. C. Wilson, C. R. Cantor, R. M. Cook-Deegan, and M. C. King. 1991. "Call for A Worldwide Survey of Human Genetic Diversity: A Vanishing Opportunity for the Human Genome Project." *Genomics* 11: 490–91.

Centre for Genome News. 1995. University of Otago, Biochemistry Department, Dunedin, New Zealand, Website.

Dill, Jordan S. 1995. In a posting to Native-L (29 October). [List serve.] To access, see footnote 1.

Dodson, Michael. 1993. "Social Justice for Indigenous Peoples." Available at http://ari-mac6.underdale.unisa.edu.au/ARI/Publications/David-Unaipon-Lecture3/text.html.

FAQ(Answers to Frequently Asked Questions). 1996. Available on the HGDP's website at http://wwwleland.stanford.edu/group/moprrinst/HGDP.html.

Greely, Henry. 1993. In a letter dated 12/16/93, available on RAFI's (Rural Advancement Foundation International) website under "HGDP Visits Guatemala." Address: http://www.rafi.ca

———. 1993. In a letter posted to Native-L (12 October). [List serve.] To access, see footnote 1.

———. 1996. "Mapping the Territory." *Utne Reader* 74: 87–89.

Grosz, E. 1989. *Sexual Subversions*. Sydney, Australia: Allen Unwin.

Gutin, Joan. 1994. "End of the Rainbow." *Discover* 15(11): 70–75.

Harry, Debra. 1994. "The Human Genome Diversity Project." *Abya Yala News* 8(4): 13–15.

Human Genome Diversity Project. 1993. *Summary of Planning Workshop 3(B): Ethical and Human Right Implications*. Bethesda, MD: HGDP Organizing Committee.

Joabquisho (Oren Lyons). 1996. In a letter from the Mohawk Council of Chiefs, posted to Native-L (17 July). [List serve.] To access, see footnote 1.

Kahn, Patricia. 1994. "Genetic Diversity Project Tries Again." *Science* 266, No. 5186: 720–22.

Kloppenburg, Jack. 1990. "No Hunting!" *Z Magazine*, September: 104–8.

Lock, Margaret. 1994. "Interrogating the Human Genome Diversity Project." *Social Science and Medicine*, 39(5): 603–6.

Marks, Jonathan. 1995a. "The Human Genome Diversity Project." *Anthropology Newsletter* April: 72.

———. 1995b. *Human Biodiversity: Genes, Race and History*. New York: Aldinede Gruyter.

McPherson, Elizabeth Clay. 1995. "Ethical Implications of the Human Genome Diversity Project." *Nursing Connections* 8(1): 36–43.

Mead, Aroha Te Pareake. 1995. In a letter to Darryl Macer posted to Native-L (29 July). [List serve.] To access, see footnote 1.

———. 1996. "Genealogy, Sacredness and the Commodities Market." *Cultural Survival Quarterly* 20(2): 46–51.

Mooney, Pat. 1993. In a letter to Henry Greely posted to Native-L (4 November). [List serve.] To access, see footnote 1.

National Research Council. "Study on the Proposed Human Genome Diversity Project: Request for Input and Notice of Public Meetings." 1996. Posted to Native-L on (June 16). [List serve.] To access, see footnote 1.

National Science Foundation. 1996. "Pilot Projects for a Human Genome Diversity Project: Special Competition." File nsf96112. Available from http://www.nsf.gov.

Posey, Darryl A. and Graham Dutfield. 1996. *Beyond Intellectual Property: Toward Traditional Resource Rights for Indigenous Peoples and Local Communities*. Ottawa, Canada: International Development Research Centre.

Proctor, Robert N. 1991. *Value-Free Science?* Cambridge, MA: Harvard University Press.

Roberts, Jenna. 1993. "Global Project Under Way To Sample Genetic Diversity." *Nature* 361: 675

Roberts, Leslie. 1991. "A Genetic Survey of Vanishing Peoples." *Science* 252: 1614–17.

———. 1992a. "How To Sample The World's Genetic Diversity." *Science* 257: 1204–5.

———. 1992b. "Genetic Diversity Project: Anthropologists Climb (Gingerly) On Board." *Science* 258, No. 5086: 1300–1.

Sherwin, Sue. 1992. *No Longer Patient*. Philadelphia: Temple University Press.

Stemerding, Dirk and Jaap Jelsma. 1996. "Compensatory Ethics for the Human Genome Project." *Science as Culture*, 5(24): 335–51.

Tauli-Corpus, Victoria. 1993. "We Are Part of Biodiversity, Respect Our Rights." *Third World Resurgence*, 36: 25–26.

Vicedo, Margo. 1992. "The Human Genome Project: Towards an Analysis of the Empirical, Ethical and Conceptual Issues Involved." *Biology and Philosophy* 7: 255–78.

Whitt, Laurie Anne. 1995. "Cultural Imperialism and the Marketing of Native America." *The American Indian Culture and Research Journal* 19(3): 1–31.

Winner, Langdon. 1991. "The Social and Professional Responsibility of Engineers." In Deborah Johnson, *Ethical Issues in Engineering*. Englewood Cliffs, NJ: Prentice-Hall.

World Media Foundation. 1994. Transcript of "Who Owns Life?: Patenting Human Genes," *Living On Earth*. Broadcast on 13 May 1994.

7

On Being a Responsible Traitor
A Primer

Lisa Heldke

Objectivity of Participants

Participants in inquiry act objectively to the extent they acknowledge, fulfill, and expand their responsibility to and for other participants in inquiry. Those trying to be maximally objective participants in inquiry would recognize themselves as members of an inquiry context, with connections to, and abilities to affect, others in that context (acknowledging responsibility). They would attempt to interact with other participants respectfully, with careful attention to their needs, desires, and interests (fulfilling responsibility). They would seek to make explicit those needs, desires, and concerns that have been implicit, and to make connections with others previously excluded from the inquiry context (expanding responsibility).

Acting objectively (responsibly) requires understanding oneself and one's connections with others, in order to make reasoned and reasonable assessments about how to respond to others' needs, desires, and interests, stated and unstated. In the absence of such understanding, one cannot be genuinely responsible; it is only when I know myself and my students well that I grade their papers responsibly. To claim it is necessary to know oneself and one's students well directly challenges the view of objectivity as disinterestedness or dispassionateness. On that view, I grade objectively only if I disregard anything I know about my students, when reading their papers.

Objectivity, so defined, has a certain quietistic sound to it; being objective may seem a lot like "being a good citizen." To reveal some of the ways this definition challenges participants in inquiry, I consider the relation between one's capacities as a participant in inquiry, and one's opportunities to be responsible.

Capacities and Responsibilities

Participants promote objectivity in ways that vary according to their capacities, the roles they play in inquiry, and the powers they have by virtue of their roles or institutional privileges. Certainly roles in inquiry are not fixed, nor does the possession of certain skills always give their possessor an advantage in inquiry. Rather, the paths open to one to be responsible will vary according to institutional and other forms of power one has in an inquiry context, the way one's role in inquiry is structured, and the institutional, personal, and other resources at one's disposal.

Someone on the receiving end of a development in medical technology will have different opportunities for increasing the responsibility of the context in which it was created than will someone doing the basic research leading to that technology. This claim is vividly manifested in the United States, where researchers hold considerable power to define research agendas and to determine how results will be disseminated, but where "consumers" of medical technology may not receive all the information they need in order to make an informed choice about whether to use a technology.

Children are able to be responsible in ways that are very different from, and generally more limited than, those open to adults. This is no doubt partly due to capacities not yet fully developed—and partly due to the paternalism of the larger society, which regards children as less than fully human in many ways. If participants are nonhumans, their ability to be responsible is even more curtailed than it is for children (for reasons both justified and unjustified by their capacities); presumably responsibility requires at least some level of self-consciousness.

To say that different participants have different opportunities to be responsible does not mean one person automatically will have "more responsibility" because she has "more power" in a given context. Clearly the institutional power invested in a research scientist is considerable, especially compared to the power of members of a citizen interest group. But nothing necessarily follows from this, about the capacity for either individual to increase the objectivity of the inquiry context. However, it might be fair to say that individuals are objective to the degree that they wield their power to increase responsibility; one cannot be expected to be more responsible than one has power to be.

On one level this statement may seem obvious—if I have no power in a given situation, I can do little to change it. On another level, it suggests an invidious hierarchy, in which powerful creators of scientific knowledge sit above less powerful recipients of it. The result is a sort of "white scientist's burden," whereby, if you have a lot of power, you can do a lot to make an inquiry context more objective, and if you don't, you can't. I may appear to be suggesting that persons of privilege, because of their special abilities, have a particularly heavy burden of responsibility to those "less fortunate" than themselves. But the relation between power and responsibility is more complicated than this. I note two complicating factors.

First, creatively and collectively wielding limited power often has effects out of proportion to the apparent insignificance of that power. Citizen action groups, and groups organized around particular medical concerns (e.g., breast cancer survivors, persons with AIDS, welfare recipients) can and sometimes do increase the accountability of researchers to a degree far greater than it "should" be, given the limitations of their budget, their access to powerful people and institutions, etc. Boycotts often raise public awareness of an issue and force companies to change their practices, without incurring significant damage to a company's financial situation.

Second, and more importantly, there is no necessary connection between possessing institutional power and overprivilege and being able to be responsible. Possessing institutional overprivilege because of one's place in hierarchical social structures does not necessarily translate into a greater sensitivity to the needs and desires of others. As I suggested earlier, such overprivilege can systematically limit one's ability to be responsible, by giving one a stake in preserving the status quo.

Following feminist standpoint epistemology, I suggest that overprivilege tends to limit one's ability objectively to understand the world. Rather than having a large and onerous responsibility because we have greater ability to understand things (the "white scientist's burden"), unreflectively overprivileged persons have the responsibility that comes to those possessing the dangerous combination of overprivilege and systematic ignorance—ignorance about the way that power shapes their understandings of the world. Such a position does not lead to those with the most power and privilege having the greatest responsibility to "take charge" of effecting change: it is rarely wise for people who are deeply ignorant about, e.g., sexism to be given (or to take) the most responsibility for overcoming sexism.

This understanding of the relation between overprivilege and responsibility lies behind the remainder of the paper. I ask, "how can one act as an objective participant in inquiry when one is systematically overprivileged by one's race, class, gender, physical ability, or other oppressive structure, and thus is inclined to favor conceptions of the world preserving that unjust privilege?" How does one challenge the overprivilege-ignorance combination that fosters irresponsibility? In particular, how do I develop an understanding of myself and my connections to relevant others that will enable me to acknowledge, fulfill, and expand my responsibilities to them? And how can my understanding change the ways I inhabit and live out the unjust privileges I receive?

Traitorous Identities

My questions above rest on the view that there always exist connections between individuals' identities and the knowledge they produce. Not all connections are obstacles, however; sometimes one's identity affords a particularly useful place from which to detect the inaccuracy of a particular way of understanding the world. It follows that reshaping one's identity in particular ways could increase one's ability to be responsible/objective participants in inquiry. (My project thus might be said to be an Aristotelian one, concerned with the character of agents.) How does a participant promote responsibility, and thereby objectivity, in inquiry? One answer is, "cultivate a certain kind of identity."

Overprivileged participants need to develop identities critical of and resistant to their privilege. Such identities would be rooted in challenges to unjust privileges, and to the ways those privileges shape their understanding of the world. Persons who develop such identities do not stop being, e.g., white men—they become white men who resist the privileges and obstacles this location affords them. They are actively becoming more objective; they are cultivating identities rooted in understandings of themselves and their relations to others that increase their ability to be responsible participants in inquiry.

Sandra Harding

In her 1991 book *Whose Science? Whose Knowledge?* Sandra Harding argues that individuals ought to develop identities that betray and resist the systems of domination that overprivilege them. Such "traitorous identities" enable occupants to develop more reliable theories about the world than those available to occupants of an identity rooted in overprivilege. In a related vein, I suggest that traitorousness is one useful means by which systematically overprivileged persons can become more responsible participants in inquiry—more objective.

Harding's argument rests on an intriguing rethinking of standpoint theory. Standpoint theorists argue that "it is an advantage to base thought in the everyday lives of people in oppressed and excluded groups" (271). Understandings of the world that emerge from the standpoints of oppressed peoples are more reliable, not only for explaining the experiences of marginalized people, but for explaining the world as experienced by privileged persons as well. It is a tenet of much standpoint theory that critically reflective understandings of the world developed by persons occupying marginalized positions in society are more reliable—true, objective—than those developed by persons of privilege.

"But," Harding asks, "is it only the lives of the oppressed that can generate knowledge, especially liberatory knowledge?" (271). Traditional standpoint theorists have often suggested that it is; wealthy people cannot develop reliable understandings of class, men cannot generate reliable understandings of sexism. Harding argues that, while this claim is compelling, the logic of standpoint analysis allows for reliable, even liberatory knowledge to be generated from other identities (273)—including those of "white antiracists, male feminists, heterosexual antiheterosexists" (271), and other overprivileged persons working against systems that privilege them.

Harding argues for these other liberatory knowledges because she holds that it is not only out of one's own oppression that one can "contribute to criticism and the growth of knowledge . . ." (278). There are connections between one's experience, identity, and knowing, but the connections are not determinative or exhaustive: "It is not necessary to have any particular form of human experience in order to learn how to generate less partial and distorted belief from the perspective of women's lives. It is 'only' necessary to learn how to overcome—to get a critical, objective perspective on—the 'spontaneous consciousness' created by thought that begins in one's dominant social location" (287). Developing the critical aspects of one's identity can enable one to negotiate or mitigate the obstacles to understanding created by one's overprivilege.

How does one form an identity traitorous to privilege? And how does such an identity make one a more responsible participant in inquiry? The two questions are deeply intertwined; answering both requires tackling the overprivilege-ignorance combination characterizing uncritically privileged identities.

Forming Traitorous Identities
Tackling Ignorance

I begin my answer to the first question with the commonplace (though certainly not unquestionable) observation that privileged, nonmarginal participants can and do learn from the understandings of the world developed by marginalized persons. Harding notes that Patricia Hill Collins insists that "people who do not have marginal identities can nevertheless learn from and learn to use the knowledge generated from the perspective of the outsiders within" (277). "Outsider within" is Collins's term for intellectuals from socially marginalized groups whose vantage point enables them to understand "both sides" of the division between, e.g., "black women's work," and "ruling work." Collins and Harding also argue that it is possible for privileged women to learn from these "outsiders within"; their insights are not comprehensible only to others similarly situated.

Indeed, Harding argues that it is not only possible but necessary for her, a European American woman, to learn from the analyses of Third World women and men. Harding's point is similar to one made by bell hooks writing about the importance of "border-crossing" dialogue between Black women and white men:

> If we really want to create a cultural climate where biases can be challenged and changed, all border crossings must be seen as valid and legitimate. This does not mean that they are not subjected to critique ... or that there will not be many occasions when the crossings of the powerful into the terrains of the powerless will not perpetuate existing structures. This risk is ultimately less threatening than a continued attachment to and support of existing systems of domination. (hooks, 1994, 131)

Harding suggests that it is more dangerous not to use analyses developed by Third World peoples than to risk using them in appropriative ways. Perpetuating one's privilege when attempting to learn from others about that privilege is harmful. But to hooks, it is at least better than tacitly supporting existing systems of domination by ignoring the accounts of "others", no matter how noble one's reasons for doing so. I suggest that learning from analyses developed by marginalized people can help overprivileged persons tackle the particular kind of ignorance that prevents them from being more responsible participants; namely, ignorance of the existence, nature, and implications for knowing of one's privilege.

One must do more than read and report on the ideas of others to develop a traitorous identity, however. Becoming a traitor means creatively thinking and acting; moving through understandings developed by thinkers on the margins, not stopping at their assessments, but using them to shift one's understanding of oneself and one's relations. When I develop a critical understanding of my own identity with the aid of analyses from theorists occupying marginalized positions in society, I do not leave other aspects of my identity—white woman with educational and economic overprivilege—in the cloakroom:

> I am to enter this discourse precisely as a European American woman—not as purportedly colorless or as a white racist but as a white woman.... The self understanding I seek is to emerge as a result of my locating myself as a European American person in the analyses originally generated by thinkers of Third World descent and then continuing in the analyses by thinking about my world with the help of the accounts they have provided—yet still out of my own different social location. (Harding, 1991, 283)

Being a traitor does not begin with "refusing to be a man." The expression comes from a book of that title by John Stoltenberg, on refusing to be white. While I can understand reasons for speaking of refusing one's identity, I still wish to emphasize the fact that, in a white racist society, I live in the world as a white woman. Thus, I am more inclined to see the process as one of dismantling an identity I inhabit, in order to rebuild it, rather than attempting to step outside that identity, in order to rebuild it from without, as it were. Traitorousness requires me to insist on my whiteness—to insist that I and others recognize my whiteness as always relevant, always a factor in the way I conceive the world and others; and to work to detect that factor in the places where it is presently most undetectable to me.

Tackling ignorance to generate a traitorous identity requires learning how to stop regarding one's overprivilege as natural and inevitable. Harding gives the example of heterosexuals, who have constructed analyses that begin from theories generated by lesbians reflecting on lesbian lives; she notes that ". . . heterosexuals have learned to 'read against the grain' their otherwise spontaneously heterosexist experience . . ." (288). Refusing to believe and act as if heterosexuality is the default sexuality becomes a part of one's identity, and one thinks, not as a lesbian, but as a heterosexual "who [has] learned from lesbian analyses" (289).

Fiddling with Privilege

Having suggested a strategy for ignorance, I turn now to the problem of privilege. It is tempting to say that unjust privilege can be tackled and diminished, just as ignorance is. To some extent, it can. Harding suggests that when an overprivileged person becomes critically reflective about her privilege, she "becomes marginal." She notes that "Some people whose sexual identity was not marginal" (in the sense that they were heterosexual) have "become marginal"—not by giving up their heterosexuality but by giving up the spontaneous consciousness created by their heterosexual experience in a heterosexist world (288–89).

As I learn more about the way that white racism has constructed the world and my understandings of it, and as that learning comes increasingly to inform the way I live in the world, I become an "unreliable" white person who cannot be trusted by other whites to "act appropriately." In a white racist society, white people who consistently reject explanations of the world presupposing the superiority of whiteness become "deviants" and "traitors." For example, for a white person to refuse to celebrate Thanksgiving or Columbus Day, to refer to Native Nations (as opposed to "reservations"), to valorize the intellectual traditions of Native peoples, and otherwise to decenter European cultures and recenter Native cultures, will, today, often earn one the label of "politically correct." Such a label marks one as a white person who cannot be trusted to do what she is "supposed to" as a white person; she has become disloyal to her race, she has ceased to be "objective" and has taken up a political ax that she has proceeded to grind. Similarly, refusing to adopt the "party line" on heterosexuality makes one a "deviant" in a heterosexist society, even if one lives otherwise as a heterosexual. Living as a traitor does erode the degree to which one will be recognized and treated as a "real" member of an overprivileged group.

But no matter how traitorous or deviant I become, overprivilege will still accrue to me. The deviant heterosexual is still a heterosexual, and the traitorous white person is still white. When I enter an unfamiliar store, I cannot shake off the positive effects of my white skin. I will regularly be given the "benefit of the doubt" because of my skin color. No amount of traitorous behavior will entirely change this.

Heterosexism, racism, and other forms of oppression are not visited upon the traitor or the deviant in the ways they are visited upon lesbians, people of color, or others marginalized by systems of oppression. As Harding puts it, "It is crucial to avoid imagining that men and people of European descent in the dominant groups really do lead marginal lives in the ways that women and people of Third World descent are forced to do" (295).

So, one's unjust privilege and power will not "go away," no matter how hard one works to become a traitor. (Of course ignorance doesn't "go away" either.) But neither can a traitor be trusted to use her privilege in the ways it is "intended." Instead, she "fiddles" with it, uses it in subversive ways and for "illicit" purposes—specifically, for dismantling the system that has given it to her. Privilege, in the hands of the traitor, becomes a tool for democracy. The traitor has an obligation (to the cause of traitorousness) to become creative in using her overprivilege to promote responsibility.

By tackling ignorance and fiddling with privilege, traitorousness provides one way for the overprivileged inquirer to address the particular obstacles to understanding that exist when one is uncritical and unreflective about the significance of one's overprivilege. Traitorous identities disrupt assumptions on which overprivilege rests, unsettle easy acceptance of the benefits of overprivilege, and spur one to investigate and challenge the ways one's understandings of the world have been shaped by unreflective privilege. In short, such identities are traitorous because they are unfaithful to and disruptive of the systems of privilege from which their holders benefit. They provide a launching pad from which to challenge the veracity of ideas about the world developed by occupants of unreflective standpoints. Traitorous identities enable us to get specific about the Emperor's nakedness.

The second question I asked above remains: How does a traitorous identity promote objectivity-as-responsibility? In the last section of the paper, I address this issue.

The Responsible Traitor

It may seem paradoxical to describe a traitorous identity as responsible. However, being "untrue" to one's unjust privilege, and to systems that bestow it, helps the traitor work at being maximally responsible. Maximizing one's responsibility not only is compatible with unfaithfulness to unjust systems of privilege; it may require such unfaithfulness.

Recall that the definition of objectivity involved three interrelated tasks; acknowledging, fulfilling, and expanding responsibility. I'll suggest how the traitor might undertake each of these tasks. I'll also show how the traitor can be understood as manifesting both responsibility for, and responsibility to, others. I begin with the latter project.

Responsibility for and Responsibility to

Harding considers white feminist writers Minnie Bruce Pratt and Adrienne Rich, who reread texts of white authors with a consciousness informed/re-formed by Black theorists' understandings, in an effort to unearth the racial assumptions written into those texts (Rich, 1979; Pratt, 1988.) Such work is traitorous to the unreflective consciousness of whites. It is also deeply responsible: the contributions of Pratt and Rich "are distinctive exactly because of the ways they have found to activate their full identities and social situations as whites and to let us see how they are taking responsibility for their identity as whites . . ." (Harding, 1991, 289–90).

Responsibility has two aspects. The first is responsibility *for*, which might also be termed "accountability." "Responsibility is responsibility for some action or judgment" (Heldke and Kellert, 1995, 8), or, as in the case discussed by Harding, responsibility for some way of being in the world. We argue that participants in inquiry "engage in actions which may fairly be imputed to them and may not be excused as involuntary. Others are right to apply evaluative categories to [them] . . . because their actions have real consequences—consequences which [they] must acknowledge and address" (8). Being a traitor involves taking responsibility *for* one's social location, and for the way that understanding flows from that location. As I have emphasized throughout this discussion, it is impossible to cease to occupy various parts of their identity. Instead, the overprivileged participant in inquiry must be *accountable* for the ways they use that identity.

The other aspect of responsibility is responsibility *to* someone or something. This second aspect of responsibility is distinct from the first in that it emphasizes the other-directedness of responsibility. "To be responsible, in our sense, involves responding—to a demand, a request, or a criticism, stated or implied" (6). This sense "draws attention to the fact that inquirers respond to those in the wider community who . . . stand to be implicated in [the results of inquiry] or affected by its application" (7). Traitorousness, to oversimplify, is responsibility to marginalized people and to the understandings developed beginning from their lives. But in being responsible to those understandings, is the traitor not betraying those developed by uncritically overprivileged persons? She is. How does she justify that betrayal? By virtue of the fact that being responsible to such understandings will never allow her to maximize her responsibility—and thereby her objectivity. Understandings developed from positions of privilege require their holders to ignore or conceal too much about how the world is understood from other standpoints; in being responsible to such a position, one must be irresponsible to too many others.

Acknowledging, Fulfilling, and Expanding Responsibility

A "minimum" requirement for the responsible participants in inquiry is that they acknowledge their responsibilities to and for themselves and others. The traitor fulfills this requirement when she recognizes that her position and understanding of the world have consequences for others, consequences both good and bad, justified and unjustified. As a traitor, I must first acknowledge that my understandings are connected to the experiences and understandings of others. In particular, as an unjustly privileged participant I must recognize the deleterious effects on others of the irresponsible descriptions of the world I develop when I occupy my privileged position uncritically.

This acknowledgment of responsibility may already count as an expansion in many inquiry contexts. The traitor acknowledges a responsibility to persons and things who seem radically outside the relevant context; part of what it means to be a traitor is to take into account the insights of persons defined as "marginal." A traitor who would be an objective participant in an inquiry project in women's biology (for example) might realize that she must attend to theories of racism developed by Black women sociologists reflecting on the experiences of poor urban Black women working as domestics. While poor Black women's experiences of racism in the homes of white women might seem irrelevant to the topic of "women's biology," they might be vital to an understanding of one's own racism, and an analysis of the way that racism shapes one's theorizing as a biologist. The traitor must become knowledgeable about her own social location: this demand requires her to acknowledge the relevance of theories and ideas from all sorts of "irrelevant" locations.

Objectivity also requires *fulfilling* responsibilities identified—or accounting for decisions not to do so. The traitor might be said to fulfill their responsibilities in part when they begin to develop their own theories, employing the theories developed by persons on the margins. In taking up and employing these theories, the traitor is working to create new theories that speak to experiences traditionally excluded. More than simply recognizing the significance of these "theories from the margins," fulfilling responsibility means operationalizing them.

Can anything be called "expanding responsibility," if even the task of acknowledging requires one to acknowledge responsibility to all sorts of persons and things "normally" considered outside the relevant inquiry context? I believe so. Expanding responsibility involves recognizing that overprivilege takes everlastingly new forms, requiring traitors constantly to reinvent themselves. In particular, traitors must recognize that they cannot "eradicate" their ignorance of their social location, because as the nature and structure of systems of privilege change, so too does that location. Tackling one's ignorance is thus an incompletable project; expanding responsibility means ferreting out ever-new ways one is ignorant.

Similarly, traitors must note the new forms their privilege takes, and the ways their attempts to subvert their privilege are themselves subverted. Any particular strategy for "fiddling" has a limited lifespan; as systems of privilege are transformed, strategies for using privilege to undermine itself become ineffectual. While they are not precisely examples of refusing an identity, consider the fate that has met the expressions "breaking silence" and "coming out," which originated with survivors of sexual assault and gay/lesbian/bi/trans persons, respectively. Such language has been coopted by all sorts of people, such that it is now possible for one to "come out" as someone who doesn't like chocolate, or to "break silence" as a perpetrator of sexual harassment (O'Connor, forthcoming). Expanding responsibility involves constantly replenishing one's repertoire of strategies for using privilege as a traitorous tool to democratize the inquiry context. It also demands working always in community with others engaged in similar projects. Such others can provide perspective on one's "horizons of ignorance" (Ferguson, 1996) and on strategies that have ceased to be effective, and can also offer much-needed support for and affirmation of the work one is trying to do—work that is often unpopular, scary, and lonely.

Becoming objective is an open-ended project, incompletable in principle. Traitors expand responsibility as they flush out new "pockets of incompleteness," and discard strategies and understandings that have lost their effectiveness.

Conclusion

I suggested that defining objectivity as responsibility acknowledges that objectivity is moral. In this paper, I explored one sense in which this is so. Implicit in my proposal for the overprivileged participant who would be objective is an ethical claim; namely, becoming more objective involves becoming a particular kind of person, working for particular social ends. Working for social justice is central to being a responsible—and objective—participant in inquiry. Developing an identity critical of and resistant to systems of oppression is crucial to being maximally objective.

Acknowledgments

Thanks to Ami Bar-On and Ann Ferguson for their helpful comments on earlier drafts of this paper. Thanks to Terry Kent and the members of the University of Indianapolis Institute on Ethics and the Educated Person, to whom I presented this work, for a very lively and helpful discussion about it. And finally, thanks to Alison Bailey and Peg O'Connor for numerous helpful discussions about the issues I discuss here.

References

Collins, Patricia Hill. 1986. "Learning from the Outsider Within: The Sociological Signifi-cance of Black Feminist Thought." In *(En)Gendering Knowledge: Feminists in Acad-eme*, ed. Joan E. Hartman and Ellen Messer-Davidow. Knoxville: The University of Tennessee Press.

———. 1990. *Black Feminist Thought: Knowledge, Consciousness and the Politics of Empowerment*. Boston: Unwyn Hyman.

Ferguson, Ann. 1996. Correspondence with the author. October 20, 1996.

Freire, Paolo. 1989. *Pedagogy of the Oppressed*. New York: Continuum.

Harding, Sandra. 1991. *Whose Science? Whose Knowledge?* Ithaca, NY: Cornell University Press.

Hartsock, Nancy. 1983. "The Feminist Standpoint: Developing the Ground for a Specifically Feminist Historical Materialism." In *Discovering Reality*, ed. Sandra Harding and Merril Hintikka. Dordrecht: Reidel.

Heldke, Lisa and Stephen Kellert. 1995. "Objectivity as Responsibility." *Metaphilosophy* 26(4): 360–78.

hooks, bell. 1994. *Teaching to Transgress: Education as the Practice of Freedom*. New York: Rout-ledge.

Lugones, Maria and Elizabeth V. Spelman. 1983. "Have We Got a Theory for You! Feminist Theory, Cultural Imperialism, and the Demand for 'The Woman's Voice.'" *Women's Studies International Forum* 6(6): 573–81.

McIntosh, Peggy. 1992. "White Privilege and Male Privilege." In *Race, Class and Gender*, ed. Margaret Anderson and Patricia Hill Collins. Belmont, CA: Wadsworth.

O'Connor, Peg. "Moving to New Boroughs: Transforming the World by Inventing Lan-guage Games." Forthcoming in *Feminist Interpretations of Wittgenstein*, ed. Naomi Scheman. State College, PA: Penn State Press.

Pratt, Minnie Bruce. 1988. "Identity: Skin Blood Heart." In *Yours in Struggle*, ed. Elly Bulkin, Minnie Bruce Pratt, and Barbara Smith. Ithaca, NY: Firebrand Books.

Rich, Adrienne. 1979. "Disloyal to Civilization: Feminism, Racism, Gynephobia." In *On Lies, Secrets and Silence*. New York: Norton.

Spelman, Elizabeth V. 1988. *Inessential Woman: Problems of Exclusion in Feminist Thought*. Boston: Beacon Press.

Stoltenberg, John. 1989. *Refusing to Be a Man: Essays on Sex and Justice*. Portland, OR: Breit-enbush.

8

Listening to Women's Voices

Rape, Epistemic Privilege, and Objectivity

Victoria Davion

This is an examination of feminist standpoint epistemology and questions of objectivity in relation to sociological studies regarding rape. More specifically, I shall examine two of Christina Hoff Sommers's objections to the Koss study (1988), the source of the well-known statistic that one in four women is the victim of rape or attempted rape in contemporary American society, which raises crucial issues concerning epistemology. Sommers argues that the one-in-four statistic is inflated because Koss counts some women who answered "No" to the question, "Have you ever been raped?" as survivors. Thus, she accuses Koss of failing to listen to women's voices. Sommers finds this ironic, because listening to women's voices is something feminist theorists say that they advocate. She also objects to the Koss study because she regards it as "advocacy research," aimed at furthering a certain political agenda rather than generating objective truth.

I shall argue that Sommers employs a naive meaning of "listening to women's voices," one that implies a problematic version of standpoint epistemology. I shall then discuss an alternative and more sophisticated account of standpoint epistemology and argue that on this version, the Koss study does listen to women's voices, and in doing so can be a source for continued important feminist research on rape. In addition, I shall address questions about the meaning and value of objectivity raised by Sommers's charge of "advocacy research." I shall conclude by using the arguments advanced in this paper to say something about the relationship between feminist ethics and epistemology, more generally. I begin with some background on the Koss study.

The Koss Study

In 1985 *MS* magazine hired Mary Koss, a professor of psychology at Kent State University, to conduct a survey on rape and sexual violation. Koss interviewed slightly more than three thousand college-age women, asking each ten questions about sexual violation (1988, 8). Anyone answering yes to the following three questions was counted as having been raped.

> 1. Have you had sexual intercourse when you didn't want to because a man gave you alcohol or drugs?
> 2. Have you had sexual intercourse when you didn't want to because a man threatened or used some degree of physical force (twisting your arm, holding you down, etc.) to make you?
> 3. Have you had sexual acts (anal or oral intercourse or penetration by objects other than the penis) when you didn't want to because a man threatened or used some degree of physical force (twisting your arm, holding you down, etc.) to make you?

According to Koss: 15 percent had been raped and 12.1 percent were victims of attempted rape. Thus, the study showed that 27.5 percent of the women surveyed were victims of rape or attempted rape (1988, 10), which translates roughly into the well-known one-in-four statistic so frequently cited. In addition, Koss asked the following question:

> Have you given in to sex when you didn't want to because you were overwhelmed by a man's continual arguments and pressure?

The 53.7 percent who responded affirmatively were counted as having been sexually victimized (1988, 10).

Sommers's Charge

Sommers is concerned because the majority of women classified as having been raped did not classify themselves as having been raped. To clarify, Koss counted anyone answering yes to the technical questions about being forced to have sex against one's will as having been raped. Yet, the majority of these women answered the specific question, "Have you ever been raped?" negatively. More specifically, 27 percent of the women Koss counted as having been raped labeled themselves as rape victims (1988, 16); 49 percent said it was miscommunication; 14 percent said it was a crime but not rape; and 11 percent indicated that they did not feel victimized (Koss, Dinero, and Seibel 1988, 12). Sommers argues that this fact, in combination with the fact that 42 percent of rape victims and 35 percent of victims of attempted rape went on to have sex with their attackers on later occasions (Koss 1988, 16), is evidence that the majority of women Koss counts as victims of rape and attempted rape were not actually victims at all.

The facts presented above are the grounds for Sommers's accusation that Koss fails to listen to women's voices:

> [A]s we have seen, believing what women actually say is precisely *not* the methodology by which some feminist advocates get their incendiary statistics. (223)

Sommers maintains that Koss presents an insulting and distorted picture of these women:

> In effect, Koss and her followers present us with a picture of confused young women overwhelmed by threatening males who force their attentions on them during the course of a date but are unable or unwilling to classify their experience as rape. Does this picture fit the average female undergraduate? For that matter does it plausibly apply to the larger community? (213)

Sommers also quotes Katie Roiphe in support of her position:

> Koss had no right to reject the judgment of the college women who didn't think they were raped. (214)

Thus, the charge of failing to listen to women's voices is clear. Katha Pollitt defended Koss, pointing out that the fact that someone might not be aware that they were the victim of a crime does not mean that they were not a crime victim. It simply indicates that they are ignorant of the law (Pollitt 1993). Sommers disagrees, maintaining that this analogy is faulty. She states:

> If Jane has ugly financial dealings with Tom and an expert explains to Jane that Tom defrauded her, then Jane usually thanks the expert for having

enlightened her about the legal facts. To make her case, Pollitt would have to show that the rape victims who were unaware that they were raped would accept Koss's judgment that they really were. But that has not been shown: Koss did not enlighten the women she counts as rape victims, and they did not say "now that you explain it, we can see we were." (214)

Hence, Sommers argues that a necessary condition for a person to be raped is that they recognize themselves as having been raped. I shall return to this point later.

Advocacy Research

In addition to failing to listen to women's voices, Sommers accuses Koss of engaging in advocacy research aimed at promoting a particular political agenda.

> The findings being cited in support of an "epidemic" of campus rapes are the products of advocacy research. . . . We need the truth for policy to be fair and effective. If the feminist advocates would stop muddying the waters we could probably get at it. (222)

And:

> High rape numbers serve gender feminists by promoting the belief that American Culture is sexist and misogynist. (222)

Thus, Sommers claims that advocacy research, designed to find many rapes, is problematic. Sommers maintains that she, and the equity feminists with whom Sommers identifies, "want social scientists to tell them the objective truth about the prevalence of rape" (225). However, advocacy research is getting in the way.

Is All Research Advocacy Research?

Sommers discusses two sources that she apparently believes are more "objective" on the subject of rape. These are Professor Neil Gilbert, of Berkeley's school of social welfare, and Nara Schoenberg and Sam Roe, reporters for *The Blade*, a small Ohio newspaper. Both sources thought that the statistics reported in the Koss study were unbelievably high, and because of this belief, they investigated the studies (Gilbert 1993; Schoenberg and Roe 1993).

Statistics aside, there is a conceptual problem here. Sommers accuses Koss and others of promoting advocacy research because they expected to find high numbers of rapes, which could be used to argue that American culture is misogynist. Yet, Sommers has no trouble accepting Gilbert and Roe and Shoenberg as taking a more "objective" standpoint. But, if expecting a certain outcome is a general objection against research agendas, it must apply equally to Gilbert and Roe and Shoenberg. They expected to find certain results, namely, that the Koss numbers were too high. The point is that all researchers enter into research projects with certain hypotheses that they expect to prove or refute. Hypotheses are necessary for the generation of any research program. Hence, Sommers cannot have it both ways. She must either be unconcerned that Koss may have expected to find high incidence of rape, or discount the people whose positions she uses to cast doubt on those studies, because they approached the issue with preconceived notions about rape as well. This discussion raises important questions about objectivity that I shall return to in later sections.

Standpoint Epistemology and Epistemic Privilege

In charging Koss with failing to listen to women's voices, Sommers assumes that the message of those voices is clear, and that listening to the voices necessarily means accepting what they seem to be saying as true. I shall argue that both of these assumptions are problematic.

Sommers provides no explicit argument that the voices of the women who indicated that they had experiences clearly falling under common definitions of rape, and who answered "no" to the question of whether they had been raped, send a clear message. Such an argument is called for because it appears that these voices are not sending any clear message, but rather, very confused messages. Their answers to the survey questions are contradictory. Sommers ignores the fact that although these women answered "no" to the question of whether they were raped, they also answered "yes" to questions that clearly indicate that they were raped. These contradictory responses call for some interpretation. Sommers charges Koss with presenting a confused picture of these women, and feminists with failing to listen to their voices. Yet Sommers herself only listens to part of the messages sent by those voices. In doing so she fails to acknowledge problems involved in trying to listen to a seemingly incoherent message. Koss does not present us with a confused picture; it is the data that are confusing.

Furthermore, although Sommers calls upon us to "listen to women's voices," her discussion of this is problematic in another way. She certainly does not want us to listen to the women who are claiming high rape statistics.

Mary Koss is a woman. In addition, Sommers appears not to give much credence to the voices of women who try to say no to aggressive men. This is revealed by the following passage from Camille Paglia, on the issue of taking a woman's "no" seriously in sexual encounters, which Sommers quotes with approval:

> No has always been and will always be, part of the dangerous, alluring courtship of sex and seduction, observable even in the animal Kingdom. (218)

I will not go into the well-rehearsed question as to just how a woman is supposed to communicate that she does not want to engage in sex, if yes means yes, and no also means yes. The point here is that there are many different women's voices on the subject of rape. Not all of them are the voices of survivors. Sommers herself chooses to dismiss at least some women's voices.

The fact that some women answered no to the explicit question of whether they were raped may indicate that they do not think that they were. As I stated earlier, Sommers's response to Pollitt suggests that in order to be raped, people would have to recognize that they were raped. On this account, we would have to be able to convince women in the problem category that they were raped before coming to a decision about their status. Thus, Sommers reduces the question of whether these women were in fact raped to the question of whether it would be possible to convince them that they were raped. In doing this, Sommers grants these women the ultimate epistemic privilege of interpreting their experiences.

Sommers does not defend this attribution of epistemic privilege. However, she maintains that feminist calls to listen to women's voices imply such privilege. Therefore, she maintains that feminists are contradicting themselves in counting those answering "no" to the explicit question of whether they were raped as rape survivors, regardless of how they answered questions that clearly imply they were raped. In reducing feminists' calls to listen to women's voices to the idea that these voices have supreme epistemic privilege in interpreting their own experiences, Sommers invokes a naive version of standpoint epistemology, based on identity politics, that most feminist epistemologists reject.

Epistemic Privilege and Identity Politics

In "Marginality and Epistemic Privilege," Bat-Ami Bar On provides an excellent feminist analysis of the problems in granting epistemic privilege based on identity politics (1993). She argues that given the existence of many marginalized groups, and given that the sources of power are multiple, isolating an appropriate group is impossible, while granting epistemic privilege to all marginalized groups makes such privilege meaningless.

According to Bar On, feminist claims to epistemic privilege have been conceptualized in two ways, both relying on the idea that epistemic privilege is generated in terms of distance from a center of power. The first involves an analogy with physical distance. She offers the following quote from Sarah Hoagland as an example:

> In the conceptual scheme of phallocracies . . . there is no such thing as a lesbian. This puts a lesbian in the interesting and peculiar position of being something that does not exist, and this position is a singular vantage point with respect to the reality which does not include her. (89)

On this scheme, heterosexual reality is theorized as the center, lesbian reality is seen as a separate space away from the center. Thus, lesbians are said to occupy a liberated space at the margins. Here epistemic privilege is theorized as analogous to physical distance from the center.

An alternative account of epistemic privilege sees it as a result of multiple oppressions. The most oppressed has the greatest privilege. Bar On offers the following quote from Barbara Smith as an example:

> Third world women are forming the leadership in the feminist movement because we are not one dimensional, one-issued in our political understanding. Just by virtue of our identities we certainly define race and usually define class as being fundamental issues that we have to address. The more wide-ranged your politics, the more potentially profound and transformative they are. (90)

Here distance is theorized as a function of multiple oppressions rather than physical distance.

Key differences of these accounts, according to Bar On, are that:

> According to one, which is a conception grounded in a single oppression and the identity and practices of those defined by it, epistemically privileged, socially marginalized subjects are horizontally distanced from the center and placed in a "liberated" space. The other, grounded in multiple oppressions and the identity and practices of those identified by them, locates epistemic privileged, socially marginalized subjects at a point distant

from the center and intersected by many axes. This too is a sort of a "liberated" space. (90)

Bar On demonstrates how both of these conceptions are problematic. The first problem is that both conceptualize power as coming from a single center. However, the generally accepted notion that oppression is not the result of the bad attitudes of individuals but of institutionally entrenched structures has resulted in a movement away from the conception of power as coming from a single core or center (Young 1990). Once the notion of a single, powerful center is abandoned, theorizing epistemic privilege in terms of distance away from it makes no sense.

Grounding epistemic privilege in the identity and practices of marginalized groups is also problematic. According to Bar On, there have been two kinds of practices that traditionally have been picked out as the source of privilege. These are practices generally associated with the group (nurturing or caring), and practices of resistance. The problem with the first (practices generally associated with the group) is that rather than working from the conception of practices as heterogenous, the project becomes one of including some practices while excluding others, presupposing that some practices more authentically express something important about the oppressed group. This results in the construction of normative ideals based on idealized versions of the practices, rather than using actual practices of people in the group. However, if it is idealized versions of the practices that are thought to generate epistemic privilege, there is no reason to grant such privilege to actual group members, who may not engage in the idealized versions at all.

Recent work attempting to construe women's special agency in terms of caring, especially in the context of mother-child relationships, demonstrates Bar On's point. For example, although Virginia Held has noted that in actuality parents do not always care for their children in the right ways, she still uses an idealized version of maternal care as a model (Held 1987). Sara Ruddick notes that maternal love is said to be gentle and unconditional, when in reality it is inseparable from anger, and fierce. Yet, she appeals to maternal thinking as a source for a gender-based disposition to nonviolence and as a gendered kind of moral agency (Ruddick 1989). Thus, if we use idealized versions of the practices of individuals in oppressed groups, and admit that actual group members do not behave according to the idealized versions of these practices, we lose any basis for attributing epistemic privilege to actual group members.

The other practices that have been picked out as a source for epistemic privilege are practices of resistance. These can be separated into two types.

The first are practices that are somehow considered pure because they either predate oppressive forces, or, although they are generated within oppressive contexts, somehow avoid such forces. The second are practices that respond to oppression demonstrating that marginalized subjects are not powerless. In the first case (predating/avoiding oppressive forces), the problem is that everything is tainted by an oppressive context. It is not plausible that practices predating oppression are not tainted by it, and equally implausible that practices emerging from within oppressive contexts could be completely free from oppressive forces. In the second case (practices responding to oppression), once again they cannot be thought of as completely free from oppressive forces. Also, the division between practices tainted by oppression and those that are not creates the sort of dualism that feminists have tried to deconstruct. Thus, the notion that marginalized subjects should have epistemic privilege because some parts of their experiences are somehow free from the tainted forces of oppression is bankrupt.

Bar On concludes that attributions of epistemic privilege based upon group identity are problematic and should be abandoned. However, she recognizes that appeals to epistemic authority justified by appeals to group-based epistemic privilege have been important in empowering members of oppressed groups. Marginalized subjects would not have this authority if all of them were equally capable of knowing their situation. Thus, appeals to epistemic authority based on group-based epistemic privilege have been an important source for demands that so-called experts should listen to the voices of marginalized subjects.

Bar On suggests that perhaps a better source for grounding the right to speak for oneself about one's experiences can be found in social justice. The claim to a privileged perspective regarding the truth has been used by dominant groups to exclude, to silence, and to command obedience to those with the "privileged perspective," the dominant group. As Bar On points out, one perspective needs to be authorized or privileged in order to command respect only when disrespect is the rule, only when silence rules. She suggests that silence is an oppressive rule that need not be obeyed, not because one has a truer perspective, but because social justice requires that people be allowed to speak for themselves.

Thus far I hope to have shown the following: Sommers's claims that (a) the women in the Koss study should be granted epistemic privilege because they are women, and (b) that feminists as a group have called for granting epistemic privilege to women based upon identity politics, are problematic. Bar On's analysis both demonstrates that feminist theorizing on the issue of epistemic privilege is far more complex than Sommers indicates, and that attributing epistemic privilege to the women in the Koss study is problematic.

In what follows I hope to show that the importance of listening to the voices of marginalized subjects need not be construed in terms of the kind of ultimate epistemic privilege called for by Sommers and critiqued by Bar On. I shall present a more sophisticated notion of what it means to listen to women's voices, and argue that, on this conception of listening, the Koss study is an important research project precisely because it does pay attention to the voices of women. This more sophisticated analysis will show also that the importance of listening to the voices of marginalized subjects is not only a matter of social justice, as Bar On suggests, but also a matter of good science.

Listening to Women: An Alternative Approach

In "Rethinking Standpoint Epistemology" (1993), Sandra Harding presents a notion of listening to women's voices, or the voices of any marginalized subjects, that does not necessarily give those voices ultimate epistemic privilege. Standpoint critiques of conventional theories of knowledge claim that knowledge is always socially situated. The failure of dominant groups to reflect the effect of their advantaged social situations on their beliefs makes their social location a scientifically and epistemologically disadvantaged one for generating knowledge. Thus, unexamined dominant locations are the most limited due to their inability to be self-critical. However,

> the experience and lives of marginalized peoples as they understand them, provide particularly significant problems to be explained or research agendas. These experiences and lives have been devalued or ignored as a source of objectivity—maximizing questions—the answers to which are not necessarily found within the experienced lives but elsewhere in the beliefs and activities of people at the center who make policies and engage in social practices that shape marginal lives. (54)

Hence, the importance of paying attention to the experience of marginalized subjects for all research projects.

It is crucial to note that Harding does not maintain that the answers to the problems are found necessarily in the experiences of marginalized persons. Harding reminds us of the crucial distinction between sociological relativism and what she calls judgmental or epistemological relativism. Sociological relativism acknowledges that people hold different beliefs.

Standpoint epistemologies are committed to taking this fact into account and to examining the beliefs of marginalized subjects. However, judgmental or epistemological relativism would hold that there is no way to evaluate the truth or falsity of these beliefs. Standpoint epistemology is not committed to judgmental relativism.

Standpoint epistemology is not only uncommitted to judgmental relativism, it is also not committed to granting epistemic privilege to marginalized subjects. Harding maintains that standpoint theories are not committed to "identity science" projects that support and are supported by "identity politics."

> Marginalized lives provide the scientific problems and the research agendas—not the solutions—for standpoint theories. (62)

Thus, according to Harding, standpoint theories are not committed to the kind of epistemic privilege Sommers calls for and Bar On critiques. Standpoint theories are not committed to the idea that the oppressed are in the best position to create knowledge out of their own experiences. Listening to the voices of the oppressed means paying attention to them as important in the formulation of research projects and agendas. While it is certainly possible for some marginalized subjects to be in the best position to create knowledge out of their own experiences, this is not a necessary commitment for standpoint epistemologies.

The analysis offered above has important implications concerning both the Koss study and Sommers's objections to it. On Harding's interpretation, the study is important because it begins with the experiences of women; therefore, it listens to women's voices in an important sense. Also, the fact that a significant number of women who had experiences that fit the definition of rape were unwilling to classify those experiences as rape can be used to generate future research agendas that try to explain this. Koss chose to count these women as survivors. I do not think this is an unreasonable interpretation of their experiences. On Harding's analysis, listening to women's voices does not necessarily mean granting women ultimate epistemic privilege, a problematic approach. Even if we wanted to grant women epistemic privilege, their voices are unclear in the Koss survey. Just as Harding suggests, by listening to the confused message, we can generate future important research projects to explain it.

Sommers offers the fact that many women reported later having sex with the men who they said either forced them or attempted to force them into sex, as evidence against counting these women as survivors. However, if rape is extremely prevalent in our society, as prevalent as Koss seems to think it is, another argument can be made. A well-known feminist argument is that we as a society implicitly condone rape and teach both men *and* women that it is part of normal male sexual behavior to try to force women into having sex; even nice men can be expected to attempt this (Stoltenberg 1990; Griffin 1971). If women learn that this is "natural" behavior, normal even for nice men, then they might indeed be willing to give their rapists/attempted rapists another chance. The hypothesis that rape is highly prevalent, and in fact considered somewhat acceptable, can therefore explain these statistics in a plausible way.

The Question of Objectivity

Before closing, I want to return to Sommers's discussion of advocacy research and her charge that feminists prevent people from getting to the "objective truth" about rape. Although Sommers is not explicit about this, she seems to be using a traditional notion of objectivity as politically neutral—in fact, value-neutral altogether. She is upset because she believes that feminists incorporate political projects into research agendas. Thus, the charge that feminists want to find high numbers of rapes to back their political agendas. As I previously argued, if the desire to find certain results is problematic in setting research agendas, the sources that Sommers cites have the same problem. They too expected to find certain results, namely, that the original data were wrong.

If having preconceived ideas about what one will find in research pollutes the research, then, it seems that all research is doomed on the value-neutral standard. In fact, this is the basis for Harding's argument that we not only need to reformulate our notions of the subjects of knowledge as disembodied and apolitical, but that we also need to reformulate the notion of objectivity as value-neutrality.

One might argue that recognizing marginal lives as important starting places for research projects is all that is needed. Doing this will allow us to fulfill the conventional goal of generating value-free objective research. We could transform the notion of scientific method while retaining the conventional goal of value-neutrality in results. However, as Harding points out, the idea that value-neutral results are untainted by the social location of subjects conducting it, is implausible given the recognition that background assumptions are present at all levels of research. This recognition leads to what Harding calls the requirement of strong reflexivity. Strong reflexivity means that subjects of knowledge must be placed on the same critical and causal plane as objects of knowledge:

> Culturewide (or nearly culturewide) beliefs function as evidence at every
> stage in scientific inquiry: in selection of problems, the formation of
> hypothesis, the design of research (including organization of research
> communities), the collection of data, the interpretation and sorting of
> data, discussions about when to stop research, the way results of research
> are reported, and so on. (Harding, 1993, 69)

Thus, strong reflexivity requires critical reflection upon and observation of
both scientists and the larger society whose assumptions the scientists share.
This critical feedback can be offered from the perspectives of those who
have been marginalized by the larger society. Thus, according to Harding,
conventional notions of objectivity are impoverished in their failure to call
for the critical identification of all of these components. This analysis illustrates that Sommers is right to call critical attention to rape researchers
themselves; however, her goal of finding objective research, meaning value-
neutral research, is problematic.

The idea of abandoning the notion of value-neutral objectivity, due to
the impossibility of eliminating all values from the results of research, appears
troubling. If we grant this, are we saying that there is no fact of the matter
about whether these women were raped? It seems that we are left with a
bunch of conflicting opinions and no value-free criteria with which to evaluate them. This would be politically disastrous for issues of social policy.

Harding suggests that we can rescue the notion of objectivity and transform it into what she calls "strong objectivity." This transformed conception
of objectivity retains some important components of the conventional one.
It can still provide a way for distinguishing between accounts of reality by
telling us which ones are less or more distorted or partial. It provides "an
important way to think about the gap that should exist between how any
individual or group wants the world to be and how in fact it is" (72). However, this fully reflexive notion of objectivity will not be value-free, it will
be value-full.

Objectivity, Truth, and Honesty

The editors of this volume suggested the following question in their book
proposal: Should feminist ethics and politics presuppose a feminist epistemology? I think the call for strong reflexivity turns this question around in
an interesting way. In order to be strongly reflexive, one must be open
about the political agendas that are driving one's research agendas. This
means not only trying to get at all of one's assumptions in order to evaluate
them critically, but being willing to be quite honest about where one is

coming from. Coming from somewhere would no longer be considered the sin that it is in the value-neutral approach. However, being strongly reflexive requires that one be honest about one's location, putting it on the table for others to critique and consider. Hence, this value-full approach to objectivity incorporates ethical values into epistemology at a core level. Understanding objectivity in this way would encourage us not to separate value theory from epistemology at all, but to recognize that value theory is represented at every stage in questions concerning science and epistemology, and vice versa. Feminist ethics and feminist epistemology are mutually dependent.

Acknowledgment

Special thanks to Chris Cuomo. Our conversations made this paper possible.

References

Bar On, Bat-Ami. 1993. "Marginality and Epistemic Privilege." In *Feminist Epistemologies,* ed. Linda Alcoff and Elizabeth Potter. London: Routledge.

Gilbert, Neil. 1993. "Examining the Facts: Advocacy Research Overstates the Incidence of Date and Acquaintance Rape." In *Current Controversies in Family Violence,* ed. Richard Gelles and Donileen Loseke. Newbury Park, Calif.: Sage Publications.

Griffin, Susan. 1971. "Rape: The All American Crime." In *Women and Values,* ed. Marilyn Pearsall. Belmont, Calif.: Wadsworth Publishing Co., reprinted from *Ramparts.*

Harding, Sandra. 1993. "Rethinking Standpoint Epistemology: What is Strong Objectivity?" In *Feminist Epistemologies.*

Held, Virginia. 1987. "Feminism and Moral Theory." In *Women and Moral Theory,* ed. Eva Feder Kittay and Diana T. Meyers. Totowa, N.J.: Rowan and Littlefield.

Koss, Mary. 1988. "Hidden Rape: Sexual Aggression and Victimization in a National Sample in Higher Education." In *Rape and Sexual Assault,* vol. 2, ed. Ann Wolbert Burgess. New York: Garland Press.

Paglia, Camille. 1990. "Madonna I: Animality and Artifice." *New York Times,* December 14.

Pollitt, Katha. 1993. "Not Just Bad Sex." *New Yorker,* October 4.

Roiphe, Katie. 1993. *The Morning After: Sex, Fear, and Feminism.* Boston: Little, Brown.

Ruddick, Sara. 1989. *Maternal Thinking: Towards a Politics of Peace.* New York: Ballantine.

Schoenberg, Nara and Sam Roe. 1993. "The Making of an Epidemic." *The Blade,* October 10, p. 4.

Smith, Barbara and Beverly Smith. 1981. "Across the Kitchen Table: A Sister-to-Sister Dialogue." In *This Bridge Called My Back: Writings by Radical Women of Color.* Watertown, Mass.: Persephone.

Sommers, Christina Hoff. 1994. *Who Stole Feminism?* New York: Simon and Schuster.

Stoltenberg, John. 1990. *Refusing to Be a Man.* New York: Meridian.

9

Remembering the Resistant Object
A Critique of Feminist Epistemologies

Renee Heberle

Introduction

Feminist epistemology draws upon women's historical experience to locate sites of knowledge production that will contest the oppressive qualities of traditional Western epistemological models (Hennessy, 1993: 67). It thus encourages us to look in unexpected places and practices in the social world to develop emancipatory knowledge claims (Collins, 1990). Further, feminist epistemology argues that looking to women's experience suggests a reconfigured self/other relation in modernity obscured by the traditional privileging of abstract knowledge of otherness in the approach to truth. For example, the qualities of "women's work," concrete and necessary for the reproduction of life, are said to engage her in a qualitatively different relationship with the object than that made possible by the qualities of "men's work" as it is carried on in the abstracted, public sphere (Hartsock, 1983).

In this essay I argue that feminist epistemology mirrors traditional epistemology in privileging the subject at the expense of recognizing the constitutive, resistant qualities of the object of knowledge. This obscures the political impulses engendered in the always immanent tension between subject and object that resides in any practice of knowledge production, including those of feminism.[1]

The critical theory of Theodor Adorno suggests a way of conceptualizing the subject/object relation that does not subdue or obscure the traces of critique that may exist in the (unpredictable) excess or difference immanent to the object. Adorno speaks to my concerns about how feminist epistemology sustains the controlling or stable subject even as it reconfigures its boundaries vis-à-vis the object in the production of knowledge.

Feminist Standpoint Theory and the Situated Subject

Feminist epistemology furthers the materialist tradition that argues for a sustained sense of self and location as one makes a claim to know the world. In the tradition of Marxian critical theory, and therefore attentive to critiques of objective reality as an ideal form or substance that exists prior to historical construction, feminist epistemologists argue that the *material* situation of the subject is central to her potential to create emancipatory theory. The state or situatedness of the subject in any given theory thus bears upon the relevance of that theory for social transformation (Benhabib, 1992; Hartsock, 1987). Drawing out women's historically constituted experience as authentic subjects in the object world will render the foundations of specifically feminist knowledge.

This overriding concern with women as subjects can be traced to the recognition among feminists that the historical and political position of "woman" in general and of "women" in particular vis-à-vis dominant culture is that of the object—that which is to be changed, but which is to have no effective historical role. The domination of woman or women as objects of male desire/knowledge is said to follow from the dominant epistemological tradition that simultaneously excludes the subject as an effect in knowledge claims while situating the object as that which is natural and therefore reified as unchanging or, alternatively, that which is controlled and manipulated through knowledge. Their enforced status as object leads to extraordinary harms perpetrated against women in the name of stabilizing patriarchal dominance and control.[2] Object status thus becomes the problem and subject status an (at least partial) achievement of political struggle.

Feminist epistemology thus contributes to feminist struggles to bring women onto the historical screen as subjects for ethical and historical reasons. But woman will not just become subject among other historically neutral, abstracted subjects. Feminist epistemologists argue that women's historically constituted differences will cause them to have essentially different relationships as subjects to the object world than those represented by the masculine subject. They offer a powerful rejoinder to Michel Foucault's (in)famous question as borrowed from Samuel Beckett, "What does it matter who is speaking?" For Standpoint feminists, the who is exactly what is important. It is not the transcendent "who" of the idealist tradition, however. It is a historically and materially embedded, potentially collective "who" that is significant for politics (Hartsock, 1983). In fact, it could be said that in more recent articulations of the value of epistemological inquiry, it is the "where" or the material situatedness of the subject, that matters as much as the "who" (Haraway, 1991).

I argue that the attention feminist epistemology pays to the question of the subject and subjectivity in epistemology precludes attention to the resistance of the object, be it motherhood or women's experience more broadly construed, to being known and therefore to representation and control, by patriarchy *and by* feminism. As we struggle to reconfigure a more just, liberatory relationship between subject and object in epistemology, we must *in general* pay more attention to the resistance of the object to the control and manipulation said to be its fate in modern epistemic models. This involves revisiting the possibilities of dialectical theory that I will argue are increasingly obscured in contemporary versions of feminist epistemology. The dialectical theory I revisit is that of Theodor Adorno. Adorno was unremitting in his pessimism about the cognitive subject and the state of the object world in modernity. But he found hope for redemption, for a different future, in the traces of difference present in the resistant objects of knowledge. Further, it becomes the task of the subject, not to establish a more "organic" or continuous connection to the object, as I will argue feminist epistemologists advocate, but to find ways of living at the edges of subjectivity and allowing the always resistant, sometimes antagonistic object of knowledge to emerge in its historical effectivity.

In each of its permutations, feminist epistemology continues the task Lukacs sets out for philosophy, that of "creating the subject of the creator" who will be positioned to overcome relations of domination (Lukacs, 1967). Lukacs theorizes the standpoint of the proletariat as a way of conceptualizing their emergence as historical actors who expose and contest the terms of a reified, commodified world. Feminist standpoint theory adapts his insights about particularly situated actors in history to argue that women's knowledges are potentially revolutionary in relation to patriarchal ideologies and beliefs. Following Lukacs, standpoint feminisms argue the necessary partiality of perspective and knowledge and show us that the powerful, those with a vested interest in the status quo, have reason not to see the boundaries or limits of their own positioning in the world. In fact, "Reason" as a historical construction is deployed precisely to render their knowledge unbounded by historicity or by concrete, material conditions.

Making those boundaries visible from the perspective of the subjugated illuminates the processes by which relations of domination become rationalized in the social world, exposing them to a crisis of legitimacy (Harding, 1993).

Thus, in an article that serves as an influential touchstone in the historical development of standpoint theory, Nancy Hartsock argues that women's life activity in the world offers more complete ways of understanding social power that defy the otherwise fragmented and alienated world of modernity (Hartsock, 1983). Broadening the Marxist understanding of "work" as activity that creates the social product, the feminist standpoint will ground itself in the daily lives of women, their roles as reproducers, and the relationship they develop in their daily lives as material organizers of family and community survival and well-being. These relationships are said to shape, if not determine, the interests of women and therefore the parameters of feminism. Women's particular experiences as gendered subjects are placed in a necessary relationship to what they will know and do as political subjects. The socially determined connection of woman to the body, to necessity, and to the object world grounds her epistemological perspective.

Thus, Hartsock argues that "woman" is in the position of subject-object of history *because of* her naturalized identity in historical relations of reproduction (Hartsock, 1983: 118–122). Woman's proximity to her object of concern is always already closer than man's proximity to his objects of concern.

> Women's construction of self in relation to others leads in an opposite direction [than the Hegelian relation to the other which is defined by a death struggle and competition]—toward opposition to dualism of any sort; valuation of concrete, everyday life; a sense of a variety of connectedness and continuities both with other persons and with the natural world. (Hartsock, 1983: 242)

Hartsock argues the emancipatory subject/object relationship to be "varieties of connectedness and continuities." However, it is unclear whether this image reflects an idealized version of how women *should* be according to patriarchal norms, or how women *are* in the world. Hartsock argues that the gendered division of labor as mapped onto the concrete (the feminine sphere) and the abstract (the masculinist sphere) is a historical construct and therefore variable. It does not necessarily follow from women's capacity to conceive and give birth that they become the primary caregivers. Nonetheless, it is this norm that becomes for Hartsock the ontology of specifically feminist criticism and transformation of the abstracted alienated world:

Finally, the unity of mental and manual labor and the directly sensuous nature of much of women's work leads to a more profound unity of mental and manual labor, social and natural works, than is experienced by the male worker in capitalism. This unity grows from the fact that women's bodies, unlike men's, can be themselves instruments of production: in pregnancy, giving birth, or lactation, arguments about a division of mental from manual labor are fundamentally foreign. (Hartsock, 1983: 243)

Hartsock centers a particular kind of female subject (the Mother) as representative of patriarchal norms and therefore as the representative of the feminist standpoint vis-à-vis patriarchal relations of power and domination. She thereby renders the meaning of other experiences of families marginal to the defining terms of feminist discourse. They may be looked to as models of a better quality of life, outside of or counter to patriarchal norms, but they do not occupy critical positions in and of themselves vis-à-vis patriarchy:

The organization of motherhood as an institution in which a woman is alone with their children, the isolation of women from each other in domestic labor, the female pathology of loss of self in service to others— all mark the transformation of life into death, the distortion of what could have been creative and communal activity into oppressive toil, and the destruction of the possibility of community present in women's relational self-definition. The ruling gender and class's interest in maintaining social relations such as these is evidenced by the fact that when women set up other structures in which the mother is not alone with the children, isolated from others, as is frequently the case in working-class communities or the communities of people of color, these arrangements are described as pathological deviations. (Hartsock, 1983: 245)

Hartsock's own discussion shows that the sacrificial, isolated Mother as the object (goal) of patriarchy is never constituted in its totality.[3] Whether women as mothers actively resist the idealized norms of the isolated sacrificial Mother figure in refusing to mother, in developing networks for sharing responsibilities of childcare, or are subjected to a completely different set of expectations in the material world as are single mothers or women of color, their differences defeat Hartsock's effort to pull them together, through the mirror of a singular oppressive ideal, into the subject of history. Further, their differences may tell something about the instabilities of patriarchy that is obscured by a singular focus on the oppressive ideal of Motherhood. Hartsock ultimately offers up extraordinary powers to the imaginary body of the Enlightenment thinker to prescribe emancipatory knowledge, defeating her own claim to value specificity and particularity as sources of critique.

I see a similar problem in Rosemarie Hennessy's discussion of standpoint theory. Although she offers a creative approach to developing a non-essentialist theory of gender for feminism, she does not adequately respond to the problem that theorizing patriarchy, even as a thoroughly "discursive" regime of power, necessarily abstracts from the particularity of the object. Hennessey argues there is a chain of meaning across experiences that renders the discursive totality of patriarchy coherent. She moves away from Hartsock's premise about mothering as a site of transformative potential. Hennessey argues instead that feminism should be understood as a critical, discursive practice that retains its own specificity only through its concrete task of "disarticulating" the construction of the feminine in patriarchy in all its variable forms. However, in her concurrent attempt to develop the systemic analysis that she argues feminism needs in order to sustain its specificity, she has to resort in the "last instance" to patriarchy as a defining other in order to locate a collective subject.

> [W]hile the ideological boundaries of the feminine are not limited by an essential female body, *the construction of women's reproductive capacity and sexuality as property to which masculine subjects can lay claim has been the cornerstone of a patriarchal social order whose genealogy precedes imperialist conquest and the emergence of sexuality as a discourse.* The particular articulations of this reproductive/alienated female body and the interests they serve are, nonetheless, historically variable. (Hennessey, 1993: 79; emphasis mine)

The historical variability, the resistance of those constituted as the feminine objects of male desire, is not, in the last instance, the politically significant moment for Hennessy. Rather the historical facticity of woman's reproductive capacity as appropriated by the masculine subject is the grounds for understanding feminist potential for a transformative politics. Hennessey thus sustains the habit of locating the emancipatory subject through its defining other rather than recognizing the resistance of women as objects (in this case, of property) as significant.

Hennessey argues that differences in experience and meaning can be shown to operate within a hegemonic discursive regime of the patriarchal ordering of gender identity. But can "differences in experience" be justly represented or recognized within the given horizons she argues are constitutive of patriarchal order? While Hennessey replaces the object or the material world, sustained in Hartsock's theory, with a theory of the discursive creation of meaning and open-ended possibilities for identification (and dis-identification), she relies on an ahistorical account of the condition of woman's reproductive capacity to ground feminist politics. She does not recognize as politically significant the historical practices of resistance by those she subsumes under objectified property relations. Women, in their reproductive capacity and thus in their identities as mothers, have been claimed as property of men. However, as such, women have engaged in complex modes of resistance that defeat any final identification of "woman" with the property form. For example, as mothers, slave women engaged in complex practices that resisted the Master's claim on their reproductive capacities and that remain constitutive of how Black women presently mother (Collins, 1990).[4] Their modes of "mothering" remain important sites of resistance to patriarchal norms and constitutive of an important difference from the identity of white mothers as property.

Donna Haraway comes closer than Hartsock or Hennessy to mapping out the historic uncertainties and instabilities of feminist subjectivity, given the vagaries of the object world. She agrees with the general principles of standpoint theory, but approaches epistemology through the differentiated pathways of what she calls an "informatics of domination." Haraway sets up the terms of a postmodern age in contrast to the terms through which we understood the world as modern or Enlightenment subjects. Through this imaging of the contemporary social world, Haraway displaces the subject/object hierarchies of traditional epistemology. She describes the condition of possibility for a postmodern "cyborg" feminism that we, as ironically modern subjects or "situated knowers," may engage in. She advances the value of these ironically situated knowledges.

Haraway's theory of "situated knowledges" shifts the feminist epistemological focus from the subject to the project of realizing knowledge through embodied objectivity. "We need to learn in our bodies, endowed with primate color and stereoscopic vision, how to attach the objective to our theoretical and political scanners in order to name where we are and are not, in dimensions of mental and physical space we hardly know how to name" (Haraway, 1991: 190). Her metaphor of the connection between the knower and the world is the prosthetic device, the scanner, the eye that does not have a necessary essence guiding its judgment but is certainly invested in the world in particular, identifiable ways. Haraway claims that there does exist something like "the view from below" as a difference that matters in social analysis. She therefore argues for an embodied vision, but a vision that sees its own boundaries and in its reflexive knowledge production sees a value in its partiality rather than a limit or a deficit. With other standpoint theorists she argues that "partial" knowledge is not somehow less real but actually a better representation of how the world works, especially in post-modern historical conditions. For her, partial connections are always more honest than those that assume total knowledge.

Haraway thus categorizes her knowers by arguing that subjugated know-ers are "more likely" to reject identitarian, "God's eye knowledge." She adopts aspects of Hartsock's work to ground this claim. But Haraway ren-ders the claim less foundational as she argues that "[s]ubjugation is not grounds for an ontology; it might be a visual clue. Vision requires instru-ments of vision; an optics is a politics of positioning. Instruments of vision mediate standpoints; there is no immediate vision from the standpoints of the subjugated" (Haraway, 1991: 193). Her work thus has a more speculative, experimental quality to it than that of other standpoint theorists. Her emphasis on the non-innocence of any knower as they engage with the otherness of the world defeats the standpoint feminists' implicit claim that some subjects may stand outside of participation in or investment in the relationships of domination whose terms they articulate through their material existence.

However, it remains unclear whether Haraway's theory of affinity and oppositional identities avoids the questions I've raised about the subject/object relation in projects whose goal is to "pull together the sub-ject (no matter how temporarily) of history" in the fragmented world. Haraway suggests that "women of color" represent a site of contingent and subversive potential for being a subject/object of history in postmodern, decentered conditions. Their self-identified multiple affinities and multiple loyalties defeat any notion of the unified political subject of modernist feminisms that rely on the uniformly gendered subject whose gaze is on the "horizons of patriarchy." Haraway refers to "women of color" as a materialist counter to the essentializing tendencies of white feminists who forget their multiply situated (at least partially dominative) selves in favor of assuming the role of essentially oppressed *gendered* subjects. Joan Scott critiques Haraway's argument on grounds that she deploys the notion of "women of color" as an identity that opposes imperialist marking of oth-erness. This repeats the "old/new left's" tendency to romanticize or reify the struggles of "the most oppressed" as if they represent a more authentic site of struggle than other identities (Scott, 1989). I argue further that this tendency to romanticize the given condition of otherness is due to a fail-ure to understand others, or objects of knowledge, as always already in a dialectical, constitutive position vis-à-vis the concept, in this case "women of color."

The above developments in standpoint feminisms approach the constitu-tive limits of the "situated self" and the horizons of feminist identity, both temporally and spatially. But they do not adequately explore the possibilities of the dialectical theory that informs their work. Each finally sustains a correspondence between being and knowing and assumes a necessary relationship between social identity as given in the world and critical politics. Each finally wants to theorize the objects of Western historiography, the Mother, the feminine principle, the woman of color, into a critical subject of history.

Negative Dialectics as a Limit Theory of Knowledge

The negative dialectic of Theodor Adorno suggests the limits of theory that privileges the subject as the necessary site of emancipation. The specifically modern privilege of subjective knowledge ignores the immanent limits on forms of representation and communication available to the subject of modernity. Adorno's negative dialectic resuscitates the Hegelian dialectic but critiques its telos. Identity formation as understood in the tradition of Hegelian dialectics involves the double movement of desire to engage an other as a means to the end of creating the boundaries, or consciousness, of one's self. Adorno argues through and against Hegel that the logic of identity, the creation of boundaries for the self and other, is historical yet *becomes* a fact of nature. If we theorize the reconciliation of identity and difference in any given institution or form of social life (as I have pointed out, standpoint feminists respectively point to how reproduction, work, or the family fulfill this role), what is actually still a moment in history, and potentially affected by the movement of consciousness, becomes naturalized.

In "Subject and Object" (1988) Adorno argues that the separation of subject and object in thought expresses the real dichotomy of the human condition. This duality reflects our alienation, from experience and from our Selves as objects of knowledge. But critical thought must neither hypostatize that separation or wish it out of existence. Adorno describes subject and object as historical terms and argues more explicitly than do standpoint theorists the necessity to preserve both sides of the dualism, albeit in a transformed relationship.

Adorno argues for a subject that recognizes its power through rather than in spite of its contingent relations to objects of interpretation. The various truths that emerge in history must be deciphered and critiqued in relationship to the object. His notion of constellations provides a working image for this cognitive process (Buck-Morss, 1977). As cognitive beings we must relentlessly place concepts in relationship to the object. Adorno uses the language of "deciphering the object" rather than "identifying the object." One must not only recognize the historicity of that object, but remember that one's own embeddedness in objective history is affecting the knowledge created.

Adorno's theory of constellations is not the same as perspectivalism. According to the simple form of this latter theory, competing truth claims are resolved on the basis of power or an instrumental purpose that can be rendered increasingly transparent through critique. Neither does constellational social theory imply a form of relativism, because for Adorno, there are temporally bound social and historical truths to be unlocked in the object. Objects are not stable in their historical constellation of meaning. Emancipatory truths lie in the ongoing process of interpreting and positioning of objects in constellations, not in the immediacy of the object in-itself. Truths are not discovered, but emerge as one places ideas, objects, or moments in juxtaposition to one another with the intent of interpreting yet another idea, object, or moment.

Adorno thus understands concepts as historical productions that can be placed in relationship to an object in order to center it and illuminate its contradictory positioning in a world characterized by reification, the exchange principle, and identity thinking. "Authentic philosophic interpretation does not meet up with a fixed meaning which already lies behind the question, but lights it up suddenly and momentarily, and consumes it at the same time" (Adorno, 1977: 127). The object as otherness is always in a process of being objectified and interpreted. Remembering this will enforce a sense of distance from it and defend against repeating the habits of the controlling, Enlightenment subject. The recognition of the many-sidedness of the object as it influences interpretation sustains the critical and ethical edge of cognition.

This is not the fluid relationship of connectedness between subject and object as, for example, is argued by Hartsock to characterize women's experience as mothers or caretakers. Adorno argues that critique lives in the tension-filled spaces at the limits of subjectivity. Persistent critique of the limits of cognition may keep the moment of objectification temporary while sustaining the distance between subject and object that defeats the smothering requirements of identity thinking.

> Unbroken and all too human slogans lend themselves to new equations between the subject and what is not its like. . . . The reconciled condition would not be the philosophical imperialism of annexing the alien. Instead, its happiness would lie in the fact that the alien, in the proximity it is granted, remains what is distant and different, beyond the heterogeneous and beyond that which is one's own. (Adorno, 1987: 191)

For Adorno, resistance to the integrative forces of the world requires distance between self and object or other. This is not the distance of disinterested objectivity, which implies that as subjects we can remove the moment of mediation from our relationship to others. It is the distance of respect, of "identifying with" rather than resting with prior classifications of otherness. It is the distance encouraged by the method of knowing in constellations that perpetually illuminate those sides of the object, of the other, that traditional means of knowing disregard as a burden or as insignificant to the conclusions the knower is obliged to reach for instrumental purposes.

If we read Adorno for a feminist politics of knowledge, we will not find a feminist subject at the end of the inquiry as Hartsock and Hennessy find the Mother and Haraway finds women of color. We will not find a final diagnosis of patriarchal desire or the hidden mechanism that leverages masculinist power.

> He who interprets by searching behind the phenomenal world for a world-in-itself which forms its foundation and support, acts mistakenly like someone who wants to find in the riddle the reflection of a being which lies behind it, a being mirrored in the riddle, in which it is contained. (Adorno, 1977: 127)

Feminist epistemology argues that the closer women are to the object world—the more "situated" they are—the better access they will have to the realities "behind" patriarchy or invisible to the ruling class. They thus risk mirroring rather than deconstructing that reality in the name of locating a foundation for social transformation.

Because historical women always exceed the terms on which patriarchy identifies and controls otherness, women's experience will become political as it illuminates the integrative function of norms, previously invisible, that dictate gendered identities and roles. This makes it impossible for those norms to function in the same way or with the same legitimacy as they did prior to the exposure. This politics does not depend upon the collectivity of women in their sameness as Mothers or as offshore workers, but assumes the relevance of their differences and particularities to an ongoing project of knowledge production.

For Adorno, traces of difference in the resistant object illuminate critical knowledge. He argues that moments found in the uniqueness of experiential traces and knowledge of difference can subvert the dominative logics of identity. These traces are no less significant for critique for not being foundational. Their apparent obscurity in the modern, administered world of exchange relations speaks to the fragility of critique but also to the threat it poses to the stability of dominance in its (as yet unrealized) potential.

It is through a complex process of recognition, one allowing for the constitutive agency of the object, that we might come to know ourselves and others. This "coming to know" implies an iterative and reflexive process of understanding that is receptive rather than assimilative of the other's experience. Asha Varadharajan describes this relation as "an-other knowledge that involves not the annihilation of the subject but its reformulation in confrontation with a resistant object" (Varadharajan, 1995: 27). In other words, we do not have to dismantle the subject in order to bear witness to the constitutive qualities of the object world or of the reality a "we" is claiming to know. Feminism itself must recognize the significance of the resistance of its own objects of analysis to encapsulation in thought.[5] Ethical engagement with the object world means recognizing its excesses as critical and always potentially political rather than considering them to be merely incidental to the project of unity or the "pulling together of the Subject of history."

Notes

1. Postmodern critics of feminist standpoint theory argue it is regressive to sustain a commitment to theorizing the knowing subject within postmodern social conditions. Rather, they suggest we assume the demise of the sovereign subject and theorize the multiple and layered historical and discursive sites through which subjectivity and/or "women's experience" are produced as such (Butler and Scott et al., 1993). Sandra Harding suggests this is a historically premature move for feminism (Harding, 1986). I would take a slightly different approach, to argue postmodern theory sustains an optimism about the disintegration of subjectivity that is unwarranted.

2. For example, feminist critics have argued that the objectification of women's bodies necessary to the representation of women in pornography is in itself a form of violence against women. The fact of this objectification is argued to lead to actual violence against women.

3. See Steedman (1987) for a story of mothering that is too complex to figure into this essay but that places a woman who both fails at and actively resists Mothering in its ideal form at the center of analysis, thereby illuminating the contradictions and fissures of patriarchal power rather than positing it as monolithic. For another approach to theorizing the significance of differences among Mothers, see Collins (1990) and James (1993).

4. I should point out that I cite Collins here because of the descriptive power of her discussions of mothering in Black communities as a mode of resistance, not because I agree with her epistemological privileging of Black women as Subjects. We could also read Toni Morrison's book, *Beloved* (1987), for a brilliant literary representation of practices of mothering as resistance to property relations under conditions of slavery.

5. Again, I refer the reader to Steedman's *Landscape for a Good Woman* (1987).

References

Adorno, Theodor. 1977. "The Actuality of Philosophy." *Telos* 31, 120–33.

———. 1987. *Negative Dialectics*. New York: Continuum Press.

———. 1988. "Subject and Object." In *The Essential Frankfurt School Reader*. New York: Continuum Press.

Alcoff, Linda and Elizabeth Potter, eds. 1993. *Feminist Epistemologies*. New York: Routledge.

Brown, Wendy. 1991. "Feminist Hesitations, Post-Modern Exposures." *Differences* 3(1).

Buck-Morss, Susan. 1977. *The Origin of Negative Dialectics: Theodor Adorno, Walter Benjamin and the Frankfurt Institute*. New York: The Free Press.

Butler, Judith and Joan Scott, eds. 1993. *Feminist Theorize the Political*. New York: Routledge.

Collins, Patricia Hill. 1990. *Black Feminist Thought: Knowledge, Power and the Politics of Empowerment*. Boston: Unwin Hymen.

Haraway, Donna. 1991. *Symians, Cyborgs and Women: The Reinvention of Nature*. New York, Routledge.

Harding, Sandra. 1986. *The Science Question in Feminism*. Ithaca, NY: Cornell University Press.

———. 1993. "Rethinking Standpoint Epistemology: 'What is Strong Objectivity?'" In Alcoff and Potter, *Feminist Epistemologies*.

Hartsock, Nancy. 1983. *Money, Sex and Power*. Boston: Northeastern University Press.

———. 1987. "Rethinking Modernism: Minority vs. Majority Theories." *Cultural Critique* 7 (Fall).

Hennessy, Rosemarie. 1993. *Materialist Feminism and the Politics of Discourse*. New York: Routledge.

James, Stanlie and Abena P. A. Busia. 1993. *The Visionary Pragmatism of Black Feminism*. New York: Routledge.

Lukacs, Georg. 1967. *History and Class Consciousness*. Cambridge, MA: MIT Press.

Morrison, Toni. 1987. *Beloved*. New York: Knopf Publishers.

Scott, Joan. 1989. "*Commentary*, Cyborgian Socialist?" In *Coming to Terms*, ed. Elizabeth Weed. New York: Routledge.

Steedman, Carolyn Kay. 1987. *Landscape for a Good Woman: A Story of Two Lives*. New Brunswick: Rutgers University Press.

Varadharajan, Asha. 1995. *Exotic Parodies: Subjectivity in Said, Spivak and Adorno*. Minneapolis: University of Minnesota Press.

Three

Identities and Communities

On Puppies and Pussies
Animals, Intimacy, and Moral Distance

Chris J. Cuomo and Lori Gruen

Feminist attention to the permeability of certain categories, such as "personal" and "political," or "private" and "public," allows us to ask important questions about the relationships between them. When category boundaries cease to be rigid, the apparent distances among previously categorized entities diminish and the possible connections between them become important sites of inquiry. Sexuality, for example, when no longer seen as behavior that is merely privately formulated and acted upon, can be understood as strongly influenced by both social power and personal desire. Questions about the political significance and appropriate expression of sexuality and sexual desire outside the bedroom then become central.

We would like to continue the discussion of the "political" relevance of "personal" interactions by exploring the positive political implications of our intimate relationships with companion-animals. This discussion is motivated by a belief that these "personal," or "private" relationships receive inadequate attention as sources of moral knowledge, particularly from environmentalists. It is also motivated by our belief, for which each of us has argued elsewhere, that animals and other nonhuman beings and entities are morally valuable, though they are most commonly inadequately valued by humans. When members of the nonhuman world are not thought to be morally considerable, human relationships with them are typically constructed as either completely insignificant, or as unquestionably private, and therefore hardly ethically relevant. They are thus relegated to the background of human ethical and political life. We aim to foreground this aspect of "private" life by considering how affectionate bonds with particular animals might be relevant to more general inquiries about the ethics of human relationships with nature.

Moral Distance

We are looking for entry points that can help us bridge *moral distance*, an accidental or intentional lack of spatial or emotional proximity that prevents us from adequately knowing or caring about whole categories of beings who are affected by our lives, actions, and decisions. The problem of moral distance is particularly pertinent in the context of global economies and communities. The far-reaching implications of even the typical American's ethical, economic, and environmental involvements across miles and borders raise important questions about how to enact responsibilities to people, societies, species, and ecosystems about which we know very little, or with whom we are never in contact in ways that seem direct or immediate.

In the face of the ugliness of oppressive postindustrial, technocratic, media-driven cultures, we might be inclined to say that moral detachment can be a justified rational response. When overwhelmed by the far-reaching implications of our everyday actions, or confronted with instances of moral horror, it is easy to respond in ways that are disengaged from the contexts and consequences of our choices. Clearly, such responses may result from certain noncognitive processes, perhaps not unlike dissociative psychological responses to trauma. But while it may be true that moral distancing can have noncognitive, or psychological, origins, moral distance can also result from cognitive choices. As such it might be interrogated, analyzed, and ultimately altered or prevented.

Moral distance is problematic insofar as it separates moral agents from morally considerable beings, and maintains epistemic gaps in our understandings of actions and outcomes. It entails some lack—of information, of sentiment—that can be accidental, purposeful, or avoidable, and that keeps one removed from a situation that warrants some sort of moral response. When we do not have, or choose not to have, the information or the emotional responses that bring responsibilities into our field of attention (or keep them there), we fail to be motivated toward certain members of our moral universes. This failure matters even if we evaluate moral actions through strictly consequentialist considerations, because so often we are prevented, through our own choices or through the complexity of institutional and psychological mechanisms, from having a rich awareness of the consequences and implications of our actions.

The problem of moral distance is particularly acute for environmental ethics. How familiar are we with the ecosystems into which the byproducts of our lives are dumped? What do we typically know about the effects of our decisions on nonhuman individuals and species, locally and globally? How impossible does it seem to obtain such knowledge? In the face of human-centered histories and presuppositions, the impact our actions have on nonhuman life are not easily recognizable. When moral relationships do not seem obvious or obviously important by what count as "standard" ethical means, such as anthropocentric values, or concerns with rights and justice, they are often unrecognized as moral relationships at all. Yet, despite the fact that these relationships are underexamined and willfully ignored, human moral agents are constantly, significantly effecting and affected by natural matter and beings.

Moral distance and detachment also lead to the creation and perpetuation of oppressive practices and institutions. Indeed, ecofeminists and others have long pointed out how detachment serves as a mechanism for domination. The creation of "others" entirely separate from oneself or one's community allows otherwise compassionate human beings to engage in stunningly destructive practices. Men's detachment from women's lives and interests, for example, is endemic to sexism and patriarchy. Horkheimer and Adorno discussed how a "logic of domination" affects both the natural world and some humans, and emphasized that the split between nature and history, or culture, and the elevation of the latter over the former requires detachment or separation (1979). This detachment denies us a great deal of knowledge concerning our continuity with nature, and thereby limits human experience. It also enables the kinds of cognitive, psychological dispositions that allow for oppression, ecocide, and genocidal domination. Moral distance is part of what allows the animal "researcher" to torture animals in the name of science and maintain a cheerful, friendly relationship with the animal who shares her home.

In many instances the phenomenon of moral detachment involves making decisions about what to see, or take seriously, as part of one's moral universe. In fact, it is not unusual to cut up the world into those actions, behaviors, attitudes, and beings that are considered morally relevant and those that are not. We might think of one's take on the world, and on what in the world ought to be taken into account as ethically relevant, as her moral *orientation*. The development of a moral orientation is related to the development of character, and to the acquisition of ethical rules and concepts through education, life experiences, and the digestion of cultural norms. As such, moral orientations are very specific dispositions toward our environments. They are built on, and in turn provide, a sense of what is and is not morally salient, and what contributes to or detracts from the richness and goodness of life. Prejudices, identities, definitions, physical responses, and a myriad of other specific factors contribute to our moral orientation—our "map" of what matters and what does not. A highly exclusionary ethos, such as a human-centered orientation, will likely result in a map that includes only those things that are immediate, obviously knowable, familiar, or understandable. As a result, those actions, behaviors, attitudes, and beings that are thought to be difficult to understand, unknowable, or unfamiliar elude the moral gaze. From within such an orientation, it is difficult to even perceive, care about, or familiarize ourselves with that to which we seemingly have little connection.

One ethical problem that concerns us here is the fact that moral agents can be *wrong* about who and what is morally relevant. When we fail to perceive and thus gain knowledge and understanding of nonhuman members of our environments, we inevitably remain cut off from those things and beings with whom we are intimately, ecologically, connected. We also fail to engage those very responses that make us moral agents: our caring, our sense of duty, our responsibility, our pain, our anger, our affection, and our sense of righteousness. If these responses are not innate traits, but are the kinds of things that require some amount of education, practice, skill, commitment, and consistency, then their disengagement is likely to have a negative effect on moral agency and community.

Marilyn Frye argues that when women develop erotic and perceptual orientations toward other women, women become more fully visible, and, as perceiving subjects, women also can gain insights about ourselves and the contexts in which we exist (1983). What is in the background becomes capable of being seen, and as seers we develop more comprehensive pictures of the world. Like sexual or erotic orientations, transgressive moral orientations might involve the conscious development of lines of attention that allow typically undervalued beings to be perceptible and relevant. With increased acuity, it becomes possible to better perceive unique and familiar traits and qualities in the objects of our affections, and to develop appreciation and respect in our encounters. Human-centered moral orientations see nature as the backdrop upon which morally salient (human) events, attitudes, behaviors, and beings become visible. In the process of giving attention only to humans and their interests, the backdrop becomes virtually invisible. If such moral orientations cannot accomodate the scope and range of beings and entities impacted by our actions, they are inadequate. In order to develop more comprehensive, inclusive, and adequate moral orientations with regard to nonhumans, we have to pay close attention to what is in the background as well as what is more clearly visible, and ensure that the background is not ignored.

Bridging Moral Distance

In the example mentioned earlier, a scientist might have a moral orientation that does not include nonhuman animals whom she encounters in the lab, despite the fact that it does include pets. Perhaps here it is a sharp division between public and private, or emotion and rationality, not a lack of familiarity, that keeps laboratory animals out of her moral purview. Nonetheless, if the needless torture of animals in laboratories is wrong, and a limited moral orientation is part of what enables the scientist to engage in the practice of torturing animals, then questions about how to shift or expand moral orientations are central to the ethics of human–nonhuman relations. We are curious about how moral orientations might be expanded from the inside—how attention to intimate connections might broaden one's moral purview.

If it is true that our moral orientations can and sometimes should be expanded, then it is important to unearth clues about what deserves attention and to develop ways of shifting attention to include other things. Drawing ethical attention to moral subjects and problems that seem beyond our emotional reach requires empirical reminders about what we are impacting, including rich stories about the consequences of actions, practices, and ways of being in the world. It also requires "ins," or epistemic and emotional entry points, for considering the interests and value of unfamiliar entities. These entry points can be models, analogies, or emotional magnets that enable us to widen our moral purview to include what may seem incomprehensible, or unimportant. These "ins" can lead to shifts in both our affective and epistemic responses to moral problems across distance.

One way to frame questions about bridging moral distance is in terms of ethical "starting points." Some feminist and ecofeminist philosophers use holism as a starting point, following, in certain important respects, Aldo Leopold's Land Ethic (Kheel, 1993). Leopold recommends what we might think of as a shift in ethical starting points—from thinking of ourselves as members only of human societies and as conquerors of the land, to "plain member(s) and citizen(s)" of ecological communities (1966, 240). He emphasizes the subtlety of biotic interdependence and the far-reaching, if incomprehensible, effects of even minute manipulations of the biotic community and its members. Recognition of the interconnections of actions, and of beings, is an ethical starting point because these interconnections dictate considerations of values based on connection *and* distinction, as well as the long-range, far-reaching consequences of actions. The complexity of connection recommends an attitude of humility and awareness of human ignorance concerning biotic interdependencies, a point that is also stressed by Leopold.

Holism is one way of beginning with connection. A possible alternative to holism entails beginning with intimate connections between and among relational selves, that is, individuals who recognize themselves as necessarily related to others. Intimate, local, face-to-face relationships provide specific forms and instances of connectedness as points of departure when moral distance seems overwhelming or insurmountable. Intimate relationships can provide "ins" for moral relationships outside intimate, or comfortable, spheres by giving information and inspiring emotional responses that motivate and justify choices across spatial, emotional, and epistemic distances. What we see and experience in those we love and care about, and how we recognize those qualities in those we don't know, helps set the stage for concern with social and ecological justice. In our intimate relations we are often made aware of the ways that our own individual interest, projects, and happiness are entangled with the interests, lives, and flourishing of others. Reflection on the interrelation of interests with those close to us can reveal how the interests of others affect and are effected by our own. In addition, the quandries and dilemmas we are faced with in our intimate relations and the processes by which we sort out the responsibilities we have to ourselves and our loved ones can provide important insights into the development of moral skills. Instead of focusing only on holistic systems and biologically necessary connections, we suggest also emphasizing successful intimate relationships in order to call to mind those contexts in which we are routinely called to be whole moral beings.

Relationships with Nonhuman Animals

Over the last twenty-five years, many philosophers have been concerned with human interactions with animals, especially human mistreatment of other animals, and have sought to develop appropriate ethical positions regarding human-animal interactions (Singer, 1975; Midgely, 1983; Regan, 1986). These discussions have most often focused on the application of general principles, such as the principle of utility or the principle of respect for subjects of lives. Many feminist theorists have resisted the abstract application of general principles, and instead focused on the insights that ethical, political, and epistemic agents can glean from preexisting relationships and modes of moral discourse and interaction (Kittay and Meyers, 1987; Card, 1990). What we are specifically interested in here is the usefulness of women's relationships with animals in conceiving of ethical interspecies relationships that are not alienating, oppressive, exploitative, or harmful, and that promote ecological and human flourishing.

In asking such questions, we do not mean to imply that power imbalances between humans and domesticated animals ought to be taken at face value. Many have suggested that the imbalance of power between humans and their pets, or companion nonhumans, provides compelling reasons to avoid such relationships. Some believe that women who have pets promote speciesist, alienating, and exploitative practices and institutions, despite the very best of intentions. Given that most of these relationships involve tremendous exploitation, it may seem absurd to think that human relationships with nonhuman animals can or should serve as a model of moral interactions. Since most humans consume the bodies or bodily byproducts of nonhuman animals, some ecofeminists argue that the power dynamics between humans and animals are intrinsically and inescapably unequal. Most humans benefit from the exploitation of animals, through labor and abuse that is often deadly, and nearly always incredibly taxing. Many humans consider animals to dwell outside the realm of full moral consideration, and therefore don't give nonhuman animals categorical ethical consideration that is equal to, or even approximates, their treatment of other human beings.

It is certainly true that most, if not all, relationships can be characterized by an imbalance of power. But not all human interactions with nonhuman animals are exploitative, and even some of those that *are* might be worth investigating for insight about why we ought to take nature seriously, and how to accomplish this in the face of wide epistemic impasses. We believe it is possible to be responsible ethical agents in our relationships with companion animals, and to act within them in ways that aim meaningfully toward the transformation of other relationships with nonhuman life. Instead of describing all human/nonhuman relations as equally repugnant, we wonder how to live attentively and responsibly within inescapably unequal power relationships, especially when we aim to resist oppressive practices. Rather than strive to avoid such relationships, if that is even possible, we might instead turn our moral attention to them and begin to analyze our negotiations of power in order to alter it. Here we can challenge obvious imbalances of power, and also directly engage in struggles to shift imbalances by treating relationships as sites for learning how to be good moral beings, friends, and members of communities.

Perhaps it is from *within* the contexts of some unequal power relationships that we might better understand how to bridge moral distance. What might successful transgressions and creative connections across power imbalances tell us?

Friendship

In many cultures, human affectionate relationships with nonhuman animals are incredibly common, and even common parlance acknowledges the centrality of nonhuman life in human community. Ecological feminists ought to think about how to tap into this fact, this history, this fruitful foundation for thought that breaks out of anthropocentric norms, in ways that build on its affective and epistemic power, especially if we can avoid anthropomorphizing projections onto animals and nature.

Janice Raymond argues that friendship can be a site for education about shared injustices, and also about the value of other persons in general (Raymond, 1986). Raymond's thesis raises important questions about the role of women–animal *friendship* as a vital factor in the creation of ecological consciousness. Although not all women interact with nonhuman animals (even their pets) as friends, the point is that positive, consciously intimate attachments with animals ought to be taken seriously as relationships with radical political implications. Women who have close companionship with nonhuman animals have an emotional and epistemic foundation for concern about environmental issues. An effective environmental ethic or movement must acknowledge the history, meanings, and importance of human bonding with nonhumans, and an ecological feminism ought to pay particular attention to women's relationships with animals. It may then even begin to ask about the significance of intimate relationships with the land.

Is it possible to have friendship with animals? Friendship is reciprocal, and most nonhuman animals are not able to reciprocate as friends in the manner we generally deem acceptable for humans. Because nonhuman animals do not communicate linguistically, they cannot share confidences, give advice, understand jokes, or discuss worldly affairs. They are not able to provide money or empathic reflection on uniquely human concerns. In fact, it is questionable what, if anything, nonhuman animals understand or know about human reality. However, friendship between and among humans is not merely a rational, linguistic relationship. Many describe friendship as a heartfelt connection that includes feelings of warmth, loyalty, and respect.

Friends are companions, and their companionship is sometimes most appreciated when it is a subtle, quiet presence.

Given an expanded description of friendship, it is certainly true that many women experience friendship with some animals—usually (but not always) their pets, or companion-animals. These nonhuman animals clearly provide much of what we seek in friends: companionship, opportunity for self-reflection, inspiration, lessons in love, caring, patience, and loss. Although such relationships are not identical to our friendships with other humans (and which two of these are identical?), numbers of persons participating in them do not hesitate to label them "friendships," and to healthily devote themselves to their maintenance.

> Over the last fifteen years I have, somewhat reluctantly, shared my life with many cats and for the last seven years have had a primary relationship with Dooley who is a dog. With them, I have learned a tremendous amount about love, commitment, companionship, trust, loyalty as well as death, betrayal, and loss. I have also learned how difficult respecting differences can sometimes be, and it is through my relationships with these nonhumans that I have been faced with some of the most immediate and seemingly intractable moral dilemmas I have ever faced. (What should I do when, after losing her bell, one of my cats brings home a maimed bird? If the only way to keep Jeremy alive and healthy is to feed him other animals, should I do it? Should I subject them to cross-country travel? Should I encourage or discourage their dependency on me by including other primary humans in their lives?) Grappling with and ultimately (although perhaps not satisfactorily) resolving these dilemmas has expanded my moral orientation. I have come to appreciate the beauty and tragedy of non-standard relationships of all sorts, and I have come to respect others who I view from afar in their struggles with seemingly intractable moral dilemmas and to admire their courage in handling such dilemmas. [Gruen]

Friendships can be sites of forms of knowledge that are particularly useful in shaping moral orientations and responding to moral distance. Of course, such knowledge is not strictly propositional or verifiable, and is not captured by characterizations of knowledge, widely criticized by feminist epistemologists, as an objective, objectifying, distanced kind of seeing. Rather than conceiving of all knowledge as something a subject has about an object, Lorraine Code suggests that knowing can be a subject-to-subject relationship. She recommends characterizing intersubjective knowing as nonobjectifying vision—as a locking of eyes, as making eye contact (1991,

145). Once we know even some other animals as Code recommends, the possibility of friendship is opened up. And friendship can lead to other radical revisionings.

When we call a nonhuman "friend" we begin to conceptualize that being in ways that are unusual. We predicate certain qualities to a being, qualities that we normally don't associate with that type of being, qualities that we are supposed to restrict to our proximate human relations. Rather than viewing this sort of predication as a category mistake, as some critics might suggest, we believe such predications are not only accurate, but can expand our conceptualizations of the moral universe. For example, acknowledging that the dilemmas faced in interspecies friendships are *moral* dilemmas allows us to shift our moral attention to previously unchartered regions. Focusing on these relationships thereby helps us to develop and expand our moral orientations and cultivate new sensitivities within our environments. Developing these sensitivities is crucial for perceiving the valuable members of our environment and sorting out what is important in particular contexts.

> Part of my experience living with cats is seeing how their small furry faces express emotions, desires, preferences, pain. My knowledge of my cats' faces is in significant ways, the same kind of knowledge that I have of a human friend's face. I've seen that expression before. I've watched the eyes alert and attentive, or slowly closing in the wake of slumber. I've felt a stretch of restlessness from across a room and have responded unconsciously, without knowing or remembering my own reaction. Like the faces of my human friends, that face is similar to but also not at all like mine. I find the emotional and physiological responses that are evidenced in that face and that body to be both like and unlike mine. I see an opossum in the wild. Briefly, I catch a glimpse of her furry face. Its texture, its difference from mine, its unconcern with my language, its round alert eyes remind me of my cat. I feel a connection, a caring, a recognition and respect not unlike my sense of distanced affection when I walk the streets of another city and am passed on the street by two women holding hands. I think (of the possum, of the dykes): they live here, they move through this space with familiarity, they find their community and their dinner here. And they are ultimately, intimately connected with the things and the beings that have no face, or no face or personality that I can understand. [Cuomo]

Friendships with animals can give human ethical agents a sense of the value of familiar types of beings, as well as an appreciation for the unfamiliar, a sense of environment as place, as home, as familiar stomping grounds, as a differently scaled universe viewed through what we imagine nonhuman eyes to see. Friendships with nonhumans can provide a different sense of scale, of beauty, of purpose, and of community. Once we begin to face nature, that is, to perceive nonhuman life as an important part of the context we inhabit, we can begin to shift our moral orientation, and our very notion of ourselves as moral beings.

Some feminists have argued that putting too much emphasis on what our particular experiences can tell us about the rest of the world can be problematically generalizing or universalizing. However, such a move can coexist with recognition of and appreciation for difference and particularity that reduces the dangers of a totalizing gaze. The main problem with the universalizing notion that "those people over there are just like us" is not the fact that similarities are noted, or even constructed, but that particularities and relevant differences are flattened or ignored and the gaze is constructed as unidirectional. The tendency to make community, to forge bonds, to cognize about others based on our local experiences with intimates and well-known others is not inextricably connected to the colonizing tendency with which it typically appears.

On Eating Our Friends

The suggestions we make here are about how to obtain knowledge and form strategies, and how to use our private relationships and experiences as political information. If the moral backgrounding of nature helps fuel anthropocentrism, then highlighting our connections, through friendship, with members of the background can enable radical transformations of our orientations toward nature. Good, face-to-face relationships with animals tell us new things about the possibilities for moral community and about our own ethical attentiveness to that which is not human. They can ground the kind of world travelling recommended by Maria Lugones, and help shift moral orientations (1987). Emphasizing these kinds of relationships, and connecting them up to relationships with faceless entities, can open up discourses on the moral relevance of the faceless world.

Our emphasis on intimate, local, and face-to-face relationships as a starting point from which to close moral distance is consistent with the views other ecofeminists have expressed about moving beyond moral distance. Chaia Heller, for example, notes that we "are curious, social creatures with the need to taste, see and dance in the world. We have a desire to know and be known, and to explore the perimeters of our imaginations and abilities.... The ecology movement will not be truly radical until we radicalize our idea of what it means to love, know and care for nature" (1993, 240–41). Recognizing and cultivating affection in our relations with nonhumans is one way to radicalize an otherwise human-centered moral orientation. Carol Adams has also highlighted the need to address moral distance and estrangement from the effects of our actions, by arguing that most people, including feminists, remove "any associations that might make it difficult to accept the activity of rendering a unique individual into a consumable thing. Not wanting to be aware of this activity, we accept this disassociation, this distancing device of the mass term 'meat'" (1990, 202). Awareness of the ways in which we further moral distance through our choices, along with the willingness to expand our moral universes, can shift our moral orientations to include those nonhumans with whom we have intimate, face-to-face relations.

The development of expanded moral orientations through relationships with particular nonhuman animals provides ways to think about and act towards those nonhumans with whom we have no personal connection. The most obvious example here is the case of eating other animals. When we learn to see nonhumans as beings that deserve our moral perception, when we shift from viewing them as background or mere food to seeing them as enablers of our own abilities to bridge moral distance, to cross boundaries, and to expand our moral orientations, the feminist case for vegetarianism becomes even stronger. As Carol Adams suggests, eating animals relegates animals to the background of reality, and requires the creation and maintenance of moral distance.

We do not want to ignore the fact that there are particular moments in which it will be useful or practical to seek moral distance, or when particular political ends require prioritizing moral responses and responsibilities. This may describe the situations faced by some feminists, such as women organizing against cultural imperialism, racism, and xenophobia, who argue that traditional animal-based diets are vital for cultural maintenance and resistance. However, moral distance might be avoided by acknowledging the weight of the decision to slaughter sentient animals for food, or of the price of prioritizing. In ecofeminist spaces, where the point is to try, together, to model new ways of being, it might be possible to assist each other in the development of creative and new moral orientations. In spaces in which we hope to think about and act toward our environments in more harmonious and just ways, the serving and eating of dead animals can only be seen as a failure of moral imagination.

Concluding Thoughts

Feminist ecological consciousness calls for ways to give life to the links and resemblances within the variegated field of our moral imaginations. Many have difficulty wrapping their conceptual toolboxes around calls to respect nature, to value ecosystems for their own sakes, and to protect species and biotic communities with which many are completely unfamiliar. Human experience of cross-species friendship, intimacy, companionship, attraction, and respect can provide "ins" for the kinds of radical ethical shifts that ecological feminists recommend. These "ins" can also be used explicitly to argue for extensions of moral orientations when decisions and policies are being considered.

Because we are using human intimate relationships with nonhuman animals as a point of departure, some disparaging things might be said about attempts to "put a face" on nature. Environmentalist critics of "extensionism"—the view that takes some given human-centered ethic and then extends moral concern out from there—may suggest that by focusing on human, intimate relations with nonhumans, by "putting a face on nature," we are engaging in a hopelessly human-centered approach to valuing the nonhuman world. Although our discussion does indeed rely on certain prior moral and epistemic relationships with humans and other beings with faces, our project is meant to highlight beginnings or starting points, in order to locate ways of moving from the familiar, or intimate, to the less familiar. Certainly this is not the only way to widen the scope of one's moral appreciation, but it is a way to bridge moral gaps using common ethical tools and models. The development of skills that enable shifts in moral orientations may help us become more attentive and integrated moral beings in a constantly disintegrating world.

Acknowledgments

The authors would like to thank Bat-Ami Bar On and Ann Ferguson for their support and assistance. In addition Chris Cuomo would like to thank Lori Gruen for being such an insightful and inspiring co-author.

References

Adams, Carol J. 1990. *The Sexual Politics of Meat: A Feminist-Vegetarian Critical Theory.* New York: Continuum Publishing.

Adorno, Theodor and Max Horkheimer. 1979. *Dialectic of the Enlightenment.* London Verso.

Callicott, J. Baird. 1989. *In Defense of the Land Ethic.* Albany: State University of New York Press.

Card, Claudia. 1990. *Feminist Ethics.* Lawrence, KS: University of Kansas Press.

Code, Lorraine. 1991. *What Can She Know?: Feminist Theory and the Construction of Knowledge.* Ithaca, NY: Cornell University Press.

Cuomo, Chris J. 1992. "Unravelling the Problems in Ecofeminism," *Environmental Ethics,* 15(4): 351–63.

———. 1997. *Feminism and Environments: An Ethic of Flourishing.* London: Routledge Press.

Frye, Marilyn. 1983. "To Be and Be Seen." In *The Politics of Reality: Essays in Feminist Theory.* Freedom, CA: The Crossing Press.

Gaard, Greta. 1993. *Ecofeminism: Women, Animals, Nature.* Philadelphia: Temple University Press.

Gruen, Lori. 1993. "Dismantling Oppression: An Analysis of the Connection Between Women and Animals." In *Ecofeminism: Women, Animals, Nature,* ed. Greta Gaard. Philadelphia: Temple University Press.

Heller, Chaia. 1993. "For the Love of Nature: Ecology and the Cult of the Romantic." In Gaard.

Kheel, Marti. 1993. "From Heroic to Holistic Ethics: The Ecofeminist Challenge." In Gaard.

Kittay, Eva Feder and Diana T. Meyers, eds. 1987. *Women and Moral Theory.* Savage, MD: Rowman and Littlefield.

Lugones, Maria. 1987. "Playfulness, 'World'-Travelling, and Loving Perception," *Hypatia* 2(2).

Midgley, Mary. 1983. *Animals and Why They Matter.* Harmondsworth, England: Penguin.

Raymond, Janice. 1986. *A Passion for Friends: Toward a Philosophy of Female Affection.* Boston: Beacon Press.

Regan, Tom. 1986. *The Case for Animal Rights.* Berkeley, CA: University of California Press.

Rolston, Holmes, III. 1988. *Environmental Ethics.* Philadelphia: Temple University Press.

Singer, Peter. 1975. *Animal Liberation.* New York: New York Review Books.

Warren, Karen J. 1987. "Feminism and Ecology: Making Connections," *Environmental Ethics,* 9: 3–20.

———. 1990. "The Power and Promise of Ecological Feminism," *Environmental Ethics,* 12: 125–146.

11

Displacing Woman
Toward an Ethics of Multiplicity

Jane Flax

Historical Context

Some feminists argue that ethical discourse and the elimination of gender-based domination require uniform concepts of gender and subjectivity. It is politically necessary to assert the existence of "women" as an undifferentiated category. Women can be defined by similarities in their material activities, inequalities, and oppression across race, class, and geography (MacKinnon 1987; Okin 1994). These similarities provide a base for the construction of feminist viewpoints and emancipatory politics. Ethics and claims to justice require a uniform class (women) and a capacity for agency and consciousness that can arise only out of an unsplit subject. The possibility of feminist agency is undermined by fluid and fragmented postmodernist subjectivity (Hartsock 1990a, 1990b).

These claims regarding subjectivity, "woman," agency, and justice are mistaken. The felt need for a solid "identity" as the ground of political action and warrant for its legitimacy is a consequence of enmeshment in liberalism, the dominant political discourse of contemporary Western states. The realization of the emancipatory potentials of feminism requires the destabilization, even the refusal of its originary subject, "woman," as a definable category and identity. In the contemporary West, effective feminist politics and ethics require neither homogeneous subjects nor uniform collective standpoints. They do entail attention to intra- and intersubjective multiplicity, taking into account each subject's multiple, interwoven locations as authority, resistor, and determined subject who articulates and is spoken by specific social vocabularies. Multiplicity represents a refusal of identity and difference, treating them as poles whose meanings are determined by a singular logic. Paying attention to this generative context is a necessary aspect of the project of creating alternatives to, not reproducing, its discursive consequences.

My intent here is to contribute to the development of ethical practices for contemporary multiple subjects by dispelling some effects of dominant discourse. No claim applies outside my geographically and temporally restricted contexts. Furthermore, I only discuss the internal logic of delimited components of post-seventeenth-century Western liberalism—Lockean notions of natural rights and individualism and Kantian concepts of reason and ethics. This focus reflects the continuing influence these beliefs exert on current Western politics (including aspects of contemporary Western feminism). I will first summarize my claims and then backtrack to develop individual points.

The Disputed Subjects of Feminism: Summary of Argument

Contemporary identity politics and its integral resistant/complicit partner—difference discourses—are consequences and effects of Lockean and Kantian liberal discourses. These discourses construct identity through two homogeneous, fixed, and exclusive categories: same and different. Identities are determined by the sharing of universal, uniform qualities. The existence of the same is dependent upon its abstraction and isolation from all other elements. The call to honor difference, while often motivated by an attempt to escape the limits of liberal discourses, recreates them. "Difference" is the remainder, the excluded, what the same is not; it is as fixed and homogeneous in its heterogeneity as the same. Adoption of either pole leaves undisturbed a problematic background context of assumptions concerning subjectivity, agency, and political action.

Dominant liberal notions of identity cannot do justice to the multiple, "impure" (Lugones 1994), overdetermined yet determining subjects of postmodern society. Within liberal discourses abstract individualism functions as a defense to ward off assigning race/gender "difference" and particularity to dominant groups (Lam 1994). Acknowledgment that difference reflects power relations, not objective qualities, would destabilize the identities of such groups and the social institutions they anchor and legitimate.

Moves to conceptualize subjectivity as multiple represent attempts to escape the homogeneity and circularity of same and different. Rather than redeem "difference" to open space for "other" forms of identity, all subjects are viewed as mutually and multiply constituted. Once race and sexuality are integrated into accounts of all modern Western subjectivities, no unitary concept of woman is available. In contemporary Western societies, no "woman" exists who has experiences unmarked by race and sexuality. These relations are not identical, or one thing, but mutually constituting, unstable, conflicting, constantly mutating, interdependent, and inseparable processes. In contemporary Western cultures, gender is always raced, and race is always gendered (Higgenbotham 1992). Presumptive heterosexuality structures discourses of gender and racial development and identity (Rich 1980; Fuss 1989; O'Connor and Ryan 1993; Calhoun 1995). Whatever their genealogies, in the contemporary West, race, gender, and sexuality blur and bleed into each other. Only interwoven, fluid concepts can delineate contemporary subjects (Molina 1994; Lugones 1994; Friedman 1995). Such concepts treat subjectivity as a verb rather than a noun. Analysis centers on locating the multiple and often conflicting relationships, practices, and processes through which contemporary subjects are constituted and in which these same subjects remake and resist their constituting activities.

The complexity and instability of any form of contemporary Western identity ("marginal" or dominant) renders claims made from it or on its behalf temporary, fragile, and suspect. Identities require a background context of discourses and practices to exist and become coherent. Simultaneously, to be coherent, these identities require the suppression of much of their generating background. For example, racial identity assumes the stability and meaningfulness of racial categories and of "race" itself. However, analysis of "race" exposes its arbitrary and historically destabilizing changing content. Multiply raced subjects destabilize existing racial categories and illuminate the politics of categorization (Friedman 1995).

Furthermore, contemporary subjects occupy more than one social location. These locations entail contradictory relations to power, privilege, and to other subjects and aspects of one's own subjectivity. For example, as a professional, white, Jewish, heterosexual woman who is the mother of a white, heterosexual, Jewish male, I am implicated in multiple histories, positions of relative power and powerlessness and ambiguous future possibilities. Since none of these locations are hermetically sealed and isolated, and some constitute, support, and undercut the status of others (for example white/woman), finding any simple, unconflicted, or unproblematic homogeneous intrasubjective space is a quixotic task. Further dimensions of complication appear when the context-dependence of identity is recognized. As a teacher, I occupy a position of power relative to my students; as a single, small person in a dangerous part of the city, quite another. Western postmodern subjects are moving rather than resting objects (through physical and cyberspace) and occupy multiple social, geographic, and subjective spaces. Our exposure through mass media to multiple modes of life and subjectivity makes it more difficult to deny the partiality and temporality of one's current positions.

Backtrack One: Tracing the Geneaology of Woman

Feminism's root is femina, woman. In some variants of feminist discourse, the existence of its subject and agent, "woman," is assumed. Woman's identity arises from her membership in a group constituted of homogeneous individuals. Woman is a plural, collective, singular, composed of individuals who share definitive, particular, exclusive, and exclusionary characteristics. By virtue of these shared characteristics, persons are recognized by themselves and others as belonging to this singular group.

What are these shared characteristics? Ultimately, underlying or weaving through a variety of discourses, the foundation, the constant, is "biological difference." The difference that counts are those anatomical features that define woman and man, her descriptive and prescriptive partner: bodies with a penis/bodies with a vagina and a uterus. These differences (not coincidentally) are ones without which human reproduction and heterosexual intercourse could not occur. The difference is sometimes said to speak for itself, as in "anatomy is destiny." However, *meanings* of ("real") difference appear increasingly problematic. They are socially constructed, effects of social practices that humans "hang on," attribute to, or read as "biology." This realization made possible the important feminist distinction between sex and gender.

Feminist analysis has begun to go further, to challenge the inevitability of "sexual difference" itself (Butler 1990, 1993; Nicholson 1994). "Sexual difference" cannot remain located in the "biological/natural" if this is understood as immune from social forces. The organization of "anatomy" into "sexual difference" is a social process. The significance, salience, and meanings of particular organs or biological processes reflect social concerns and practices. While there are bodily processes that exceed or exist independently of our discursive practices, categories such as "sexual difference" are human artifacts. The mere presence of our genitals does not cause or warrant concepts of sexual difference, gender identity, or sexuality (de Lauretis 1987; Laqueur 1990). Such concepts reflect and contribute to the reproduction of particular social organizations of organs and embodiment.

In the contemporary West, gender is produced by and expresses asymmetries of power and socially constructed meanings. It bears no necessary relation to "sexual difference," which is itself a social and not a biological fact (Laqueur 1990; Nicholson 1994). Without socially constructed "sexual difference," woman, man, and gender would not exist. Given this genealogy, what gain could arise from a project of reconstituting rather than destabilizing, deconstructing, and resisting gendered identities?

Woman is also a political status. Modern Western discourses of feminism, from the eighteenth century on, have not existed outside their relations of tension and dependence on liberal political theorizing. Liberals claim all individuals possess rights "by nature," prior to and outside any state. The legitimacy of political institutions rests on the agreement of these individuals to temporarily cede some of their "natural" rights and powers to the state. The state promises to protect such rights. It must not exceed the powers ceded to it.

Liberal subjects are equal, e.g., uniformly situated in relation to rights; therefore, they are entitled to equal treatment. Claims to justice must be made based on principles applicable to, binding on, and recognizable by all. They must be disinterested in the sense that they are made in the name of all—not any particularized part. Uniform oppression of a homogeneous group is necessary for it to count as injustice. Sexism, too, must affect a homogeneous category in uniform ways to be taken seriously as a form of injustice. Here we see a theoretical root of identity politics.

Modern Western feminism is initiated by the potential contradictions between the premises of liberal discourse and its practice (Wollstonecraft 1967). Liberal states initially refused to include woman within the class of rights holders and thus excluded then from possessing and exercising citizenship. Feminists fought to have woman recognized as an individual, for her to have an independent existence rather than as a "femme couverte," subsumed under and represented by the man/husband. Until woman was an individual, she could not possess rights. Until she possessed rights, the state could not recognize her existence. She could not be party to any contract with the state or make any claims on or against it.

The early slogan of modern Western feminism might well have been, "ain't I an individual?" Many feminists fought for inclusion as individuals within the liberal state; they wanted the "rights of man" extended to them. Recognition by the state required the assimilation—or disappearance—of woman as a marked social category with specified political differences. Feminists could only make demands on the state within the discourses available to them. These discourses required that a woman become an individual, like a man. Since man was a neutral universal, this did not appear intrinsically contradictory. However, to claim individuality on the behalf (and in the name) of a class whose identity is constituted collectively assimilates certain paradoxes that will haunt later feminists. The idea that "man" and individual might not coincide—or could be problematic—will only occur much later (Pateman 1980).

Backtrack Two: Race Matters

While many contemporary feminists would agree that modern Western feminism initially arose within and was motivated by liberal individualism and Kantian ethics (universalizable principles/subject), we disagree about the current effects and desirable disposition of this inheritance. Some argue that a simultaneous claiming and critique of liberalism are necessary and productive for feminist theorizing and practice. We require something like the liberal subject to exercise agency and some collective universal category (the name of woman) for feminist politics to be coherent and effective. Since modern Western states claim to honor rights and individualism, refusal to make use of their discourses for feminist ends is self-destructive (Okin 1989).

However, such claims require a problematic assumption that gender generates and can be understood as a simple binary opposition composed of two categories: man/woman. This is problematic, because internally undifferentiated concepts of woman place all women in a similar (oppressed) condition. Simple dichotomies obscure the equally important relations of domination between women. Furthermore, not all women are situated identically in relation to men. Such claims foreclose exploration and acknowledgment of our conflicting positions in contemporary networks of power. They misconstrue the meaning and miscalculate the significance and effects of race and sexuality for all contemporary Western women and theorizing practices.

In our ability to ignore the effects of racism, white women differ radically from racialized ones. While for all women, "issues of gender are always connected to race" (McKay 1993, 276), racially unmarked women can avoid recognizing this. "And although black feminists, even radical black feminists, have been trying to impress the significance of this truth on white feminists for more than twenty years, some still do not understand" (McKay 1993, 276). Most discourse concerning racism still focuses on its horrifying effects on its objects. While this is absolutely necessary, another aspect of racism is often ignored—"the impact of racism on those who perpetuate it" (Morrison 1992, 10). We must analyze what racial ideology does to "the

mind, imagination and behavior of masters" (Morrison 1992, 12). As Nellie
McKay writes:

> Speaking specifically of the experiences of Black and white women in the
> USA, for Black women there is a long and painful history embedded in
> the differences that separate them from white women. This history begins
> with the first African slave woman who encountered a white woman on
> this continent.... [T]he "often *violent* connection pitting black female will
> against white female racism" is a condition that penetrates all of American
> cultural and literary consciousness. (McKay 1993, 273)

Denial of multiplicity and relations of domination among women renders claims of solidarity suspect. Neither white nor black women can find
racially neutral spaces of gender identity or unity outside "the anguish of
racial differences inscribed in the complexities of race, sex, rage and power
in Black and white women's relationships" (McKay 1993, 273). Perhaps we
could construct them, but that could only be the consequence of difficult
struggles hardly begun (hooks 1984; Martin and Mohanty 1986).

Backtrack Three: Troubled Subjects

The multiple constituents of feminism and gender require complex, hybrid
subjectivities and ethics of multiplicity. Theorizing must move beyond
metaphors of intersections or multipliers to those of "creolization, mestizaje
and hybridity, pollution and impurity . . . cultural mutation and restless
(dis)continuity that exceed racial discourse and avoid capture by its agents"
(Gilroy 1993, 2; see also Anzaldua 1990; Lugones 1994; Molina 1994).

Such discourses posit multiple subjects occupying complex and contradictory positions. This approach violates the logic of dominant social constructions. These logics produce binary choices as if they were exclusionary
pairs. For example, we are expected to choose a gender (male/female), a
race (white, black, asian, hispanic, etc.), and a "sexual" preference (heterosexual/homosexual). Attention to the binary pair obscures the arbitrariness
of the logic that generates it and the dependence of both positions upon it.
For example, neither homo- nor heterosexual object choice constitutes a
fixed or secure identity; both are contingent organizations of desire. Both
identities are dependent upon socially constructed organizations of desire
through which all subjects must define their practices and self-constructions. Heterosexuality is no more "natural," unconstructed, or unproblematic than homosexuality.

Identity politics operates within the logic of abstract individualism. One aspect of complex subjectivity is abstracted from its many constituting elements; it is treated as uniform and definitive of the subject's identity. Secure in this purity, its contradictory and excluded elements recede. For example, if I abstract "woman," I can focus on my lack of power in relation to "man." However, if woman (and man) is always complicated with race and sexuality, my sense of my location and my relation to my own political demands will be much more constrained and suspect. I will hesitate before saying "X" is something all women share, because I must pay attention to the varied meanings and multiple practices X might express. In the United States, rape, for example, is located not only in relations of power between men and women but in complex histories of racial domination and gender struggles among dominant and racialized men and between dominant and racialized women. In thinking through feminist politics of rape, one would have to consider these multiple, contradictory subjects and histories and, given these complexities, the complex and heterogeneous consequences any approach to rape might have.

Backtrack Four: Toward an Ethics of Multiplicity

Our liberal heritage does not equip us to imagine or practice a politics of multiplicity and conflict that is simultaneously governed by a mutual desire for justice (Young 1990). Inherent within liberalism is an alterity of abstract individualism and particularity as modes of subjectivity. The assignment of determining locations such as race or gender to marked others allows the liberal individual to be "free" or to acquire objectivity behind a Rawlsian veil of ignorance (Rawls 1971). According to liberal philosophies, the possibility for justice depends upon these undetermined, objective subjects. However, since no such subjects can exist, marked social characteristics such as race are projected outward or denied. Unlike rational subjects, the others this generates are embodied, historically situated, raced, and gendered (duCille 1994; Lam 1994).

Interest group politics replicates rather than breaks out of this circle. The logic of such politics requires its practitioners to define themselves as homogeneous subjects who are simultaneously possessors of several unitary "interests." There is a sovereign abstract "I" that can identify and put forth claims based on these bounded interests; for example, as a mother I am interested in child care; as a patient, I am interested in health care. A group is an aggregate of sovereign individuals who share an interest. However, the subject cannot be merely an aggregate of its interests; it possesses a capacity for autonomy and choice among them. The subject possesses but is not possessed by its "interests." None of these are understood as actually constituting the subjectivity of the chooser. Furthermore, as countless critics of pluralism have discussed, the existence of these "interests" is treated as unproblematic social fact. Neither the conflict and relations of domination that may produce a felt interest nor the fluid and contradictory aspects of subjects and their practices are incorporated within pluralist politics. To the pluralist, subjects are rational individuals who know what is in their interest; these subjects and their interests are not internally heterogeneous, multiply determined, uncertain in effect or internally contradictory.

An ethics of multiplicity requires new modes of discourse and understandings of subjectivity. Contrary to a liberal, Rawlsian, or Kantian view, justice requires attention to one's determinations, not detachment from them. The search for or claim of an Archimedean point, whether via the original position or another approach, impedes rather than fosters the pursuit of justice. Since creation of marked others is essential for the "free" subject's constitution, we cannot operate within liberal discourses without reproducing their constituting relations of domination.

Rather than deliberation about objective rules of procedure or universal norms, such ethics requires first that relatively privileged people develop the capacity to engage in different ways of listening. This mode of listening is quite different from the one a Rawlsian veil of ignorance supposedly institutes. Behind the veil of ignorance, Rawls's method of reflective equilibrium requires that one impartially takes up one point of view after the other; one imagines a variety of circumstances, relationships, or rules as binding on the self. The requisite attitude is impartiality. Although one subjects one's own given moral beliefs to scrutiny in the process, they are not assumed to be constitutive of the self, nor is the self implicated in their existence. This is why they can be outside, subjected to rational scrutiny, and are adopted or rejected depending on whether they meet the condition of universalizability. The dialogue is between reason and an external position, belief, experience, or rule presented to it.

The mode of listening I have in mind is quite different. Learning to listen is a complex process in which one must rethink one's own position and try to see oneself through the eyes of others. Among the relatively powerful, adopting such a position requires empathy and a willingness to see oneself as a contextual, situationally determined subject. One must understand oneself as not outside the relations that constitute the other; one's own identity is dependent on being in relation to her. It requires an uncomfortable, shifting vision that is more difficult for the privileged than subordinates, since the latter usually have had to see through the eyes of the dominant for self-defense.

Those who are the marked bearers of "cultural differences" have long experience with this. One's survival requires seeing oneself as others do and understanding how the others see themselves. The other's view cannot be purely alien or external, since it has constituting effects. One must struggle with and against it, and the struggle becomes part of one's subjectivity. As with the effects of the unconscious, one can never be fully aware of the effects of the other's view and the relations of power that potentiate this view and render it salient. Even ideas or aspects of subjectivity that seem exempt from the other's determination remain suspect. One can never be fully at home with or trusting of oneself. Decentered, partially estranged, multiple, overdetermined subjectivity is not a postmodernist conceit. Colonized and culturally, racially, or sexually defined "others" have long been familiar with it (Du Bois 1961; Fanon 1967; Minh-ha 1989; Williams 1991; Lam 1994).

Relatively privileged persons also are multiply constructed, but we have more social supports for projecting or denying unwanted or uncomfortable aspects of our subjectivities. The supposedly solid agents some feminists (Hawkesworth 1989) argue women need to emulate to attain and exercise political efficacy have the power to construct myths about themselves and shift their determined aspects to others. One of these myths is that they possess a stable identity and that their actions reflect the freedom, authority, and autonomy of this self rather than their privileged positions within asymmetric relations of power. Modern Western narratives about the sovereign subject reverse the relations between rationality, autonomy, authority, freedom, and power. Despite their own claims, such subjects can impose their wills upon the world because they possess power, not because they exercise the capacity for agency grounded in a stable identity. The *appearance* of stability, autonomy, and identity is generated and sustained by relations of domination, denial of aspects of subjectivity, and projection of contradictory material onto marked others. "The concept of subjecthood" has become problematic as the marked others attempt to "name themselves," but not because the privileged wish to avoid extending the subject's capacities to others (Hartsock 1990b, 163). While the privileged are reluctant to abandon their favorable positions, attempts to claim subjecthood by subordinates also expose the limits of the narratives the dominant tell about themselves. Their dominance rests on far less flattering bases than subjecthood. They never had the "subjecthood" that some others now wish to claim. What subordinates need is their power.

The success of feminist projects does not depend on the acquisition of an autonomous agency some white men can pretend to exercise. The possibility of just practices depends instead on fuller recognition of our multiplicities, mutuality, and antagonisms, and their often tangled and bloody histories. Feminist ethics must attend to and address relations of domination among women in the United States and elsewhere. White women are often tone-deaf to the voices of others and blind to the constituting effects of multiplicity within our own subjectivities and politics. Unless fuller explorations of our hatreds and divisions and of the multiplicity of our positions as oppressor and oppressed are integrated into them, any claim of intrasubjective, intersubjective, or group identity must remain suspect.

The politics of identity cannot be immune from a wish to control others and a denial of the past and current conflicts that pervade the contemporary United States. The assertion of identity entails the normative regulation of subjectivity and often the exclusion of aspects that would dislodge one's own privilege or victimization. For example, when gender is excluded from race, black men can challenge the "race" loyalty of black women and simultaneously protect their (racially constrained) power (hooks 1990). White women can deny our (gender constrained) race privilege while emphasizing the universality of gender oppression.

Justice is undermined by domination, not multiplicity (Young 1994). Lack of attention to multiple positions blocks "our" ability to articulate just principles. Innovative theorizing can emerge once we no longer assume it is necessary to claim a position of purely oppressed victim or utilize abstract reason to articulate ethical principles, resist oppression, or engage in just practices. Concern for inequities among women strengthens claims to gender justice. To have mutual futures, we must cultivate new, un-Kantian loves: of diversity, instability, heterogeneity, conflict, and that which is not solidly or uniformly grounded. How these loves might be fostered among the dominant is a complex question and one that cannot be answered outside particular contexts. Nor can an ethics of multiplicity provide general rules for deciding among competing intra- or intersubjective desires. It requires first an attitude of suspicion and distrust each subject adopts toward her own wishes and a deep skepticism toward the innocence of any political or subjective position. It involves a change in attitude toward all subject positions. Rather than producing entitlement, they instigate inquiry into both the relations that make entitlements possible and into our responsibilities for them.

Further development of such ethics requires arguments far beyond the scope of this paper (Flax 1993; compatible projects include Reagon 1983; Mouffe 1992; Brown 1993; Lugones 1994; Molina 1994; Friedman 1995). My hope here is to reduce the constraining influence on feminist discourse of a problem (identity/difference) that is an effect of a mode of thinking (liberalism), so that our efforts to imagine better politics can be more productive.

References

Anzaldua, Gloria, ed. 1990. *Making Face, Making Soul—Haciendo Caras: Creative and Critical Perspectives by Women of Color.* San Francisco: Aunt Lute.

Butler, Judith. 1990. *Gender Trouble: Feminism and the Subversion of Identity.* New York: Routledge.

———. 1993. *Bodies That Matter: On the Discursive Limits of 'Sex'.* New York: Routledge.

Brown, Wendy. 1993. "Wounded Attachments." *Political Theory* 21(3): 390–410.

Calhoun, Chesire. 1995. "The Gender Closet: Lesbian Disappearance Under the Sign 'Woman.' " *Feminist Studies* 21(1): 7–34.

de Lauretis, Teresa. 1987. *Technologies of Gender.* Bloomington: Indiana University Press.

Du Bois, W. E. B. 1961. *The Souls of Black Folk.* New York: Fawcett.

duCille, Ann. 1994. "The Occult of True Black Womanhood: Critical Demeanor and Black Feminist Studies." *Signs* 19(3): 591–629.

Fanon, Frantz. 1967. *Black Skin/White Masks: The Experiences of a Black Man in a White World.* New York: Grove.

Flax, Jane. 1993. *Disputed Subjects.* New York: Routledge.

Friedman, Susan Stanford. 1995. "Beyond White and Other: Relationality and Narratives of Race in Feminist Discourse." *Signs* 21(1): 1–49.

Fuss, Diana. 1989. *Essentially Speaking: Feminism, Nature and Difference.* New York: Routledge.

Gilroy, Paul. 1993. *The Black Atlantic: Modernity and Double Consciousness.* Cambridge: Harvard University Press.

Hartsock, Nancy. 1990a. "Rethinking Modernism: Minority vs. Majority Theories." In *The Nature and Context of Minority Discourse*, ed. Abdul R. JanMohamed and David Lloyd. New York: Oxford.

———. 1990b. "Foucault on Power: A Theory for Women?" In *Feminism/Postmodernism*, ed. Linda Nicholson. New York: Routledge.

Hawkesworth, Mary E. 1989. "Knowers, Knowing, Known: Feminist Theory and the Claims of Truth." *Signs* 14(3): 533–57.

Higgenbotham, Evelyn Brooks. 1992. "African-American Women's History and the Metalanguage of Race." *Signs* 17(2): 251–74.

hooks, bell. 1984. *Feminist Theory: From Margin to Center.* Boston: South End Press.

———. 1990. *Yearning: Race, Gender, and Cultural Politics.* Boston: South End Press.

Lam, Maivan Clech. 1994. "Feeling Foreign in Feminism." *Signs* 19(4): 865–93.

Laqueur, Thomas. 1990. *Making Sex: Body and Gender from the Greeks to Freud.* Cambridge: Harvard University Press.

Lugones, Maria. 1994. "Purity, Impurity, and Separation." *Signs* 19(2): 458–79.

MacKinnon, Catherine A. 1987. *Feminism Unmodified: Discourses on Life and Law.* Cambridge: Harvard University Press.

Martin, Biddy and Chandra Talpade Mohanty. 1986. "Feminist Politics: What's Home Got to Do with It?" In *Feminist Studies/Critical Studies*, ed. Teresa de Lauretis. Bloomington: Indiana University Press.

McKay, Nellie Y. 1993. "Acknowledging Differences: Can Women Find Unity Through Diversity?" In *Theorizing Black Feminisms: The Visionary Pragmatism of Black Women*, ed. Stanlie M. James and Abena P. A. Busa. New York: Routledge.

Minh-ha, Trinh T. 1989. *Woman/Native/Other.* Bloomington: Indiana University Press.

Molina, Maria Luisa "Pupsa." 1994. "Fragmentations: Meditations on Separatism." *Signs* 19(2): 449–57.

Morrison, Toni. 1992. *Playing in the Dark: Whiteness and the Literary Imagination*. New York: Vintage.

Mouffe, Chantal. 1992. "Feminism, Citizenship, and Radical Democratic Politics." In *Feminists Theorize the Political*, ed. Judith Butler and Joan W. Scott. New York: Routledge.

Nicholson, Linda. 1994. "Interpreting *Gender.*" *Signs* 20(1): 79–105.

O'Connor, Noreen and Joanna Ryan. 1993. *Wild Desires & Mistaken Identities: Lesbianism and Psychoanalysis*. London: Virago.

Okin, Susan Moller. 1989. *Justice, Gender and the Family*. New York: Basic Books.

———. 1994. "Gender Inequality and Cultural Differences." *Political Theory* 22(1): 5–24.

Pateman, Carole. 1980. *The Disorder of Women*. Stanford: Stanford University Press.

Rawls, John. 1971. *A Theory of Justice*. Cambridge: Harvard University Press.

Reagon, Bernice Johnson. 1983. "Coalition Politics: Turning the Century." In *Home Girls: A Black Feminist Anthology*, ed. Barbara Smith. New York: Kitchen Table Press.

Rich, Adrienne. 1980. "Compulsory Heterosexuality and Lesbian Existence." *Signs* 5(4): 631–60.

Williams, Patricia J. 1991. *The Alchemy of Race and Rights: Diary of a Law Professor*. Cambridge: Harvard University Press.

Wollstonecraft, Mary. 1967. *A Vindication of the Rights of Woman*. New York: W. W. Norton.

Young, Iris Marion. 1990. *Justice and the Politics of Difference*. Princeton: Princeton University Press.

———. 1994. "Gender as Seriality: Thinking about Women as a Social Collective." *Signs* 19(1): 713–38.

12

El Pasar Discontinuo de la Cachapera/Tortillera del Barrio a la Barra al Movimiento

The Discontinuous Passing of the Cachapera/Tortillera from the Barrio to the Bar to the Movement

María Lugones

Necessary Admonitions: Guidelines Into the Landscape Para Saber de Quien Hablamos y que Queremos Decir por "Hablar" Glossary

- *Ambiente*: Latino/a spaces where homoeroticism is lived. Lived Latino homoeroticism constitutes the spaces as ambiente. Gente de ambiente: jotos y tortilleras.
- *Una conversación*: a word, a look, a gesture, directed out, anticipating a response that anticipates a response in turn without closing out meaning not already contained in the expectations; without pulling by the roots tongues that break the circle of expectations. Our creativity lies in our putting out gestures, words, looks that break closed cycles of meaning en un desafío erótico.
- *Silences*: attentive silences, refusal to speak silences, tongue cut out silences, provocative silences, refusal to listen silences, intimate silences.
- *Signifying and representing*: words that have come to me from the language of gangs and hip hop culture: graffiti writing, tagging, wearing colors, are examples of signifying and representing. The conversation I have in mind needs to include words whose sense has been disrupted and sometimes,

no words at all, as jotas signify and represent ourselves in relation, disruptively, when "ordinary" conversation shuts our mouths.

• *Nombres*: cachaperas, jotas, tortilleras, patas, mita y mitas, marimachas.

Para su Información (Nuevas/*News*)

1. Gays and lesbians march in New York City in a joyous parade that brings together the city's enormous diversity of homosexual life. Participants, including white, Puertorican, African American, Asian, Dominican gays and lesbians, are asked about their wishes and dreams for the year 2000. Each responds, echoing everyone else like a chant: "an end to AIDS-equal rights for gays and lesbians." No matter the location: "an end to AIDS-equal rights for gays and lesbians." Nothing else informs the politics and dreams: "an end to AIDS-equal rights for gays and lesbians" (Lynn, 1994).

2. As the people of Cincinnati were preparing themselves to vote on whether to keep or repeal the city's antidiscrimination ordinance that includes gays and lesbians, right-wing opponents of the ordinance produced a video in which spokespeople for the African American, Latino, and Native American communities spoke against what they saw as "special rights" for gays and lesbians. In the video one can follow the right wing's manipulations of lesbian/gay and particularly African American, but also Latino and Native American identities, histories, struggles. But the video also documents and exploits the disconnection and fragmentation within and between those identities and struggles. The video begins with scenes from the Civil Rights March on Washington, including King's delivery of his "I Have a Dream" speech. The images of the March on Washington are mixed with and overwhelmed by images of the Gay and Lesbian March on Washington. As the images depict the displacement, spokespeople for the African American, Native American, and Latino communities decry the use of civil rights rhetoric by a group of people they identify as outsiders to their groups and struggles and whose lifestyles turn that use into an abomination. "There are no African American, Latino, Native American gays and lesbians" is part of the message. This is a declaration. The question I ask is whether there are any tortilleras, jotas, marimachas.

3. A tortillera is putting up posters in Tucson for an event sponsored by several organizations. As she asks a shop owner whether she can put a poster in his shop, he says: "Yes, if you cut out that sponsor," pointing to "Lesbianas Latinas de Tucson." La tortillera says, "What, are we not part of la raza?" "Not of my raza" says the man (Camacho, 1996).

The Landscape: La Geografía Discontínua

I begin this dangerous reflection with an evocative and problematic text, one that has accompanied me even as I have reflected on its nostalgic, romantic quality: "La geografía de mi barrio llevo en mí. Sería por eso que del todo no me fuí" (Blazquez, 1987). (*I carry the geography of my barrio within me, maybe that's why I have not left altogether.*)

I bring this text to mind because my reflections are about geography, sexuality, and subjectivity in a society where the geographical memory of Latino homoerotic subjects is sharply discontinuous. My intention is to disturb the complacencies that uphold the fusion of heterosexuality and colonization. I see these complacencies as unwitting or careless or tyrannical collaborations between Latino nationalisms and the contemporary U.S. Lesbian Movement in its various versions and enclaves.

Entonces quiero hacerle el try al hablar de una serie de pasos y piezas que nos lleven hacia una conversación comunal latina sobre autodestrucción y sexualidad: Una conversación y where we can signify and represent the urgencies that torture the relation between sexuality and politics in la vida latina, in and out of el ambiente, breaking the circle of ossification and destruction. La relación entre política y sexualidad, una relación osificada, peligrosa, leading one easily to move between self-betrayal and escape, dos lados de la misma moneda. La lengua misma una ambiguedad erótica, un tierno instrumento de tortura: lengua bífida sin ser híbrida, bífida como la lengua de la serpiente, pero tragando veneno. (*So I want to try to speak of a series of steps and pieces that can lead us to a communal Latina conversation about self-destruction and sexuality. A conversation where we can signify and represent the urgencies that torture the relation between sexuality and politics in Latina life, in and out of the ambiente, breaking the circle of ossification and destruction. The relation between politics and sexuality, a dangerous, ossified relation, leading one easily to move between self-betrayal and escape, two sides of the same coin. The tongue itself an erotic ambiguity, a tender instrument of torture: bifid tongue that is not hybrid. Bifid like a serpent's tongue, but swallowing poison.*)

Pasos Discontínuos/*Discontinuous Passing-Steps*

Primer paso

Las butches in sutes, con vests de raso. Imposing, como en un drama, quietas, muy en papel, hieráticas. Cerveza con limón en la boca, in the throat, on the tongue. The steps quick, solid, precise, graceful. The handling of the femmes all contained flirtation. Las femmes con boquitas pintadas, the hair una mata rebelde purposefully trained wild, tacones bien altos. Short, tight, skirts that show off the precision and quickness of the step, the boldness of so much leg. Can I speak here about the meaning of máscaras worn after sun down? Qué, lo digo en español, in my femmes ear, como un bolero? (*The butches in suits, with satin vests. Imposing, as in a drama, still, very much in their roles, hieratic. Beer with lemon in the mouth, in the throat, on the tongue. The steps quick, solid, precise, graceful. The handling of the femmes all contained flirtation. The femmes' mouths lipstick red, the hair a rebellious bush purposefully trained wild, very high heels. Short, tight, skirts that show off the precision and quickness of the step, the boldness of so much leg. Can I speak here about the meaning of masks worn after sundown? What? Do I say it in Spanish, in my femme's ear, like a bolero?*)

Segundo Paso

Y mañana al jale. Con traces de la barra in the movements of the hips, the pursing of the lips to point to things, the taste for love and style directed strictly inward, toward a point inside that is locked beyond meaning. Como si fuéramos simplemente mujeres. Not even bothered by the conversations ordered by heterosexual domesticity. Qué va, si a una ni se le ocurre pensar en ninguna lengua, ni con ningún conjunto de cicatrices y palabras, algo como "ordered by heterosexual domesticity." Oh, a veces se lo piensa, como algo abstracto, taking a step back, like taking a picture for posterity. ¿Y si mi mamá es tortillera? ¿Dónde? ¿Aquí, entre las casadas y por casar, que saben tanto de showers para mujeres y beibis? No tiene sentido. Su ser femme aquí no puede ser para mí. Tortillera es para el mitote, cosa que se dice en susurritos, cosa sucia, invertida. ¡Ay que asco que se besen en la boca! ¡Ay virgencita, ni me lo cuentes! (*And tomorrow to work. With traces of the bar in the movements of the hips, the pursing of the lips to point to things, the taste for love and style directed strictly inward, toward a point inside that is locked beyond meaning. As if we were simply women. Not even bothered by the conversations ordered by heterosexual domesticity. It doesn't even occur to one to think in any language, nor with any set of scars and words, something like "ordered by heterosexual domesticity." Oh, sometimes one thinks about it, like something abstract, taking a step back, like taking a picture for posterity. And if my mother is a tortillera? Where? Here, among the wedded and to be wed, who know so much about showers for brides and babies? No, it doesn't make any sense. Her being a femme here cannot be for me. Tortillera is for gossip, something said in whispers, something dirty, inverted. How revolting that they kiss each other on the mouth! Holy mother of God, don't even tell me about it.*)

Tercer Paso

And there we are, having come from all parts of the city, Belmont Stop in the L, Boystown, everything gay and lesbian dominating the streets, the talk, the buying and the selling. A middle-size room in Horizons. Once a week. All Latina Lesbians getting together to be Latina Lesbians in some half way between the bar and the closet, una penumbra. Trying to find a voice, saying something or other, just to hear "español/lesbiano" spoken at a distance, public style. Boystown frames the scene: the movement brought you this possibility! All the way from the barrio or your escondites (*hiding places*) in the suburbs to la polis homoerótica, where lesbian voices can speak their things at a discrete distance from each other, public style, in any language, all the way across a room, among themselves, far away from las comadres mitoteando su homofobia en susurros (*far away from women gossiping their homophobia in whispers.*)

Fourth Step

Busy, together, articulate, proud, flamboyant, Latina emphasized in the tone, the style, the direction of the lesbian politics. Brazen, self-confident, radical. Influential in the movement, quick to point out the racism, the ethnocentrism, the classism. Fun, intense, warm, no nonsense, fiery, red hot angry presence among lesbians. Planning and risking. Way out, bien asumida, en la sociedad grande, far away from the barrio. Oh sometimes almost touching hands with barrio organizers in marches against 187, almost seeing herself in their eyes as she moves with the fleeting lesbian presence. Not wanting to stop long enough for a good look of herself in those eyes, which may well be her own.

¿Y Qué?/*And So, What Is It to You? To Me?*

Pasos y piezas. Movements in and away from different contexts. La cachapera se mueve (*she moves*) to avoid passing; to avoid becoming a figment of the Anglo imagination consumed by and reduced to protesting ethnocentric racism; to avoid being silenced; to avoid being socially reduced to her construction en el mitote. ¿En qué lugar y en qué desplazamientos es que la cachapera, la jota, la pata, la marimacha, puede encontrar respuestas a sus gestos y palabras, respuestas que se regodeen en la abundancia de su significar? (*In what spaces and through which movements can the cachapera, jota, pata, marimacha, find responses to her gestures and words that take pleasure in the abundance of her meaning?*) I want to take you inside the Latino

Nations and inside the Lesbian Movement, so you can witness that those are not los lugares de la conversación (*those are not the places for the conversation.*) De aquí pa'llá sin encontrar su ground, the ground of her possibilities. (*From one place to the next without finding her ground, the ground of her possibilities.*)

De Aquí/*From Here*

Moving in, inside the nations, rehearsing over and over the lessons of the sacrosanct place of heterolife as she (the cachapera?) affirms her place among Latinos. The idea of Nation brings the logic of the colonizer inside Latino life. The logic of modernity that "unifies" the disparate elements that face the colonizer oppositionally prevents them from creating disruptions of traditions in their encounters with domination. A unified front is itself a commitment to a logic of self-destruction: Nationalism leaves colonialism undisturbed when it places different Latino practices, values, traditions, and limits outside of critique and re-creations; when what is old forms the substance and grounds of "our" rebellion and possibilities. Nationalism leaves colonialism undisturbed when it affirms a line of connection between the colonizer and the colonized in their weddedness to heterosexuality, a line of connection that tightens around la marimacha y la asfixia.

La tortillera passes as heterosexual, a status that is accorded to her face to face. She may be spoken about as a tortillera, but she is not spoken to as such. Heterosexual is a status that she may actually seek through her manner of presentation, including her speech, her compliance, and allegiance to heterosexual norms, including explicit displays of homophobia. Or a status that she allows to be hung on her, like a sign that negates what in her announces her transgression. She does not speak as and in a social sense, because in an outspoken, public social sense she is not a tortillera. Si me dices que no hay lesbians en nuestra comunidad, también quieres decir que "jota," "tortillera," "marimacha," "pata" are not names pa' la gente, dentro de la raza? ¿Y entonces porqué susurras mi presencia entre nosotros behind my back? Los hombres se gritan el insulto, "¡joto!": como drill sergeants entrenando a sus bros en la masculinidad. (*If you tell me that there are no lesbians in our community, do you also mean that "jota," "tortillera," "marimacha," "pata" are not names for our people, within la raza? And then, why do you whisper my presence among us behind my back? Men shout the insult to other men, "¡joto!": like drill sergeants training their bros into Latino masculinity.*)

"Lesbian oppression," says Sarah Hoagland, "is not a relation" (Hoagland, 1988, 4). Heterosexualism denies lesbian existence. That which does not exist cannot relate to anything or anyone else. La tortillera exists en la comunidad only as a pervert. Perversion constitutes her and marks her as outside of countenanced relationality. Her sociality is alive and constructed en el mitote (*in gossip*), in her absence. Pero si la tortillera no habla—aún cuando entra en la iglesia vestida como un chamaco—la gente la considera, le dirije la palabra. ¿Cómo podría hablar excepto en su silencio, sin descubrir su marca? ¿Cómo podría hablar un sentido que no la traicione, que no se le eche pa' trás? (*But if the tortillera does not speak—even when she enters the church dressed in men's clothes—people respect her, they address her. How could she make sense except in her silence, without uncovering her mark? How could she speak a sense that does not betray her, that doesn't turn against her?*)

So, en la comunidad, under the reigns of nationalism, la cachapera is silent, her meaning is made by others. El mitote imagines her as most vividly social and anomalous, but the anomaly is tamed through lack of direct address, through a denial of dialogue. As a woman with a speaking tongue, her tongue is twisted against her name as she passes as heterosexual.

Pa'llá/*To There*

Moving away, away from comunidad Latina to the inside of the Lesbian Movement. Movement toward movement. Our movement guided by a dislike for pained stasis, looking for voice outside the confines of our tongues. Fantastic flight from our possibilities. Because we do, definitivamente, we do, pose a threat to our Nations. Nations that stand on the textured and fragmenting ground of unchallenged, uncritical, complacent, heterosexuality at their own peril. La cachapera: a threatening promise. Instead of cultivating her company toward impure shatterings of colonized communions, la cachapera becomes the Latina/Lesbian. As the Latina/Lesbian she plays out her sexuality uncritically and flamboyantly in ways that combine the idea of closet and colony. These sensual rehearsals take place inside the territoriality of the Lesbian Movement.

Lesbian Movement: in white landscapes, locales, geography. Movement that does not move into Latino communities except fleetingly and without engaging in a contestation of meanings over sexuality and its ossification in Latino life. Movement that lacks a taste for conversations inside locales and ways that risk its complicity with colonization, with our cultural and material erasure. Movement that does not take our integrity seriously because it affirms the confines of its own territoriality.

Oh, we are inside of it, somos la sal sin ejercitar una disrupción de los límites. (*Oh, we are inside it, we are the salt without exercising a disruption of its limits.*) We are inside it, negatively, in a peculiar absence of relationality. Movement that averts its eyes from the split lives of tortilleras/cachaperas en los barrios de Chicago, Los Angeles, New York City, and in the small and middle-size villages, towns, and cities of Arizona and New Mexico.

Latina/Lesbian is an oxymoron, an absence of relation. Latina/Lesbian lacks a hyphen. The territoriality of the movement erases the hyphen. Latina/Lesbian necessarily speaks with a bifid tongue. ¿Cómo podría saber the tones of a hyphenated, hybrid, tongue when she is committed and confined to a negation? The Latina/Lesbian is a critic in the Movement. The Movement can only hear her speak when it sheds the purity that permeates its domain, its geography.

The movement of the tortillera into the Lesbian Movement is a fantastic flight because as she flees the confines of nation in search of substance, range, and voice she becomes an oxymoron, the Latina/Lesbian: two terms in extreme tension. No hyphen: no hybridization. The Latina/Lesbian moves within a Movement that lacks a sense of its geography and becomes aware of territoriality only when it stops outside the Nations. A Movement that lacks a sense of geography finds in the Nations both imagined and real, a fierce sense of geography in resistance to colonization, a sense that "justifies" the Movement's retreat.

The movement of the tortillera into the Lesbian Movement is a fantastic flight because she comes out to a forced speaking in a bifid tongue; because the eyes that see her coming out, remake her in their own imagination. A bifid tongue; split, speaking out of both sides of her mouth. A tongue whose sense is made only in response to the closed sets of meanings of interlocutors whose tongues dictate her own into conversations where she must collaborate with the fusion of nationalism and colonianism. How could the tortillera come out in and into the Movements—movimientos nacionalistas, the gay and lesbian movements—given the closed conversations?

Because of the geography of the Lesbian Movement—all of whose versions stay away from the borders of Latino communities—the Latina/Lesbian is a split, fragmented self that speaks with a bifid tongue and cannot deploy techniques that lead to hybridization. Simple occupancy in the domains while calling the racism does not resolve the split, nor does unveiling one's own mixed raced/mixed culture quality, nor does discussion of hybrid productions that doesn't call into question the where and among whom the conversation takes place, within what geographies. The logic of modernity, of unity, takes a characteristic turn in the geographical setting of boundaries of the Lesbian Movement: "Lesbian" becomes ideologically "unified" even against much protesting and soul searching. The "unification" is produced by avoiding border encounters. All encounters are within the geographical limits of master territories. There, the one who has left the politics and geographies of the Nations gets to protest the Movement's racism while enjoying the "freedoms" of white/Anglo homoerotic landscapes. She gets to change all her relations, a change so profound that she comes to believe in the logic of unification. And isn't it a wonder that this ideological move also leaves the social structures of the Latino Nations undisturbed? La cachapera who wanted voice, gains voice as the Latina/Lesbian and becomes articulate in the logic of modernity, keeping her split self and animating a self that is imagined.

I cannot see any possible justifications for the Lesbian Movement's staying away from border contestations: from engaging the great number of Anglos buying and reselling our geographies, edging their artistic communities into ours and then replacing artists with wealthy lovers of the refined; from engaging the police state flying low over our geographies in helicopters, surrounding them with armored vehicles and armored men, invading them with a will to kill us for being brown, whatever our sexuality.

Can the cachapera gain voice in the Movement? Not unless we take seriously the need to question the geography in which the "we are fa-mi-lí" is to be lived and the colonial induction of cachaperas into the traditions of Anglo-European sapphists (with a difference of course): What's in a name? What's in a place?

¿Es que Acaso la Tortillera Existe en Alguna Parte?/*Does the Tortillera Exist Anywhere?*

La barra is where I see "máscaras worn after sundown." I have the sense that maybe la mujer en la barra is the real thing, la tortillera muy asumida en su ambiente and at the same time I have this inclination to perceive masks in the bar, en el ambiente. Is it that I think there could be someone else underneath the mask waiting to speak? La tortillera is not really "she" who spends her days passing: being seen and not disrupting the being seen as heterosexual, practicing the words and logic of Latino heterosexuality. Does "she" (the passeuse) know the one she is after sundown outside the strict and rather limited rules of comportment of the bar, the limited repertoire, the being seen in such limited circumstances? Does she (la de la barra) know "her" (the passeuse) apart from heterosexual rehearsals? Who sees her? Other tortilleras who, in the light of day, collaborate in the daily production of the passeuse? Does she know "her"? Where? In the midst of what sociality? As someone she betrays in silence? Who betrays whom?

She can be her own possibility to the extent that she can shake the interpretive hold over her movements that reduce her to someone imagined both by the Latino heterosexual imagination and the Lesbian imagination.

She can be her own possibility to the extent that she can be part of a moving that does not diminish her subjectivity, a moving that is geographically devoted to her unbounded inhabitation.

Buscando Dirección/*Looking for Direction*

The passeuse, the Latina/Lesbian, the tortillera in the bar are all "real," constrained, fragmented, all coming to life in problematic geographies. I want voice as a jota, un repertorio amplio en las cosas diarias entre la gente. (*I want voice as a jota, a wide repertoire in daily things among people.*) It is my ground, my own sense of walking in some direction rather than wandering aimlessly and without sense in terrains prepared to swallow me whole or in parts, that we, cachaperas, can move away from the frozen states in which the encounter of colony and Nation have imprisoned us. We can exercise ourselves in the encounter at the geographical limits, where change is bound to happen. Our threat and our promise es que podemos amasar la dirección del cambio (*is that we can knead the direction of the change*), we can make tortillas. We can exercise ourselves confronting our cultures as anomalous beings, as beings denied from within the depths of traditions that also define us. We can exercise ourselves in the encounter with the colonizing cultures in a re-creation of our cultures, bringing our cultures away from the death of conservative clasping into hybrid life. The transformation of the cultures that make us cachaperas, patas, tortilleras, jotas, marimachas, needs to be itself an exercise of those cultures, an exercise that would leave them and us changed.

The crucial and confrontational point here is that to exercise oneself culturally in a live culture is not to repeat over and over in tired combinations the traditions that "constitute us as a people" even when these iterations are presented as defiant refusals of mimicry of the colonizer/dominator. The confrontational and enticing point is that, in the border encounters, we can negotiate in a lively cultural mode that takes issue with domination in tense inside/outside/in between conversations. We, cachaperas, patas, marimachas, can become fleshy tongue, sound out loud, el cuerpo y los gestos significando y representando ampliamente que estamos bien plantadas en la vida diaria, en los encuentros diarios con la colonización y las tiranías de nuestras tradiciones. (*We, cachaperas, patas, marimachas, can become fleshy tongue, sound out loud, the body and the gestures signifying and representing amply that we are well grounded in daily life, in the daily encounters with colonization and our traditions.*)

It is in this way that we can come to conversations that have a suspension of the given in the making of sense. Right now we have ways of silence, in mitote, in negation, in passing; passing as Latina/Lesbians in the Movement and as implicitly or explicitly heterosexual in the Nations. We are also constrained in invisible locations—la barra y las organizaciones de Lesbianas Latinas—where our rehearsals and creations leap geographically out of the border contestations.

It is the tortillera, la pata, la marimacha, la jota, la cachapera, the non-speaking subject, the one who needs voice, movement, who can negate, decry, the torturings of Latino nationalisms and Anglo colonialisms. No one can speak for her but with her. I am suggesting that the production of a hybrid culture is itself an exercise of our cultures. It is in responding to ways, practices, beliefs, that are intrusive, dominating, in a Latino cultural vein, a way that is a taking-in and also a dismantling—of the invading culture that hybrid Latino cultures come to be our cultures. This is a wordly task that we can undertake as cachaperas as we battle, well placed geographically. It is in this way that our tongues acquire the hyphen.

I don't wish to be healed. I feel sensual loving and healing as politically different. I am looking for carnal disruptions. Compromisos íntimos. Una política sexual against the tortures of colonization and Nation.

Acknowledgments

A las marimachas en mi vida, gracias de corazón por la conversación. Gracias especiales a Julia y Laura. Gracias a Kelvin, Isra, Suzanne y a la Tamañota. A Helena Maria Viramontes gracias por organizar "El Frente: U.S. Latinas Under Attack and Fighting Back" at Cornell que me permitió el primer sentido de la posibilidad de conversación y a las Latinas presentes por la conversación. A Aurelia Flores y todas las miembras y miembros de La Familia gracias por organizar la discusión en Stanford. Thanks to the lesbian women in SWIP for the town meeting/discussion of the issues. Gracias a Sarah.

References

Anzaldua, Gloria. 1987. *Borderlands/La Frontera*. San Francisco: Spinsters/Aunt Lute.

Bhabha, Homi K. 1994. *The Location of Culture*. London: Routledge.

Blazquez, Eladia. 1987. "El Corazón al Sur," words and music. *El Corazón al Sur*. Buenos Aires: Elli-Sound S.A.

Camacho, Julia Schiavone. 1996. Personal conversation.

Conmoción: revista y red revolucionaria de lesbianas latinas Number 1. 1995. 1521 Alton Road #336, Miami Beach, FL 33139.

Hoagland, Sarah Lucia. 1988. *Lesbian Ethics: Toward New Value*. Palo Alto: Institute of Lesbian Studies.

Lugones, María. 1994. "Purity, Impurity, and Separation." *Signs* 19 (2): 458–79.

Lynn, Don. 1994. *1993 Gay Parade (NYC)*. Unpublished video.

Moraga, Cherríe. 1983. *Loving in the War Years: Lo que nunca pasó por sus labios*. Boston: South End Press.

Ramos, Juanita, ed. 1987. *Compañeras: Latina Lesbians*. New York: Latina Lesbian History Project.

Rosaldo, Renato. 1989. *Culture and Truth*. Boston: Beacon.

Minh-ha, Trinh T. 1995. "No Master Territories." In *The Post-Colonial Studies Reader*, ed. Bill Ashcroft, Gareth Griffiths, Helen Tiffin. London: Routledge, pp. 215–18.

Trujillo, Carla, ed. 1991. *Chicana Lesbians*. Berkeley: Third Woman Press.

13

Inquiry into a Feminist Way of Life

**Kathryn Pyne Addelson and
Helen Watson-Verran**

Doing Things Together

A feminist ethics has to be suitable for a feminist way of life. If an academic theorist devises the ethics, then there may be two ways of life at issue—the feminist way of life in the world and the academic way of life in which the moral theory is made. For although feminists may work to change the academy, the academy and its disciplines do not practice a feminist way of life. This raises questions that must be answered, about the theorist's participation in the feminist way of life in the world, the theorist's participation in academia as a feminist, and the relation between the two. We see this as the "double participation" of the feminist theorist.

In this paper, we make a proposal for a feminist moral theory that takes the double participation into account by considering ways of life in three sites: Jane Addam's Hull House; a community organization called Wellspring House that operates, as one of its efforts, a family shelter; and an Aboriginal community in Yirrkala in the Northern Territory of Australia. We participate in the latter two communities and our proposal arises out of our work. The proposal includes guidelines for moral theories that feminists make in the academy: that the theories should not prescribe what is to count as a "moral scheme" or a feminist way of life; and they should not prescribe a method of conflict resolution. These guidelines contain pre-scriptions we suggest to our academic coworkers—that our theories should not prescribe certain things about feminism in general. We make them as participants in the common, academic work, not as a prescriptive part of theory. Accepting these guidelines requires changing the methods used in philosophy and some other fields as well as changing the relationship of the academy and ways of life outside the academy. Because of this, we believe the issues we raise shed light on the nature of feminist commitment within the academy.

We'll introduce our discussion with two "scenes."

Scene 1:

Kathy Addelson is a professor at Smith College in Massachusetts. She first drove out to Wellspring House in Gloucester, on Cape Ann in Massachu-setts, in May 1990. Gloucester has been a fishing town since Colonial times, but in recent years, many of its fishing boats lie useless because fish stocks are depleted. Many of the processing plants have closed. Cape Ann suffered terribly from the recent recession and it has not yet recovered. Jobs are gone and housing has been priced out of the market for low- and middle-income households. Some families have no home to call their own.

Homelessness was not a public problem when Wellspring House was founded in 1981, though it became one soon after. Public policy solutions to homelessness assume that the homeless are strangers, like the drunks on skid row, the bag ladies, the drug addicted, or those forced out of institu-tions. Or it is seen as a problem of the poor, who cannot manage for them-selves, who slip through "safety nets." Public policy offers solutions to homelessness when it is defined by seeing the homeless as strangers, out-siders versus the rest of the normal people of the society. The homeless become clients of the social welfare bureaucracies, which are designed to handle these outsiders.

The founders of Wellspring House used a different definition of home-lessness and so had their own solution. They bought the rambling house on Essex Avenue and moved into it, making it their own home. In their eyes, it was a place to work out a vision of *community*, out of a mission of *hospitality* (a basic idea in the vision). One of their thoughts was to offer hospitality to people in need by taking them as *guests* in their own home, and to make this home a part of the community. *Guests* not clients, *home* not shelter. Wellspring House also began to make a home in the community for the many volunteers and other residents in Cape Ann. Their motive sprang from a feminist spirituality that had its early beginnings in the Gospels' talk of the possibility of *transformation*. The feeling was that the project was both part of *the return home* and part of *the experience of exile*, both taken from biblical metaphors. Homelessness was something shared by all women, exiled from home in the earth, home in community, and home in sisterhood.

As the years passed, the vision of hospitality and community became clearer in the day-to-day experience of sheltering families and living and working with the people of Cape Ann. Over the past fifteen years, the organization has established a community land trust to provide affordable housing, an economic venture in marketing underutilized fish, and an ambitious educational program. Today, Wellspring House is integrated into Gloucester and has the support of men and women in all walks of life.

A principle of reciprocity operates at Wellspring House, under which those who give are also to receive. Everyone needs cherishing and a home in the community. For people who volunteer their time at Wellspring, this reciprocity includes cultural and educational workshops. Among the offerings were Kathy Addelson's "work and vision" workshops.

Scene 2:

Helen Verran first came to the school at Yirrkala in the mid-1980s. Yirrkala is a small town in the far northeast corner of Australia's Northern Territory, and most of the residents are Yolngu Aboriginal Australians. The settlement as well as a school were established by Presbyterian Church missionaries (with Government support) in the 1930s. During the 1960s, the state took direct control of Aboriginal schooling, driven by notions of equal opportunity to universal schooling. The bureaucrats spoke of a moral duty to provide young Yolngu Aborigines with a "proper" education: English, mathematics, history, and geography. Under this policy of assimilation, Yolngu input was reduced to Friday afternoon "cultural activities."

Helen Verran is a feminist and a philosopher at the University of Melbourne—an academic professional. When she arrived at the school, she was welcomed in the principal's office by a large, red-faced white man who saw her as a colleague in the task of "civilizing" these people. Helen worked with Yolngu people to develop an educational approach that integrated the Yolngu way of life with the Western curriculum.

In September 1995, Gulumbu, a middle-aged woman, an elder in a community about two hours' drive south of Yirrkala, and a teacher in the community school, stands barefoot in her good clothes facing an audience of seventy or so, assembled in the grassy square of Yirrkala School. Beside Gulumbu is what she calls a "latju min'tji" (a fine design), a map of the school curriculum. She refers to its four areas often; she is explaining how the Yolngu conceptual domain of *djalkiri* can form a basis for children to learn about Western mathematical concepts of space, and how the notions embedded in the Yolngu discourse on *gurrutu* can help Yolngu children get the idea of number. "Djalkiri, space, gurrutu, number" is like a litany.

Booklets line the walls of the school's literature production center, reporting past workshops with community elders, teachers—both Yolngu and *Balanda*—and sometimes academic participants—and of course with the schoolchildren.[1] Put together, these booklets mark the bumpy passage of this group as they struggled toward developing the curriculum Gulumbu is at present elaborating, and which the students' and teachers' work expresses.

Gulumbu's feet are planted wide as she talks of "luku," her metaphorical feet planted firmly in her culture and her own Gumatj lands, which inspire and direct the life of her community. She talks of her commitment, as a teacher paid by the state, to plant the feet of the children of her community firmly in Yolngu life and culture. "Only when this ground is firm and rich can our children effectively take in the Balanda understandings they need." Gulumbu is elaborating what she sees as her moral duty to provide young Yolngu people with a fully fledged contemporary Yolngu education.

A Philosophical Challenge

What are we to make of these two scenes?

Some feminist theorists might see the first scene as involving a "white," "Christian" feminist organization fighting for the rights of the disadvantaged, particularly women and the poor, under capitalist patriarchy. Some feminist theorists might see the second as involving an oppressed indigenous group struggling against the imperialism of "The West." These terms—rights, disadvantaged, capitalist patriarchy, oppression, imperialism—are theoretical terms of feminist political analysis that do not appear among the italicized "folk" terms in the two scenes as we presented them.[2] Yet the folk terms are those that shape the past and future practice in the two scenes. Does this mean that the feminist theorists are prescribing what is to count as a feminist way of life or a method of conflict resolution? If so, what grounds their authority to do so? And what about the presence of the academics in the two scenes? What is their place and their responsibility? These are all questions about what a feminist moral theory is, and what it should be. They are also questions about what philosophical moral theory is and should be.

The *Encyclopedia of Philosophy* divides ethics into three categories: ethics as a way of life; ethics as a code or rules of conduct; ethics as inquiry about ways of life and codes of conduct. Let's look at the first category, ethics as a way of life. The feminist theology of Wellspring House is certainly in conflict with the Presbyterian approach of the 1930s, and though both are Christian, they differ radically in doctrine and in way of life. Our own feminist view is that *doctrine is not separate from the way of life in which it is embodied*. On the philosophical side, this was Wittgenstein's point about language games. But it is also the foundation of feminist criticism of male dominance. Taking women's experience seriously requires understanding how the doctrines associated with male dominance play out in the way of life. Categories one and three are two sides of a coin.

What of category two? Particularly, what about professional ethics? Here we must also assume that the "professional code," since it is a doctrine, has its meaning in a way of life, but this time, it is the professional way of life. We might ask what "code" is appropriate for academics, but for feminists it is better to ask what "way of life" is appropriate for academics who are trying to do "the characteristic philosophical task?" The philosophical task for feminists must be embedded in a way of life for theorists who have one foot in the academy and another outside. The academic way of life includes the teaching; the departmental and university duties; the luncheons and conferences; the friendships and social gatherings with colleagues; presentations at professional meetings (including feminist ones); feminist research; and of course, formulating feminist theories.

We each take part in the scenes we described above, but we also take part, in the very writing of this paper, in the academic way of life. We have a "double participation" in both scenes, as participants at Wellspring House or Yirrkala, and as participants in the academy. It is this double participation that allows the work to be feminist in the sense that feminist theory is aimed at changing society. Feminists who restrict their work and their friendships to the academy make their contributions through the machinery of the academy, and that machinery is heavily implicated in the ruling apparatus, as Dorothy Smith (1987) calls it. A theory is not to be detached from a way of life any more than a doctrine is. And a way of life is not to be detached from the day-to-day intimacy of doing things together.

We'll begin illustrating our approach with another "scene," this time out of United States history—the story of Jane Addams and the founding of Hull House. In this story, Jane Addams was a moral theorist who resisted academia and chose to be a central activist in the feminist way of life. Beginning with this story allows us to show concepts and methods of our moral theory leaving aside, for the moment, the complex issue of the relationship of double participation. We'll then move on to take up double participation by continuing our discussion of the two scenes in which we are participants.

Hull House

When Hull House opened in Chicago in 1889, the United States was suffering the birth pangs of becoming a modern nation. It was submerged in the public problems named in the history books—urbanization, immigration, labor unrest, terrorism, rape and pillage by banking and industrial barons, corrupt governments unable to govern an ungovernable democracy. There were also problems suffered by ordinary folk, particularly women, problems of illegitimate births, abortion, abusive husbands and fathers, prostitution, disease, hunger, poverty, and in general the terrible dangers of anarchic and immoral cities. The Women's Christian Temperance Union attributed the cause of many of these problems to alcohol, and their solution was temperance. Other "purity" reformers found a solution in censorship and changes in the law, a route supported by many women but one that had to be spearheaded by men because women did not have the vote, and they could not hold political office (Pivar, 1973).

These were days of the division in practice between the public and domestic spheres, men's sphere and women's sphere. At the time, there were women fighting to enter the professions where they would, in effect, use the ways of men's sphere to contribute to resolving the conflicts. Addams took the home to be the original center of civilization. The home was a center for care for others, for the education of children, and for enjoying music, art, literature, and beauty of all sorts. The home was a place where there was acceptance and love and commitment to others. Addams wrote that a new *social ethic* was needed to extend women's moral perspective out of its parochial focus on the family to the larger world. She was writing not only a new social ethic but a new politics.

The new social ethic required altering the boundary between men's and women's spheres, not a change of mind but a change in way of life. She expressed the change in terms of becoming a neighbor to the poor. By becoming a neighbor to the poor, she hoped that class conflict might be eased and class walls worn down.

Becoming a neighbor to the poor was understood in the tension with more traditional practices. It was not helping the poor through charity or delivering humanitarian aid. It was not renting an apartment and helping out the people next door. It was not modeled on a religious ideal of divesting oneself of possessions and becoming like the poor to live a good Christian life for the sake of one's soul. Being a neighbor to the poor was increasingly understood in the course of the collective passage through which the new way of life came to be, out of tension with the old ways and the newly forming ways of the raw city of Chicago. Addams understood becoming a neighbor to the poor in accord with the slogan, *The doctrine must be understood through the deed.* This was something she took from Tolstoy and (later) Gandhi, but it was also the principle of the American anarchists of her time. Neighbors, the volunteers, the charismatic leaders, philanthropists, politicians, and even academics were involved in the process of making Hull House. This process was a collective passage made with the participation of all these people.

Addams and others became neighbors to the poor by founding and living in Hull House, the original settlement house. They changed their own ways of life, and their immigrant neighbors changed theirs, through all of them participating in the neighborhood activities. At one time or another, the settlement house included catering service, child care, a kindergarten, a coffee house (an alternative to bars as a social place), an art gallery, a library, concerts, and regularly scheduled talks and discussions by speakers who ranged from soap boxers to professors. There was also health education and emergency aid for neighbors in crisis.

Hull House provided the neighbors with a place of their own, allowing the older folk to talk about history, and the younger to record present and past times before they were lost. The immigrants, after all, had brought with them the cultures of the various European peoples. There were also research projects aimed at understanding the city and neighborhood. They included "mapping" the neighborhoods according to population, family type, occupation, and income, with the maps posted at Hull House (not locked away in the University of Chicago library). There was a two-volume report, produced by insiders—stories about themselves, their customs, experiences, and hardships. The University of Chicago tried for years to take Hull House under its aegis, believing that the settlement house offered "a window on the slum" for academic studies and students' training, but the Hull House regulars resisted the effort. All of this was part of the collective passage in which the new "people of the United States" was to be born. It was education, but not in the way that education was offered in school.

Addams' social ethic was also a new politics that had its root in dissolving the public/domestic wall. It was community-based and grew out of women's work and concerns in the family and home neighborhood. It was not a politics of rights and liberties, though she did work in the necessary tensions with city, state, and federal government. It was not a politics of class conflict. In fact, she intentionally offered it as an alternative to the bloody class warfare between labor and capital.

In our story of Hull House, we have introduced a number of the notions of our moral theory. The basic unit of our theory is that of a *collective passage*—rather than the more usual notions (in Anglo-American ethics) of individuals, principles, virtues or character, moral reasoning, codes, cultures, human nature, dominance and oppression, and the like. "Becoming a neighbor to the poor" was a *folk concept* embedded in the way of life at Hull House, so that in the passage in which they made the way of life, the participants were sensitized to what it meant. *Passage* is a notion of our theory meant to sensitize our readers to the dynamic aspects of ways of life. *Social problem* is another concept we have used. Our idea is that social problems are constructed in ways that set the range of possible solutions. Participants in Hull House defined the social problems differently from both the politicians and the good Christians who offered charity. The tensions within which Hull House operated emerged from these differences.

Folk concepts are bound up with the everyday life and the politics of community groups, and with different groups, and in different times and places, the folk concepts are different. Folk concepts offer a foundation for moving on into the future amid the tensions of the present. Our next two cases, that of Wellspring House in Gloucester, Massachusetts, and of the Yolngu in Australia involve different folk concepts, but some of the sensitizing concepts we use as researchers are useful talking about the differences in situation and politics in their passages.

Wellspring House

The folk concepts of the feminist ethics practiced at Wellspring House include those of *hospitality, home, guest*. Hospitality has its core in the behavior of householder to stranger—in the requirements placed on host and guest for peoples in hard lands, the obligation to open the home even to strangers and to provide food, drink, and shelter even though there is barely enough for one's own. Hospitality in this sense requires risking oneself. It gives a very different definition of the problem of "homelessness" from the official definition of the social problem in the United States, which seems to mean, "without a roof over one's head," not "without a home." The social welfare bureaucracies that offer the solutions to the problem defined in this way provide a protective wall between "normal" citizens and the homeless—"normal people" need not risk themselves as hosts in a hard land.

In their initial choice of buying Wellspring, the founders challenged the definition of home by making the notion of home include Wellspring—a home in the community, not a homeless shelter. Wellspring House is part of the shelter system in Massachusetts; families are referred by social service agencies, and Wellspring receives a portion of its operating budget in this way, but it leads to serious tensions because social service agencies must define guests as clients, using a rights and entitlements vocabulary.

Wellspring House exists in the midst of these and other tensions, including those of the market and government. The tensions form not only the arena for its survival and success but the arena for social change as well. Working within the tensions is how the new way of life is born within the old.

I, Kathy Addelson, had done volunteer work with community organizations on and off since 1972, and I had worked with other feminists in the academy since that time as well. In the spring of 1990, I met Rosemary Haughton, a feminist theologian and one of the founders of Wellspring. We exchanged our books, and a short time later I paid an overnight visit to Wellspring and began to know the house and its ways, and they began to know me. Rosemary and another founder, Nancy Shwoyer, and I got along well together and shared much of our feminist outlook as well as our understanding of political methods—their understanding was far better grounded in political practice than mine, while mine included the research in women's history and politics that my academic position had allowed. We decided that I should try offering workshops for the volunteers—eventually they came to be called "Work and Vision Workshops" because they explored ideas and possibilities for making a different future through the way of life at Wellspring. Vision came from imagination grounded in practice, work was necessary to test and effect vision. Over the next three years, I did four to six workshops a year in which we discussed issues like class and race, community, market, state and civil society, the nature of social problems, Reaganomics, and some economic history. By some act of synchronicity, I chose Hull House as the topic for the first workshop. People at Wellspring had not known of Jane Addams's work, although their efforts were similar in some ways.

After the first workshop, the topics were selected in discussion with the workshop members, or in a planning discussion that covered a series of workshops with two of the founders and the director of volunteers. In a planning meeting for the third-year workshops, I asked the three what they believed were the functions of the workshops. According to notes I took at the time, they said:

> The workshops are one of the circles of reflection about Wellspring practice. They are primary in the sense that those who attend may explain and carry to other places a harmonious development of theory, analysis, and understanding. Otherwise people are let down and the influence for transformation is lost. They should be able to answer, when people ask them, "Why do you go to Wellspring to volunteer?" The workshops help that.
> The workshops offer an opportunity to think aloud and push ideas forward. Raise questions we haven't thought of yet.

The workshops offer a dialog where people deepen their awareness. It's a place of reflection on action that's going on, at the same time that it moves the action forward. People's minds get energized for the action as well.

The workshops build community—it's an intellectual search together. A personal and spiritual search are satisfied.

The volunteers were enthusiastic participants at the workshops, eager and excited about exploring how history and economics related to problems Gloucester was facing and how they might, together, have the vision and do the work to make the future. My own academic work had to change to fit the needs of the group and Wellspring's community work—quite different from work designed for the academic classroom. Even the theoretical problems I faced were different.

With the Yolngu

The Yolngu Aboriginal community at Yirrkala in Australia's Northern Territory aspires to *self-reliance, self-sufficiency*, and *self-determination*. These are the folk terms that the community uses to explain itself. The community sees itself as needing to control its own future, to be remade in ways that are informed and inspired by stories of its Yolngu pasts. But this is not a form of apartheid. At all levels in the community it is recognized that non-Aboriginal people are important in making Yolngu futures. The community sees their endeavor as being as much about promoting change in "mainstream Australia," as it is about imagining a Yolngu future. And this is a risky business on both sides, but perhaps more so on the Yolngu side.

One of the most important sources of inspiration is the homelands movement. This began in the 1970s as the various Yolngu clans began to actively work toward establishing permanent settlements in their own clan lands. Being Yolngu is living in your lands and through your everyday life, and ceremonial life, paying homage to those spiritual ancestors who created the land. In contemporary times this involves hunting, fishing, and collecting food, and singing and dancing in ceremonies; it also includes bores for permanent water supply, road and air transport, medical facilities, and schooling. It is schooling that is the most perplexing. It involves a profound re-imagining of contemporary education and of traditional Yolngu notions of education, which center around participation in ceremony.

Schooling here is perplexing both for bureaucratic, mainstream educational institutions and officials, and for Yolngu institutions and cognitive authorities alike. The classroom life that comes into being in the Yolngu schools is brought forth *working with* and through *on-going*. The minute-to minute life of Yolngu classrooms grows from the tensions between the alternative knowledge traditions that teachers are seeking to mobilize. What/how are the teachers to teach?

From the time of the establishment of the first school in the region, the Yolngu community has voiced a need for Yolngu teachers. The entire problematic of Yolngu education took on new dimensions when, in the mid-1980s, clan leaders finally convinced teacher education authorities of the efficacy of community-based teacher education. Yolngu teachers stay in their communities, and visiting teacher educators work with them there. Curriculum development, both for schools and for the teacher education program, was taken as central in this new endeavor. And it was through this newly established, community-based Yolngu teacher education program that I, Helen Verran, came to the community in 1986. I was a visiting research fellow at the university providing the teacher education program, one of the few there with extensive cross-cultural experience.[3]

Having the teachers remain in their communities during their teacher education enabled community elders, as local cognitive authorities, to intervene in and contribute to their education as contemporary Yolngu teachers. But we soon came up against a problem. The interventions and contributions needed to be public events; private tutoring of individual student teachers would not produce public knowledge and constitute curricula. This endeavor needed to produce accredited knowledge as well as sensitized (trained) teachers.

Out of this tension between public and private knowing, *galtha* workshops were devised as a forum for producing public knowledge that worked both Yolngu and Western knowledge traditions together. And the making of galtha workshops was explicitly informed by particular understandings from both Yolngu and Western knowledge traditions. Here is how Raymattja Marika, a senior Yolngu teacher, describes the origins of galtha workshops in Yolngu knowledge traditions.

> In starting our research we have to negotiate our starting point and our direction in our work. We need to fit this into our Yolngu understanding of ways to do this. Galtha helps us answer these questions: In a Yolngu school where do we start? Do we start from curriculum documents that are sent to us from outside the community? Do we negotiate together a starting point and direction on the basis of where we are, who we are, who is with us, and how we can use the laws and traditions of our ancestral leaders and our community elders?

We considered the example of situations when there is to be a ceremony. Ceremonies must be planned so that all the correct interrelationships are taken into account. Negotiations take place to find the right place to start and the right direction to follow. This negotiated starting point is called the galtha.

So a galtha workshop is in some ways like a Yolngu ceremony. It is a public expression of knowledge involving all those who have a legitimate claim to be involved. And a galtha workshop, like a ceremony, is an expression of a negotiated way that all those (often opposed) interests can work together. What emerges from a ceremony (or workshop) is called *garma* (stabilized) knowledge. In a traditional ceremony this is re-presented in the form of dance, song, and painting. In a galtha workshop the stabilized knowledge is re-presented in the form of a written text, a booklet reporting and evaluating the episode. All those present are expected to contribute a text of some form for the booklet. Participation in a galtha workshop is expected to be a transforming experience, and it is expected that this transformation will show in the texts that constitute the booklet. Galtha workshops are distinguished by the very wide range of teachers and learners who participate, from children to senior elders, school teachers, and teacher educators and curriculum officials. The mix can vary, but it is important to have all those there who should be there. I am treated as an elder on the Balanda side. I both learn and teach.

Contributions from Yolngu and Balanda alike are valued, and these contributions are made within a structure that has been extensively negotiated over the several preceding weeks. The focus of the first workshop in 1988 was recursion. We looked at what gurrutu (the formal Yolngu kinship system) and number held in common. We had lecturers on the Yolngu side and I was the lecturer on the Balanda side. We actively negotiated ways of talking of recursion in this context, through finding ways to teach each other. Yolngu language and English were both used, but there was no official translation.

Since 1988 workshops have been held on a very wide range of topics, and we have come to a formalized way of representing curriculum as the four areas: gurrutu (the formal Yolngu kinship system, a recursive formation), number (also a recursive formation), djalkiri (the analog notions that mobilize space in Yolngu life) and space (the digitalized version of space common in Western life).

Galtha is a folk concept of contemporary Yolngu life, but its "substantive" content is made anew in each ceremony, and now in each workshop, each instantiation of this theory of knowledge making. As a folk concept, galtha has been drastically extended. The garma curriculum has accreted in the form of booklets reporting and evaluating galtha workshops. Those of us who have been to many galtha workshops know what to expect; we are sensitized. Galtha workshops have become a standardized and standardizing form, and out of them new concepts are routinely produced, and old concepts extended. A robust and coherent curriculum is coming to life. In addition Yolngu knowledge authorities understand themselves as cognitive authorities in new ways, and the academy of the Balanda world also has possibilities, for understanding itself in new ways.

As an academic philosopher I tell a conceptual story about this work, and this conceptual story involves technical terms like "folk terms" and "tensions." But, like the term "galtha," these terms have content only in their instantiations in particular times and places.

Feminist Ethics as Moral Theory and Way of Life

At the beginning of this paper, we presented two guidelines for feminist theorists in the academy: our theories should not legislate what is to count as a moral way of life nor should they legislate the method of conflict resolution. We have located moral ways of life in the three communities we described. The methods of "conflict resolution" were contained in the practices within each group and captured in their central concepts of "becoming a neighbor to the poor," "hospitality," and "galtha." We use various terms of our moral theory in doing this, including those of "a passage," "social problem," and "tension." We have discussed these notions elsewhere, and we'll say only a little here (Addelson, 1994; Watson-Verran 1990, 1990a).

The concepts of the folk communities at Hull House, Wellspring House, and Yirrkala are lived in the collective life. The concepts of our moral theory presuppose two ways of life for their meaning. One is the professional, disciplinary, and academic way of life, while the other is the way of life in the folk communities. The theoretical notions must be useful both in the folk communities and in the academic communities. They are elements in the relations between the two ways of life that concern the intellectual and moral responsibility of the academic theorists. Among the most important of the notions of our moral theory is that of a passage. That concept is meant to sensitize the theorist to seeing ways of life (including the academic way) as dynamic and changing, as arising out of a past and reaching into a future. Passages as we have discussed them here are fundamentally collective, and whatever balance there is must be worked out within tensions, tensions being the way of the social and natural world. Concepts and theories have no existence outside the life of knowing communities, and we hope our moral theory is versatile enough to connect up academic life with communities outside academia and to let those other communities change academic life by way of changing its practice and theory.

For the sake of intellectual responsibility, academic theories require test. Feminists (and others) have conclusively criticized the old requirements of testing against empirical instances with the observer located at a neutral, "Archimedian point." We believe the test of any theory should be whether it is useful to ways of life outside the academy. For a feminist theory, being useful requires allowing women with experience, women involved in action toward a feminist way of life, to create the folk concepts necessary to change—this rather than prescribing them in the abstract theories judged solely by disciplinary standards. It also requires finding ways to allow those feminists to change the academy and its theories and practices. In the earlier days of the second wave of the women's movement, this was much more the practice than it is today, and it resulted in some significant change.

Our theorizing as part of the community of philosophers also tests our theory and often in valuable and necessary ways. Our point is that criticism by disciplinary standards alone is not sufficient—not in the humanities or the social sciences, not even in the holy halls of the science buildings.

We professionals in the academy pass through a long training and a severe discipline. The terms of our theories and our methods have been made to suit certain practices and certain audiences—the classroom, the thesis advisers, the journal editors, the participants at scholarly meetings. It's difficult to escape having our work entirely embedded in this way of life. We want to close with a remark written by Frederique Marglin in her introduction to essays by participants in the Peruvian project called PRATEC. In it, she discusses the radical moves made by some professionally trained people working in the Andes.

PRATEC was founded by three men who were members of the first generation of Peruvians from non-elite, peasant background to have access to university training, men who had reached significant positions, one in a government bureau, another in a development agency, the third in a university. They had devoted themselves to helping their people, but in the end, they concluded that the problems lay with the very idea of development that was at the base of their professions. We have not left our professional employment, but we are struggling to see with some clarity the nature of the knowledge we learned in our disciplines and to see with greater clarity the ways of life and the ways to the future that are being made outside the academy.

We have told stories about Wellspring House and the Yirrkala curriculum project, and we hope it is clear from those stories that the important concepts in ethics are embodied in the passages that constitute the ways of life. The moral concepts are self-consciously developed in the local community practice. Those are the places where feminist ethics is made, not in the academy. An academic moral theory, in the sense of category three, is feminist to the degree that it can accommodate and be useful to passages in the feminist ways of life outside the academy. Being useful requires commitment and actual participation by the theorist. An academic moral theory is feminist to the degree that the theorist acts to allow activists to change the academy and to change the very way academic theory is made.

Notes

1. "Balanda" is the Yolngu word for white Australian. It is a word that predates British settlement of Australia, a version of the Macassan "Hollander."

2. See Becker 1970 and Addelson 1994 for discussion of folk terms. Our point is that they are not the terms used for political movement in our two scenes. When theorists use them in their theories, they do not explain our scenes and they implicitly accept a political approach that is quite different.

3. I had recently returned to Australia after seven years working at Obafemi Awolowo University in Nigeria.

References

Addams, Jane. 1907. *Democracy and Social Ethics*. New York: MacMillan.

———. 1910. *The First Twenty Years at Hull House*. New York: MacMillan.

Addelson, Kathryn Pyne. 1994. *Moral Passages: Toward a Collectivist Moral Theory*. New York: Routledge.

Becker, Howard S. 1970. *Sociological Work: Method and Substance*. Chicago: Aldine.

Encyclopedia of Philosophy. 1968. New York: MacMillan.

Pivar, David. 1973. *Purity Crusade*. Westport, CT: Greenwood Press.

Smith, Dorothy E. 1987. *The Everyday World as Problematic: A Feminist Sociology*. Boston: Northeastern University Press.

———. 1990. *The Conceptual Practices of Power: A Feminist Sociology of Knowledge*. Boston: Northeastern University Press.

Watson-Verran, Helen. 1990. "With the Yolngu Community." In Yirrkala and D. W. Chambers, *Singing the Land, Signing the Land*. Geelong, Australia: Deakin University Press.

———. 1990a. "The Politics of Knowing and Being Known." *Arena*, 92: 125–34.

FOUR

Policy and Its Issues

Feminist Politics or Hagiography/Demonology?

Reproductive Technologies as Pornography/Sexworks

Dion Farquhar

> Liberated from subjection to biologico-Christian standards, pleasure must now be politically correct.
> —JANE GALLOP

> That child-bearing is no longer automatic has spawned a whole series of discourses and representations that figure forth contradictory ideologies and unconscious fantasies.
> —E. ANN KAPLAN

Technology as Pornography

While *what* pornography signifies has always constituted a site of intense contestation, Walter Kendrick argues in *The Secret Museum* (Kendrick, 1987) that it has become a locus of impassioned debate for U.S. and European feminism in the 1980s. The rhetorics that represent these conflicts over the normative and strategic valence of pornography/sexwork are isomorphically reproduced in most contemporary feminist representations of assisted reproductive technologies.

It is in recent years that the antipornography feminist gaze has turned its moralizing ire on another set of misogynist cultural practices that unequivocally harm women—reproductive technologies. This paper will show how the radically opposed norms, epistemic commitments, metaphysical assumptions, and political styles that animate *both* the pornography and the reproductive technology debates remain largely unacknowledged. Most feminist representations of pornography and reproductive technology are equally underlaid by incommensurable theories of signification: postmodernist social constructionism versus naturalist essentialism.

A few feminist writers make the homology between feminist representations of reproductive technologies and pornography/sexwork explicit

(Raymond, 1993). "The act of men buying women for sex bears a striking resemblance to men buying women's reproductive services in surrogacy. The connection between sexual and reproductive politics is no mere metaphor" (Rowland, 1991, 32). So, for example, they assert a connection between pornography and sonogram technology as analogous visual appropriations of women's private or internal experience. Women's testimony or "experience" is cited as unproblematic foundational truth criteria.

> Against the grim background of the huge pornography industry and other evidence of social misogyny, it becomes important to resist the tendency to use technology in ways that turn attention away from the woman in labor, or which devalues the pregnant woman's own felt experience of the fetus, in favor of publicly observable images on a cathode ray tube. (Whitbeck, 1988, 56)

In addition, I believe that feminist excoriations of both pornography/sexwork and reproductive technology are sustained by a constitutive moralism that is suspicious of and conflicted about any political practice that foregrounds desire—and with it, the necessary admission of ambivalence, multiplicity, contradiction, and compromise. Antipornography feminist critic Susanne Kappeler indicts the straw woman of desire-as-escape:

> Political consciousness means recognizing no sanctuaries from political reality, no aesthetic or fantastic enclaves, no islands for the play of desire. (Kappeler, 1986, 147)

It is a much unacknowledged irony that feminism's attack on compulsory natalism has stimulated contradictory fantasies, *desires*, and investments for a diversity of maternal positions and identifications. As Ann Kaplan has noted: "The feminist movement has itself contributed to the destabilizing of the mother, in turn creating a renewed *desire* to occupy the mother position" (Kaplan, 1992, 182).

Epistemic norms such as skepticism, tolerance of gender ambiguity, subcultural deviance (particularly male-to-female transsexuals), suspicion of closure and finality, and parodic appropriation all work to interrupt monological feminist excoriations. Binary antipornography and antitechnology feminist narratives divide the players neatly into "real" women and "real" men, who devolve into category exaggerations: victims and perpetrators, oppressed female technology users and profiteering male providers, coerced prostitutes and exploitive pimps.

Anti-reproductive technology and antipornography feminist discourses share a conception of "the natural" that functions to assuage contemporary anxieties over instabilities in women's reproductivity—marriage, family life, and sexuality. The posit of an idealized, pre-patriarchalized "nature" serves to police undomesticated and unruly family and sexual practices by reinventing conventional boundaries (biology-gestation). Such pumping up of ossified oppositions (nature-culture) shores up, ignores, or repairs fissures in naturalizing ideologies (maternity, nature), as well as recuperates unstable identity categories (mother) whose apparent unicity is undermined by contemporary destabilizing hybrid practices.

In this paper I argue that most contemporary feminist political struggles around women's reproductive health and pornography/sexwork have been hamstrung between two equally untenable, narrow conceptual frameworks: liberalism and radical feminism. While many theorists and activists have utilized rhetorics of self-ownership and a woman's right to control and *own* her body—often against patriarchal practices and ideologies of forced trafficking, intrusion, or commodification—these Lockean formulations have in turn been criticized by radical feminists and Marxists who argue that the liberal rhetoric of property rights and body ownership contributes to women's subjection to capitalist patriarchal institutions.

Radical feminist critiques of individualist ownership as inherently masculinist, however, themselves rely on an uncritical, essentialist embrace of feminine "difference." Rosalind Pollack Petchesky's nuanced reconsideration of the usefulness and indispensability of rhetorics of bodily ownership insists on the difference between "a rhetorical strategy for political mobilization and defining identities, *not* a description of the world" (Petchesky, 1995, 387).

Radical Feminist Representations

A "brothel model" is proposed by Andrea Dworkin in *Right-Wing Women* and endorsed by Gena Corea: "While sexual prostitutes sell vagina, rectum and mouth, reproductive-prostitutes will sell other body parts: wombs, ovaries, eggs" (Corea, 1987, 39). Pornography and reproductive technologies are condemned by opponents on the zero-sum grounds of female victimization for male pleasure (pornography) or profit (reproductive technologies). Whereas pornography commodifies *nonreproductive* sex for pleasure (the male client's), reproductive technologies commodify medical and laboratory procedures for *nonsexual* reproduction. Feminist critics of these practices oppose commodification as an appropriation that somehow deforms women's bodies from their original (essential) integrity. "Because of the Radical Feminist analysis of the oppression of women through male sexuality and power, and because of the demand *to take back our bodies*, Radical Feminism has defined sexuality as political" (Rowland and Klein, 1990, 290, italics added).

For antipornography feminists, reproductive technologies are a manifestation of patriarchal domination and greed, fueled by the ruthless exploitation of women's bodies by men envious of women's procreative power. According to the feminist misery narrative, desperate, uncritical, infertile women flock to the patriarchy's techno-medicine, the equivalent of unhappy hookers in the pharmacrats' "reproductive brothel" (McClintock, 1992).

> Technological reproduction completes the medicalization of sex begun in the nineteenth century. The sexual objectification and violation of women is made invisible because technological reproduction has turned medicalized pornography into education, made medicalized access to the female body acceptable, and transformed medicalized abuse into standard treatment. Technological reproduction is first and foremost about the appropriation of the female body. (Raymond, 1993, xxxi)

They believe that "women" are an essential group that—by virtue of being women—share an alternative oppositional set of female values based on nurturance, procreativity, and emotion. They construe pornography and reproductive technology providers and consumers monolithically—as utterly lacking in agency, will, and ability to choose or inflect their practices or take responsibility for risks they entail. Rosalind Petchesky has noted this utilization of "the language of the 'essential woman' as sexual and reproductive being . . . [in which] all prostitutes, all surrogate mothers, all wives become the same" (Petchesky, 1995, 395–96). Only such a universalizing reductionism could speak as self-righteously and confidently for *all* users and producers of these complex practices.

They deny the complexity of social construction and historical and cultural production of such values as well as their problematic long association with women's subordination. Antipornography and anti-reproductive technology feminist critiques share a universalizing impetus. They assert the harmfulness of these practices as if they were static reified objects, and not a complex of shifting practices and interactions having essentially no *inevitability* of effect or consistency of interaction. Their dire predictions assume a universality of reception, and a seamlessness of providers, clients, and resisters' intentions and appropriations. Like the narrative of women's subordination and oppression and the necessary binary implied by these concepts, male domination—what it is and how it works—is unvaryingly monolithic, stable, and self-consistent. It "is always the same" (Birke et al., 1990, 228).

Feminist antipornography and anti-reproductive technology narratives make two symbiotic, essentializing binary moves: they stipulate and then canonize "the natural" as a "found" object; and they demonize both the market and the consumer. Both strategies siphon discussion away from the complex social relations that constitute the unstable and shifting gender identities of people who provide, use, consume, contest, and staff the pornography/sexwork industry as well as the biomedical industry that mediates the delivery of reproductive technologies.

Unintended Consequences

The emergence in the 1980s of prostitutes' unions and alliances (PONY, etc.), feminist pornographers as writers, filmmakers, directors, actors, and performance artists, as well as a burgeoning list of lesbian hardcore video and sex zines have facilitated some interesting feminist interventions and appropriations. In the case of sexwork, prostitutes' advocates seek to end police and legislative harassment and bring the industry under the minimal control of the same juridicolegal norms that bring the relative benefits and protections offered by liberal corporate capitalism to most workers in that sector. Reproductive technologies, particularly donor insemination and the rise of commercial sperm banks, have likewise produced many unintended effects, including the expansion of the narrow canon of family and parenting practices from middle-class heterosexual married nuclear couples to middle-class single women and both single and partnered lesbians.

The proliferation of VCR technology and video rental stores carrying X-rated tapes has created a new (home) audience for pornography and consequently depleted the mostly male movie theatre audience. The larger home video rental market includes social groups largely absent from the traditional sleazy porn theatre audience of men alone: single females, heterosexual couples, and lesbian couples. In addition, many larger video stores (along with some feminist bookstores) devote entire sections to lesbian videos—some of which are produced by lesbian directors, actors, and production companies.

Feminist censorship advocates anachronistically configure the pornography consumer as seamlessly monolithic and self-identical. He, and this subject position is always "he," is the skulking social misfit, the proto-psycho aficionado of the male-dominated porn film theatre and peep show, directly incitable by his image consumption to rape and act violently against women. According to simplistic feminist reception theory, male pornography consumers cannot distinguish between representations and real social relations. Porn consumers are mimetic ciphers, incapable of distinguishing the monolithic representations they see in porn films or peep shows from their own (future) behaviors. Women, pure victims, must be saved from male lust and desire; they themselves have no agency or desires. The unacknowledged feminist model is Platonic (not Aristotelian *catharsis*) in its equation of representation with *mimesis* and debasement; and the solution is Platonic: authoritarian protectionism (Plato, *Laws*, 817 b–d).

Nonconsumers, on the other hand, those antiporn (all female) advocates who do not watch, and would never be turned on by, porn videos, or women who do not use reproductive technologies but reproduce "naturally," somehow transcend the manipulative representational contagion of woman-degrading imagery, freely engaging in sexual behaviors that are somehow beyond power. In alliance with the radical right and its censors, "we" all may be liberated from sexual imagery deemed dangerous via restrictive legislation under the banner of "community standards" in the near future. According to this antimarket moralizing metaphysic, however, the time and space of a before or an after to pornography not only is posited as possible, but also presumed to actually exist, outside of the economies of discourse, desire, and power.

Unintended utilizations of both pornography and reproductive technologies are both the result of changing social and economic trends and political struggles as well as the stimulus for future social consequences and the development of new sites of contestation. Along with their right-wing allies, antipornography and anti-reproductive technology feminists deny the production and productivity of emergent contestations that both pornography and reproductive technologies have engendered in contemporary culture. One antipornography theorist hectors feminists about the necessity of unitary politics:

> Political consciousness includes historical determinations as writing subject, . . . and it means owning up to one's gender and the history of that gender. It means giving up the fantasy of the literary androgyne. (Kappeler, 1986, 147)

The politics of prohibition also ignores the pro-sex contribution to sex discourses made by pornography in proliferating varieties of enthusiastic explicit sex-for-pleasure representations in an increasingly antisex and anti-safe-sex-education (including condom-distribution) milieu. Similarly, advocating a politics of suppression of reproductive technologies ignores the social possibilities inherent in dividing and multiplying social options for maternal practice (Singer, 1989). The ahistorical and acontextual representation of these practices by antipornography activists as ubiquitously oppressive and universally similar ignores their diversity, hybridity, unintended transgressive potential, and diverse appropriations and contestations.

Antipornography and antitechnology narratives constitute a genre of victim testimonials. These include the testimony of former prostitutes, on the one hand, and unsuccessful reproductive technology users, on the other hand, testifying to the degradation and suffering they endured as sexworkers or as patients and their struggles to leave the sex industry or medical treatment. One of the few feminists who has noted the commonality between feminist antipornography campaigns and religious fundamentalist movements is Elizabeth Wilson. She defines fundamentalism as

> a world view . . . which insists that the individual lives by narrowly prescribed rules and rituals: a faith that offers certainty . . . with its preacher-style harangues, its "testimony" from women who have "seen the light," its conversion rituals and its shock-horror denunciations. (Wilson, 1993, 28)

The first feminist group to articulate an explicitly feminist analysis of and opposition to reproductive technologies was the Feminist International Network of Resistance to Reproductive Technologies and Genetic Engineering (FINRRAGE), founded in 1984. At a subsequent meeting in 1989, it issued an appeal "to unite globally against dehumanizing technologies" (Rowland, 1992, 288). In contrast to the producers of such monolithic feminist panic narratives which ignore the ways that domination actually works (by producing subjects, always double-edged, including "natural" angelicly antisex and antitechnological "feminist" ones), many Marxists, critical theorists, and postmodernists argue that power creates resistances, not victims.

Narrative Strategies

Feminist opposition to pornography and reproductive technologies utilizes similar narrative strategies, as does liberal discourse's celebratory individualist *laissez-faire* defense of both pornography and reprotec. Feminist condemnation and liberal endorsement invoke equally problematic, though radically different, ahistorical and acontextual abstractions about market freedom, individual freedom of choice, privacy protection, the ascendancy of contract, etc. (Robertson, 1988, 191–93). Radical feminist opposition to pornography/reprotec criticizes liberal contractarian conceptions of the market model, correctly perceiving the limits of individual, rights-based justifications, whether in prostitution/sexwork, or in reproductive technologies. Nonetheless, radical feminists go too far in rejecting every conception of "choice" as overdetermined by self-serving male sexism or natalism (Sherwin, 1992, 136).

The feminist antitechnology narrative also configures debate as composed of only *two* opposed sides. This reduction ignores the historical discursive field on which a varied collection of divergent perspectives gather. Likewise, a minority of theorists and activists in the technology debates refuse to endorse or condemn reproductive technologies and oppose outlawing them (Duggan and Hunter, 1995). In the pornography debate, a broad spectrum of theorists and activists, including queer theorists, socialist-feminists, post-Marxists, sexual liberals, libertarians, and postmodernists (including filmmakers, actors, performers, and writers) who oppose censoring pornography and condemning the sex industry are, at the same time, critical of potentially oppressive sexist, racist, and classist dimensions of each of these sets of practices.

According to the feminist anti-reproductive technology narrative, a phallocratic conspiracy of woman-hating, womb-envying "pharmocrats" foist their high-priced, risky, invasive, and low-success-rate reproductive technologies on the class of "natural" women. Instances of women clamoring for access to these technologies (documented by year-long waiting lists for admission to some medical programs) are dismissed as false consciousness. "This individual woman is a fiction—as is her will—since individuality is precisely what women are denied when they are defined and used as a sex class" (Dworkin, 1983, 182).

The identities of reproductive technology users/consumers represented by this binary narrative are simple, fixed, and noncontradictory, undisturbed by diversity or incommensurability of context. Such feminism ignores the self-constitutive discursive moment in identity formation, mistaking identity for ontology. For all its fetishization of "women's experience," it is a legislative feminism that prescribes an abstract idealized maternity, rather than an antithetical range of maternities, as Rosalind Petchesky notes, "within [a woman's] her total framework of relationships, economic and health needs, and desire" (Petchesky, 1987, 288).

It fails to appreciate the diversity of circumstances surrounding women's and men's use and revision of reproductive technologies or, in the case of pornography, the difference of motivations and appropriations of pornography production and consumption. Anthropologist Marilyn Strathern understands that "developments in reproductive medicine do not just comprise new procedures. They also embody new knowledge" (Strathern, 1995, 348).

For example, one way that reproductive technologies are potentially transgressive of gender norms consists in their achieving the separation of reproduction from heterosexual sex. They do this by allowing us to rethink what was formerly considered unified "natural" maternity as divisible into three parts: *genetics, gestation*, and *social mothering*. The distribution of maternity (and paternity through the practice of donor insemination) offers the potential of exploiting unintended social effects of the technologies in democratic directions for resignifying family, kinship, and social relations.

As Donna Haraway has said of the lack of secure guarantees for cyborg social relations: "even technoscience worlds are full of resources for contesting inequality and arbitrary authority" (Haraway, 1990, 13). Some destabilizations of gender and identity are successful. We must ask, along with Valerie Hartouni, "What are the stories they tell about reproductive possibilities, relations, and relationships in late twentieth-century America, and what is the terrain they occupy and contest in that telling?" (Hartouni, 1991, 30). Antipornography and antitechnology critics also excoriate the market, idealizing social relations presumed to have existed in a premarket world. Egalitarian, nonphallocentric sex and "natural" woman-centered reproduction are stipulated to predate the market, serving as an idealized, nostalgic political horizon of possibility. Anticommodification and the belief in a preexistent better world are requisite elements in this essentialist narrative. "Surrogate brokers are reproductive pimps" (Rowland, 1991, 32). A Manichean world is reassuringly simple.

Both radical feminist condemnations and liberal defenses of pornography/reprotec configure freedom negatively. In the pornography debates, sexual freedom is imagined as freedom *from* male-dominated values, images, and practices; in the reproductive technology debates, "natural" maternity is configured as maternity experienced without male-dominated technological intervention. In the pornography debates, the complex, ambivalent social and historical construction of sexual desires and behaviors is left unaddressed or worse, reduced to a univocal demonization of sexual desire in the service of male domination, leaving only the canonization of one ideal type (vanilla lesbianism) as fulfilling the *telos* of (all) women's true nature.

Antipornography and antitechnology feminists define *their* positions as feminist or "women-centered" critiques (Whitbeck, 1988, 53). Their opponents get renamed nonfeminists or enemies of feminism (Raymond, 1993, 88). When the mainstream media refers to "feminist" concerns or criticisms of reproductive technologies, they usually mean the most vociferous feminist position.

Antipornography

Both antipornography and antitechnology proponents subscribe to simplistic ahistorical binaries: nature versus artifice, danger versus pleasure, and systemic male violence versus women's autonomous sexual agency. The contracting of pornography to one-dimensional "violence against women" ignores the contribution that pornography has made for some people in staking out the ground of explicit sex-for-pleasure in a repressive society as well as the existence of some nonsexist sexual images elaborated by some producers of written and cinematic pornography. Antipornography censorship of pornography would eliminate all sexually explicit material along with so-called sexist and/or violent material. The sex education function as well as voyeuristic satisfaction that pornography provides in a sexually repressive society contributes to women and men's exploration of their sexualities. Anticensorship and sexwork activists along with feminist and queer porn performers and artists have changed the nature of video, film, and written pornography production (Segal and McIntosh, 1993).

Feminist writers and filmmakers have contributed alternative image repertoires as a counterpoint to the relentless monotony of mechanistic plastic hetero-pap of mainline video and written pornography. Their alternative textual productions have challenged both antipornography feminism's prescriptivist imposition of a unitary vanilla sexual style along with the sex industry's prescriptive norms of sexual behavior.

Invoking repression in the form of censorship of pornography, however, follows logically from normative prescription of one politically correct style of sexual practice. Linda Williams has noted:

> As long as a long-suffering, victimized, and repressed natural female sexuality is viewed as the antithesis to a falsely ideological, constructed, sadistic male sexuality (or any other kind of "perversion"), practical resistance to what many women do find inimical in that sexuality is limited to the condemnation of unorthodoxies measured against an orthodox norm. (Williams, 1989, 23)

Feminist pornographic practices challenge the radical feminist hegemonic sexual style based on nongenital cuddly mutuality, one that tries to suppress *its* power relations—analogous to its idealization of a "natural" model of reproduction as noninterventionist, spontaneous, free, and self-determining (Raymond, 1993, 28).

Antitechnology

Like antiporn writers who exaggerate the effectiveness of the porn world's regnant fictions—utopic presentation, endless performance, repeatable erections (Wilson, 1993, 27), antitechnology feminists magnify the extent of their opposition's power, making dystopic projections of regnant ectogenesis, obsolesced women, self-congratulatory pharmocrats, and techno-docs.

While antipornography feminists decry the celebration of commodified consequenceless (irresponsible) sex, antitechnology feminists denounce the degradation of women's bodies by exchange relations and market conditions. Writing in 1985, radical feminist Gena Corea predicts: "Just as the patriarchal state now finds it acceptable to market parts of a women's body (breast, vagina, buttocks) for sexual purposes in prostitution . . . , so it will soon find it reasonable to market other parts of a woman (womb, ovaries, egg) for reproductive purposes" (Corea, 1985).

Narratives that focus on the threatened refuge of "the natural" work to deflect interest in the ways reproductive technologies destabilize and interrogate traditional assumptions about kinship and identity. "Through the use of the new reproductive technologies, women's reproduction is now being objectified in the same way woman's sexuality has been for centuries" (Corea, 1988, 89). The "experience" of conception through heterosexual penile-vaginal intercourse in state-triangulated legal marriage achieved without reproductive technologies is no more "natural" than an institutional medically mediated conception in a laboratory petri dish with anonymous donor sperm. The former is no more necessarily unalienated, or given, than the latter. Both "experiences" are historically overdetermined social and political relations that can be explained by a complex of cultural factors that include class, race, and gender variables.

The experience of conceiving a child with one's husband within the first few years of marriage in one's late twenties is a twentieth-century, white middle-class, contingent phenomenon. Just as the desire for a child must be explained by the overdeterminations of natalism and the limited nonreproductive options available to most women, the desire to reproduce "naturally" must also be explained. In both cases, socially and culturally different subjects are constituted through different experiences.

The Feminist Body of Nature

The posit of a break between the present and the past that is unsupported by any historical evidence serves to idealize "natural" sex and "natural" reproduction as regressive, consolatory social goals. According to this idealized worldview, the fiction of a prepatriarchal, edenic state in which women were unoppressed by sexist practices and ideologies serves as the source of contemporary feminist cultural values. So, feminist visions of maternity supposedly fuel an ideal type of contemporary maternity as the only acceptable one. From this benevolent but monolithic universalizing maternal practice, feminist values of nurturance, connection, sensitivity, etc. are both derived and extended. "Nature" and not history, biography, and society construct reproduction and sex. Such feminist hagiography of "the natural" is relentlessly essentialist.

Narratives about "natural" reproduction are themselves rooted in a construction of the empowering fertility of the pre-edenic female body as a purported source of transformative resistance to male domination. "Reproductive technologists now aim to bring forth life through 'art,' rather than nature and enable a man to be not only the father, but also the mother of his child" (Corea, 1985, 291). Antipornography/reprotec feminism always entails a lament, the loss of an imagined prepornographic or pretechnological world that existed *before* the contemporary patriarchal manifestation of commodification, technologicization, and alienation.

Feminist antitechnology discourse constructs reproductive technologies as "fidd[ling] with eggs" and "merging the woman's identity with that of the couple" (Rowland, 1991, 38). Reproductive technologies effect "a strange distortion of nature" in which passive, manipulated, formerly integral female bodies are increasingly alienated "from their bodies and from motherhood, signifying their loss of control of themselves as whole people" (Rowland, 1991, 38). The monolithic representation of reproductive technologies as "industrialized breeding" (Raymond, 1993, x), reifies the technologies and stipulates only one possible register of appropriation-oppression. Accordingly, they are represented as "violat[ing] the integrity of a woman's body in ways that are dangerous, destructive, debilitating, and demeaning, they are a form of medical violence against women" (Raymond, 1993, viii).

This universalizing feminism simplistically posits an idealized, "natural" reproductive body that requires no technological assistance or intervention. It "affirms a woman-centered, life-affirming experience of reproduction, an affirmation of women's physical integrity, the integrity of the mother-child relationship, and of pregnancy and childbirth as a personal, sexual, familial, communal experience" (Spallone, 1989, 180–81). It opposes *its* metaphor of holism and relatedness to the medical one of fragmentation and alienation that it vilifies (Martin, 1987, 1992, 56). "The new reproductive technologies reflect a view of women as decentered subjects and social beings. The material outcome of such a view is a concrete carving up of women into body parts, specifically, into wombs, eggs, and follicles" (Raymond, 1993, 204).

Fragmentation is univocally bad; holism is univocally good. Such a repertoire of static, essentialized categories is impervious to the uneven flows of discourse and history that comprise history and biography.

We have seen how radical feminism's rage against liberalism's often biased, inadequate, and narrow conceptual framework has led it to presume the beneficence of a "feminine" homogeneity, no less essentialized than the universalizing categories it critiqued as patriarchal in the first place. Until feminist theory and practice can grapple with women's huge, unreconcilable, and unstable differences of desire in regard to sex and reproduction, it will contribute less than optimally to expanding categories that welcome pleasure, multiplying utilizations that question tradition, and proliferating resistances to arbitrary stipulation. Perhaps the continuation of generating (and celebrating) the unintended effects of both contemporary pornographic practices and reproductive technologies will continue to challenge the narrowness of feminist politics based exclusively on consolatory fantasies of naturalized, holistic, and organic sex, on the one hand, or unitary maternity and family, on the other. And drive a stake through the heart of all edens.

References

Lynda Birke, Susan Himmelweit, and Gail Vines. 1990. *Tomorrow's Child: Reproductive Technologies in the 90s.* London: Virago.

Corea, Gena. 1985. *The Mother Machine: Reproductive Technologies From Artificial Insemination to Artificial Wombs.* New York: Harper & Row.

———. 1987. "The Reproductive Brothel." In *Man-Made Women: How New Reproductive Technologies Affect Women,* ed. Gena Corea, Renate D. Klein, et al. Bloomington: Indiana University Press.

———. 1988. "What the King Can Not See." In *Embryos, Ethics, and Women's Rights: Exploring the New Reproductive Technologies,* ed. Elaine Hoffman Baruch, et al. New York: The Haworth Press.

Duggan, Lisa. 1995. "Censorship in the Name of Feminism." In *Sex Wars: Sexual Dissent and Political Culture,* ed. Lisa Duggan and Nan D. Hunter. New York: Routledge.

Dworkin, Andrea. 1983. *Right-Wing Women.* New York: Perigee Books.

Gallop, Jane. 1988. *Thinking Through the Body.* New York: Columbia University Press.

Haraway, Donna. 1990. "Interview." By Andrew Ross and Constance Penley, *Social Text* 25/26.

Hartouni, Valerie. 1991. "Containing Women: Reproductive Discourse in the 1980s." In *Technoculture,* ed. Constance Penley and Andrew Ross. Minneapolis: University of Minnesota Press.

Kaplan, E. Ann. 1992. "Sex, Work and Mother/Fatherhood." In *Motherhood and Representation: The Mother in Popular Culture and Melodrama.* New York: Routledge.

Kappeler, Susanne. 1986. *The Pornography of Representation.* Minneapolis: University of Minnosota Press.

Kendrick, Walter. 1987. *The Secret Museum: Pornography in Modern Culture.* New York: Penguin.

Kitzinger, Sheila. 1989. "Introduction." In *In Search of Parenthood: Coping With Infertility and High-Tech Conception*, by Judith Lasker and Susan Borg. London: Pandora Press.

Lasker, Judith and Susan Borg. 1989. *In Search of Parenthood: Coping With Infertility and High-Tech Conception*. London: Pandora Press.

Martin, Emily. 1987. *The Woman in the Body: A Cultural Analysis of Reproduction*. New Introduction, 1992. Boston: Beacon Press.

McClintock, Anne. 1992. "Screwing the System: Sexwork, Race, and the Law." In *boundary 2*, vol. 19, no. 2.

Petchesky, Rosalind Pollack. 1987. "Fetal Images: The Power of Visual Culture in the Politics of Reproduction." In *Feminist Studies 13*.

————. 1995. "The Body as Property: A Feminist Re-vision." In *Conceiving the New World Order: The Global Politics of Reproduction*, ed. Faye D. Ginsburg and Rayna Rapp. Berkeley: University of California Press.

Plato. 1961. *The Laws*. In *The Collected Dialogues*, ed. Edith Hamilton and Huntington Cairns. Princeton, N.J.: Princeton University Press.

Raymond, Janice. 1993. *Women as Wombs: Reproductive Technologies and the Battle Over Women's Freedom*. New York: Harper Collins.

Robertson, John A. 1988. "Procreative Liberty, Embryos, and Collaborative Reproduction: A Legal Perspective." In *Embryos, Ethics and Women's Rights: Exploring the New Reproductive Technologies*, ed. Elaine Hoffman Baruch, et al. New York: Haworth Press.

Rowland, Robyn. 1991. "Decoding Reprospeak." In *MS*, May/June.

————. 1992. *Living Laboratories: Women and Reproductive Technologies*. Bloomington: Indiana University Press.

Rowland, Robyn and Renate D. Klein. 1990. "Radical Feminism: Critique and Construct." In *Feminist Knowledge: Critique and Construct*, ed. Sneja Gunew. New York: Routledge.

Segal, Lynne and Mary McIntosh, eds. 1993. *Sex Exposed: Sexuality and the Pornography Debate*. New York: Routledge.

Sherwin, Susan. 1992. *No Longer Patient: Feminist Ethics and Health Care*. Philadelphia: Temple University Press.

Singer, Linda. Winter 1989. "Bodies—Pleasures—Powers." In *differences*, vol. 1, no. 1, 45–65.

Spallone, Patricia. 1989. *Beyond Conception: The New Politics of Reproduction*. Houndmills, UK: Macmillan.

Strathern, Marilyn. 1995. "Displacing Knowledge: Technology and the Consequence for Kinship." In *Conceiving the New World Order: the Global Politics of Reproduction*, ed. Faye Ginsburg and Rayna Rapp. Berkeley: University of California Press.

Vance, Carole S. 1995. "False Promises: Feminist Antipornography Legislation." In *Sex Wars*, ed. Duggan and Hunter. New York: Routledge.

Whitbeck, Caroline. 1988. "Fetal Imaging and Fetal Monitoring: Finding the Ethical Issues." In *Embryos, Ethics and Women's Rights: Exploring the New Reproductive Technologies*, ed. Elaine Hoffman Baruch, et al. New York: The Haworth Press.

Williams, Linda. 1989. *Hard Core: Power, Pleasure, and the "Frenzy of the Visible."* Berkeley: University of California Press.

Wilson, Elizabeth. 1993. "Feminist Fundamentalism: The Shifting Politics of Sex and Censorship." In *Sex Exposed: Sexuality and the Pornography Debate*, ed. Lynne Segal and Mary McIntosh. New Brunswick, N.J.: Rutgers University Press, 1993.

15

Prostitution as a Morally Risky Practice from the Point of View of Feminist Radical Pragmatism

Ann Ferguson

Feminist ethicists share the engaged view that social domination, particularly male domination, exists and ought to be eliminated. But there are vast disagreements among feminist ethicists about what normative ethics to adopt. In this paper I defend what I call *feminist radical pragmatism*, a context-based ethical approach that can also accommodate a structural-historical critique of existing institutions and policies. I shall apply my approach to the difficult question of prostitution, an issue that has divided Western second wave feminists.

Feminist radical pragmatism differs from both modernist ethical approaches, whether utilitarian or deontological, that must appeal to general principles or goals, and those postmodern ethics that either espouse a total relativism or a so-called radical ethical pluralism. All of these positions assume either that we can make ethical judgments and policy recommendations independent of the actual political context of power, or that ethical critiques of political practices are suspect since they are intertwined with the self-interested power and politics of the critics. On the contrary, a feminist radical pragmatism sensitive to the interests and contexts of those for and with whom it speaks can build a feminist oppositional ethico-politics able at once to make ethical critiques of dominant institutions yet forge a coalitional political stance that reconfigures the interests of those involved, in a new "bridge identity politics" (Ferguson, 1996).

My position on feminist ethico-politics differs from two relevant "philosophies of suspicion" that also critique mainstream modernist ethics, that of radical feminism and Marxist feminism. Both accuse mainstream ethics of being ideological devices that hide ulterior motives in order to justify status quo political power relations, whether the ruling class in power be thought to be men as a gender class or the capitalist class. Mainstream liberal and liberal feminist defenses of prostitution ignore the structural ways that capitalist patriarchy provides forced options for women. For Marx, all production in capitalism becomes commodity production, that is, production for exchange, not use, and alienates workers from control of the process, product, and uses of production. Women in particular lack fair economic options. The sexual division of labor creates exploitative work relations for women as economic dependents for male kin in the home, as employees in underpaid, mostly sex-segmented wage labor, or as single mothers taking care of children on state welfare. Thus even if prostitution is the optimal choice for poor women, it still is a forced rather than a free choice. Furthermore, since it forces women to engage in alienated sexual acts for pay, acts that should inherently be used for intimate love relationships chosen for their own sake, prostitution should be morally forbidden.

Although I agree with these structural and moral critiques of prostitution, I do so on different grounds and with a different moral and political perspective than radical and Marxist feminists. First, although prostitution may be alienating, it is not because there are inherent goals of sexuality that connect to the universal needs of human nature, as both Marxism and radical feminism maintain (Marx, 1978; Foreman, 1977; Barry, 1995). Rather, alienation is context-specific, and depends on the frustration of historical expectations of goals associated with certain activities (e.g., sex connected to romantic partnerships in modern societies, Ferguson, 1989). From a feminist radical pragmatic position, prostitution is morally problematic when it is structured to use sexuality to undercut socially sanctioned values that benefit women in a particular historical context. But sometimes certain prostitution practices may in fact promote alternative values that promote women's interests better than those values not achieved. For example, sexworkers Shannon Bell and Annie Sprinkle see themselves as liberating women from objectified, repressed, and male-dominated sexual scripts in favor of modeling a women-controlled sexuality focused on a number of goals: spiritual feelings, immediate pleasure, a committed intimate relationship, or even a caretaking sex-therapy for the client, depending on the decision of the practitioner. The argument is that liberating sexuality from the norm of a committed intimate relationship can give it feminist value whether or not it is also a paid activity (Bell, 1994; Sprinkle, interview in Chapkis, 1997). Bell in particular sees herself as a postmodern feminist subject whose practices as a sexworker are *productive* rather than *repressive* of a woman-controlled sexuality (also Foucault, 1977).

A second objection to structural critiques of prostitution is that even where structures limit options, they do not necessarily eliminate the distinction between *coercion* and *consent*. Though all but the independently wealthy are forced to work in the capitalist system, we can still make the distinction between dangerous, unpleasant work which is so forced that one only does it because the alternatives are life-threatening, and work which individuals take to be freely chosen because there are a range of other reasonable alternatives, not life-threatening, against which they still choose this option. Since many sexworkers take themselves to have chosen their work based on this latter scenario, they are insulted that Marxist and radical feminists treat them as coerced victims. Of course there are other sexworkers who do feel themselves to have been coerced into prostitution, who support the Marxist and radical feminist structural critique of prostitution. How, then, can we account for the power of the structural critiques of prostitution yet do justice to the voices of prostitutes who insist they are freely choosing their occupation, and indeed, even argue that it is empowering to them? (Chapkis, 1997; Delacoste and Alexander, 1987).

My solution is to develop a distinction between *ideal* and *transitional feminist moralities*, with structural critiques of prostitution in the former category, and liberal feminists' defenses of prostitute rights in the latter category. An *ideal* morality gives us ideals and values with which to critique reality. It also can provide a macro-critique that can inspire women and their male allies to work for radical changes in exploitative economic and political institutions such as capitalism and male-dominated state policies and family practices. But one of the functions of morality is to provide advice, norms, and values about what individuals and governments should do in the present situation and context, even when conditions are not ideal. Thus, a *transitional* morality tells us what ought to be done to promote feminist values in our present imperfect reality, in a transition to a social reality that better meets feminist ideals. In order to deal with the ethico-political problem of prostitution, we need both ideal and transitional moralities and some way to negotiate between them.

One way to understand the controversy between radical feminists and sex radicals over prostitution is to see it as a disagreement about whether we should operate from an ideal or a transitional morality. International feminist activists such as Kathleen Barry (1979, 1995) have made structural critiques of the institution of prostitution as tied to capitalist patriarchy's exploitation of women's sexuality. Barry argues that the twentieth-century industrialization of sex as a commodity has created a coercive international trafficking in women, first by the use of rape victims of war as prostitutes trafficked across national borders, then by local women servicing foreign military bases (Enloe, 1989), and finally by planned economic development to include sex tourism and mail-order-bride businesses as a way to attract capital from the wealthy North to the poorer South. An international feminist politics of defending women's human rights as a gender class (e.g., against male violence; against exploitation; for health, nutritional, and workers' rights) has been proposed as an ideal moral solution to this problem. Women's human right against sexual exploitation has involved the international Coalition Against Sexual Trafficking in Women in a proposal to the United Nations called the Convention Against Sexual Exploitation. This convention, drafted in 1994, would bind states who sign it to condemn sexual exploitation, which is defined as any practice "by which person(s) achieve sexual gratification, or financial gain, or advancement through the abuse of a person's sexuality by abrogating that person's right to dignity, equality, autonomy and physical and mental well-being" (Barry, 1995, Appendix: 326). Prostitution is one of the named practices, which also include female infanticide, sexual abuse, and genital mutilation. States who sign the convention are bound to forbid sex tourism of any sort and to create economic programs of restitution for former prostitutes.

Although such international feminist attempts to deal with structural inequalities between men and women engaged in prostitution are important, the struggle to get bodies such as the UN and national governments such as the United States to adopt general policies against sexual exploitation will not eliminate the continuing economic and social reasons why some women will still choose prostitution as a way of life. How then can feminists frame a transitional morality that does not end up continuing the stigmatization of women engaged in prostitution? As long as prostitution continues to exist, sexworkers as wage workers surely ought to have the same rights as other workers to control their working conditions and workplace, including health and safety issues. Thus it would seem that feminist organizations and networks ought to give political support to organizations of sexworkers and prostitutes such as COYOTE, a prostitutes' rights group in the U.S. Such groups contain self-identified feminists who are attempting to create unions of prostitutes to demand the decriminalization of prostitution practices. A feminist radical pragmatism can maintain that it is consistent to support their efforts as a transitional feminist moral stand, and yet support the direction of the Coalition Against Trafficking in Women as the ideal moral position on prostitution to work for the long-run goal of eliminating institutionalized prostitution. But this long-run goal does not rule out a transitional morality that aims to decriminalize prostitution at the national and local levels to protect prostitutes' rights in local contexts.

In previous work I have argued that a *transitional morality* must distinguish between *morally basic, risky,* and *forbidden feminist practices* (Ferguson, 1984, 1986, 1989). The distinctions themselves assume a basic set of feminist set of values, such as *equality or reciprocity* between individuals in social exchanges; *freedom for self-development;* a sense of *community or social belonging* and self-worth among peers; opportunities for *democratic participation* in government, sociopolitical, economic, and environmental decisions affecting one's life; and *fairness* or *justice* in the distribution of socially acknowledged goods. With these in mind I offer the categories of *morally risky* and *forbidden* practices, which refer to those practices that fall within institutions that are subject to feminist critique for their general sexist functioning in the past and present, and are opposed to *basic feminist practices,* which are seen as supporting the values listed above. The category of *risky practices* that are not forbidden allows that in particular contexts individuals or groups have developed *practices of resistance* or survival that have allowed them the possibilities of achieving feminist values *in spite of* the dangerous institutional constraints making this difficult to do. Thus, such individual or group practices, though undertaken in a constraining institutional context, should not be *morally* or *politically forbidden* by feminists, even though the institutions may be condemned as dangerous.

Feminist radical pragmatism suggests a kind of a ethico-political compromise or mediation between radical feminists, and those who call themselves "sex radicals" or "pluralist feminists" (also called "libertarian feminists" by their radical feminist adversaries, Ferguson, 1984, 1986, 1989). Consequently, although my position is something that neither committed radical feminists nor sex radicals particularly like, I maintain that it is more helpful with the complexities of concrete ethico-political situations, and, as such, is more useful to the majority of nonacademic feminists who have to deal with these complexities in their everyday life.

Let us consider how using the tripartite distinction between *morally basic, risky,* and *forbidden practices* would change our perspective on feminist sexual ethics. *Basic* feminist *practices* include not only cohabiting, reciprocal love partnerships outside of marriage, whether heterosexual, bisexual, or homosexual, but also various forms of multiple household coparenting, joint income, and carefully negotiated domestic and non-living-together love partnerships. They also include wage labor in cooperative and feminist-managed workplaces, whether or not they are women-only workforces.

With respect to public policy, basic feminist policy would include a feminist reproductive rights public policy agenda that involves not only abortion rights, but state-supported funding for abortions, measures against sterilization abuse and against surrogate mother abuse, as well as public school sex education classes that include education against homophobia.

Consensual heterosexual marriage and prostitution are *risky practices* since they have been patriarchally controlled institutions and still involve structural dangers for women. Single-parent, women-headed family practices are also risky, since in capitalist countries such families usually lack the necessary social supports and economic opportunities to be economically and socially secure. Academic feminist practices, such as feminist philosophy and women's studies, are also morally risky since they occur in patriarchal institutions where the academic division of labor, the status of academic knowledge production and academic professionals, and the theory/practice split make it easy for feminist projects to be coopted into perpetuating the status quo.

Forbidden practices include not only coerced marriage and prostitution, but also the refusal of biological parents to assume expected parental responsibilities. Also morally forbidden for feminists, I would argue, should be managerial work positions in capitalist racist patriarchal corporations where there is no power to change the power dynamics.

Basic feminist practices also include consensual non-pain-directed sexual practices between adults (often called "vanilla practices"), while consensual S/M is a risky practice and coerced violent sex (rape), domestic battering, and violence and adult/child sex are forbidden practices.

A transitional feminist morality would critique liberal defenses of the institution of prostitution on both structural grounds and in concrete contexts. The empirical evidence suggests that a number of prostitutes are in coercive situations that they did not choose, for example, when they are controlled by pimps or in exploitative brothel work. For those who are immigrants from another country, perhaps as many as 80 percent started out as young runaways, were duped into exploitative situations, or internationally were sold by relatives into sexual slavery (Barry, 1979, 1995). However, there are contexts and situations in which individual prostitutes and other sexworkers may have achieved more economic security and control over their work situation than comparable jobs would give them, particularly in the U.S. The combination of dangerous structural features and yet some opportunities for individual resistance to patriarchal control is what moves me to define individual choices of prostitution as *risky*. However, just as I urge my daughter not to set herself up for single parenting on the basis of my institutional critique of that practice and her increased economic alternatives if she waits until she can coparent, I would certainly urge her not to engage in the practice of prostitution, since it is a very risky business, which in her context is not worth the cost.

Feminist radical pragmatism maintains that structural critiques of patriarchal institutions, such as marriage and prostitution, the sexual division of wage and heterosexual family labor provide us with moral "rules of thumb" not to engage in such practices if we can find ways around them. Nonetheless, it also acknowledges that there are always *social conflicts* or *contradictions* in such institutions that allow for spaces of counter-power to operate. For example, Marxist critiques of wage labor do not conclude that workers should refuse to engage in wage labor at all, but that workers should organize radical trade unions to fight to expand their control over the means of production. Similarly, many heterosexual feminists engage in marriage, and even prostitution, because they believe they find themselves in particular contexts that allow them to challenge and undermine the patriarchal power of the institution. They can thus be said to be engaging in *risky practices*, whose ethico-political worth must be judged by how successful they have been in the context in establishing sexual freedom and reciprocity *in that context*. If they have been successful in their individual contexts, then the moral rules of thumb against engaging in marriage or prostitution would have been shown not to apply to their cases.

A further reason that a transitional feminist morality defines prostitution as a morally risky rather than as a morally forbidden practice is that none of the ideal policy solutions succeed in protecting women. The three options that have been urged as remedies of the evils of prostitution are: *legal prohibition, state regulation,* and *de-criminalization.* But each of these alternatives is problematic. *Legal prohibition* is the situation in most countries in the world, and most states in the U.S. except for Nevada. But it still continues to stigmatize and criminilize women who engage in prostitution. Male pimps and mostly male-controlled brothels are able to avoid prosecution while prostitutes themselves are open to legal sanctions in a way that makes them even more dependent on their pimps and employers for protection against the state and subject to blackmail if they do desire to leave prostitution. *State regulation* of prostitution makes prostitution legal under the condition that prostitutes and brothels are licensed by the state, and is practiced in the state of Nevada, and Germany, among other places. The problem is that this alternative allows states to take over part of the patriarchal control of women formerly exercised by pimps and other male entrepreneurs but does not eliminate this set of parasites on women's sexual labor: the state negotiates with these latter, but does not allow sexworkers themselves to unionize and negotiate for better working conditions. *Decriminalization,* the strategy favored by Barry in her earlier book (1979) usually involves eliminating legal prohibitions against prostitution as a general practice and substituting more specific laws, for example, against forced marriages, sexual trafficking that involves force and deception, the practice of pimping, and the practice of mail-order brides. This way the activities of prostitutes themselves are not illegal, and prostitutes can turn to the state for protection against the latter sort of coercive practices.

The problem with all of these strategies, however, is that they do not get at the root of the problem of which prostitution is only one symptom: the widespread economic and social inferiority of women institutionalized in patriarchal societies by the unequal sexual division of labor, patriarchal marriage practices, and women's economic dependence on men. So, instead, a feminist radical pragmatism would support a feminist coalitional approach that negotiates both an ideal and a transitional morality with feminist activists engaged practically in working on prostitution. This would have to include the range of pro-prostitute-rights sexworkers' voices included in Chapkis and Delacoste and Alexander's networks (Chapkis, 1997; Delacoste and Alexander, 1987) as well as those who have been victimized by prostitution, as referred to by Barry (1979, 1995). Since none of the above public policy positions on prostitution (prohibition, state regulation, or decriminalization) will solve the structural problems that continue to give rise to it, we need to support local spaces for prostitutes to organize unions to demand better working conditions and to demand the decriminalization of prostitution (perhaps the best practical alternative for the working prostitute population), at the same time as we support efforts by the Coalition Against Trafficking in Women to get a version of the Convention Against Sexual Exploitation passed by the UN and signed by member states. The U.S.-based coalition, however, needs to consider more sensitivity to other feminist international organizations working to support prostitutes, for example the Dutch Foundation Against Trafficking in Women, which like COYOTE and other local prostitute organizing networks opposes that provision of the convention that would criminalize clients engaged in prostitution (cf. Chapkis, 1997).

It is important not to allow political work promoting our ideal morality to undermine the goals of our transitional morality. A *process liberatory* goal of feminist struggle around prostitution should be to value the self-organizing of prostitutes themselves as a fourth alternative to the three problematic policy approaches listed above. Support of local organizing drives by sexworkers is a way to supplement work toward decriminalization. A transitional morality based on supporting local sexworker organizing, and a radical feminist ideal morality, i.e., a revised international Convention

Against Sexual Exploitation, could allow a viable cross-class Prostitution Action Coalition to develop, which would unite working prostitutes with feminists opposed to various aspects of prostitution. Our coalition could support "bridge identity politics" (Ferguson, 1996), that is, an attempt to refuse the fixed identities given us by gender, race, class, and sexual differences by a transformative political practice. Such a political practice would have to allow feminists to agree to disagree on some political priorities, e.g., whether to work to eliminate prostitution or to reform it. It would also allow the issue to be dealt with differently in different political spaces; that is, it could support prostitute rights to demand better working conditions on the local level, yet on the international level protest the exploitation of prostitution as an economic activity benefiting states and mostly male-dominated enterprises.

References

Barry, Kathleen. 1979. *Female Sexual Slavery*. New York: Avon.

———. 1995. *The Prostitution of Sexuality*. New York: New York University Press.

Bell, Shannon. 1994. *Reading, Writing and Rewriting the Prostitute Body*. Bloomington and Indianapolis: Indiana University Press.

Chapkis, Wendy. 1997. *Live Sex Acts: Women Performing Erotic Labor*. New York: Routledge.

Delacoste, Frederique and Priscilla Alexander, eds. 1987. *Sex Work: Writings by Women in the Sex Industry*. Pittsburgh: Cleis Press.

Enloe, Cynthia. 1989. *Bananas, Beaches and Bases: Making Feminist Sense Out of International Politics*. Berkeley: University of California.

Ferguson, Ann. 1984. "Sex War: The Debate Between Radical and Libertarian Feminists." *Signs*, 10 (1) (Fall 1984): 106–12.

———. 1986. "Pleasure, Power and the Porn Wars." *Women's Review of Books* 3 (8) (May 1986): 9–13.

———. 1989. *Blood at the Root: Motherhood, Sexuality and Male Dominance*. London: Pandora/Unwin & Hyman.

———. 1996. "Bridge Identity Politics: An Integrative Feminist Analysis of International Development." *Organization* 3 (4): 571–87.

Foreman, Ann. 1977. *Femininity as Alienation*. London: Pluto.

Foucault, Michel. 1977. *Discipline and Punish*. Alan Sheridan, tr. New York: Pantheon.

hooks, bell, 1984. *Feminist Theory From Margin to Center*. Boston: South End.

Jaggar, Alison. 1994. "Prostitution" (abridged version). In *Living With Contradictions*, Alison Jaggar, ed. Boulder, CO: Westview Press: 102–11.

———. 1996, mss. "Western Feminist Perspectives on Prostitution." Women's Studies, University of Colorado/Boulder.

Marx, Karl. 1978. "Alienated Labor" (*Economic and Philosophical Manuscripts*). In *The Marx-Engels Reader*, Robert Tucker, ed. New York: W.W. Norton.

Rubin, Gayle. 1984. "Thinking Sex: Notes for a Radical Theory of the Politics of Sexuality." In *Pleasure and Danger: Exploring Female Sexuality*, Carol Vance, ed. London: Routledge.

16

Contentious Contraception

Feminist Debates about the Use of Long-Acting Hormonal
Contraceptives by Adolescent Urban Women

Sarah Begus

In the 1990s, among the many reproductive issues with which feminists struggle are the uses and abuses of newly developed birth control technologies (National Women's Health Network, 1994). Available methods of contraception continue to be imperfect, and new developments are eagerly awaited by consumers and health providers. Long-acting contraceptives are among the newest birth control technologies developed. The two most widely used as well as most controversial are levonorgesterol, a five-year subdermal progestin hormonal implant manufactured by Wyeth Ayerst under the trade name Norplant; and Depo-Provera, an injectable dose of progestins that lasts three months, and is popularly referred to as "The Shot." These two forms of birth control are now the most popular in the world. Norplant and Depo-Provera have only been available in the U.S. since 1990 and 1992 respectively, but were originally tested in the Third World (Women and Pharmaceutical Project, 1993).

Sociopolitical pressure for new forms of birth control is pernicious as well as beneficent. State-controlled contraceptive research often focuses on developing and disseminating forms that will facilitate the control of particular groups of women's reproduction, resulting in either the prevention or encouragement of birthing based on public policy rather than individual women's choices (Petchetsky, 1990). Moreover, in current U.S. public policy, the long-term health of certain groups of women, namely poor women and women of color, is secondary to the prevailing drive to limit reproductive options.

Feminist health providers, health policy makers, health activists, and theorists often disagree on the benefits of the new forms of long-acting hormonal contraceptives, particularly their use by adolescent women, poor women, and women of color. Debates on these forms of contraception, particularly Norplant and Depo-Provera, can be sharp and acrimonious. Debate polarizes opinions and can lead to bitter antagonism, which can close down communication among different groups of feminists. This essay explores this debate, describing the various polarized positions and some potential political fallout of each pole. Out of this debate arises some broad and useful ethical questions about compromise and pragmatism in feminist politics and practices.

Before focusing on the particulars of the debate over long-acting contraceptives, I would like to frame the discussion by situating my sociopolitical and theoretical perspective. I live and work in Baltimore, Maryland, which has become a laboratory for policy and ethical questions about the use of Norplant among poor and African-American young women, so that the politics of contraceptive policy are very much vibrant and current in the city. Baltimore has the highest rate of teen pregnancy in the nation: in 1992, the rate was 70.5 pregnancies per 1,000 fifteen- to nineteen-year-old women (Beilenson, et al. 1995). In addition, the majority population of Baltimore City is African-American. The use of Norplant by young urban women is thus both critical and contentious: many racially diverse feminist health providers are desperate to find ways to help young urban women control their reproduction, and many people, with diverse political perspectives within the African-American community, are critically concerned about the availability of long-acting contraceptives in public school health clinics. As a result, in this essay the focus is on Norplant rather than Depo-Provera, which is less widely used among urban Baltimore women.

In addition, my research on women's health issues is grounded in my position as a theorist who believes that theory must be tested and refined in practice. Experience during twenty-five years of political activism in U.S. second wave feminisms has shown me that theory without practice quickly becomes irrelevant to women's lives, while practice without the benefit of rigorous theoretical analysis can become parochial and myopic, oblivious to critical issues of history and social situation (Bunch, 1983). My current political work and research involves me in neighborhood and community debates among health practitioners and activists in the Baltimore African-American community.

The overall concern in this essay is not to settle the question of whether long-acting hormonal contraceptives, in particular Norplant, are safe and, in some cases, optimal methods of contraception, or, whether it is *ever* possible to offer Norplant in a noncoercive manner to adolescent and young poor women who rely on Medicaid or public health clinics for their reproductive health care. Rather, the central question is how feminist health practitioners, activists, and advocates, who have the same professional goal—the securing and provision of high-quality, woman-controlled, low-cost and freely chosen reproductive health—can hold such diametrically opposed views on Norplant. Illuminating this debate and exploring the issues involved could help develop some wider ethico-political principles for solving conflict among feminists who have similar political goals but differ sharply on particular issues. Examining the public health conflict among feminist health providers and activists on Norplant might reveal similarities with other conflicts in feminist politics. Certainly, a feminist theoretical analysis of politico-ethical questions ought to shed light on the very real and often critical controversies that affect the lives of many women.

Two different but sometimes overlapping groups with opposing points of view are referred to in this essay. The first is feminists of differing races, classes, and nationalities who differ along the lines of practitioners versus theorists and policy analysts. Generally, feminist health practitioners—medical doctors, midwives, nurse practitioners, etc.—differ in their views regarding long-acting hormonal contraception from feminist health policy advocates. Another group with differences of opinion is composed of members of the African-American community—feminist health providers, community activists, and policy makers who also disagree sharply on whether new forms of injectable long-acting hormones should be made freely available to adolescent African-American women. The points of view of these two overlapping groups are explained in the following discussion.

As in other cases of debates within feminisms, each differing position claims some strange political bedfellows. For example, in Baltimore the side in favor of providing Norplant to teen-age women in school-based clinics includes the white, socially conservative former governor, a feminist African-American ob/gyn with a large clinic practice, and feminist members of the state legislature representing Baltimore city. Meanwhile, in opposition are a feminist member of the city council, the medical director of the Nation of Islam, and a coalition of conservative male African-American ministers. This situation is analogous to the debates on sexuality and pornography that polarized the U.S. women's movement the 1980s and produced a similar schism with tremendous bitterness and political paralysis among theorists and activists who purportedly were working toward the same goal, i.e., the empowerment of women. During that time, Ann Ferguson suggested ways in which feminists could re-frame the issues so that dialog could continue and feminist political work go forward. Ferguson argued for a "transitional feminist morality," that could define contested terms in such a way as to allow for creative tensions and differences within feminist sexual practices without political or theoretical ostracism of competing position (Ferguson, 1983). Ferguson expanded these ideas and defined a "feminist radical pragmatism," an ethical position that can be helpful in adjudicating conflicting ethical claims. It is useful to rehearse briefly her discussion since it is applicable in the case under review here (1996).

In trying to sort through competing claims about which sexual practices feminists assert are detrimental to the empowerment of women, Ferguson argues for a "transitional feminist sexual morality" (Ferguson, 1989, 210). Ferguson defines three categories under which practices can fall: basic, risky, and forbidden. "Basic practices," involves behaviors where feminists could agree that there is little involved that might contribute to the domination of women. "Risky practices," are those behaviors where women would be taking risks because, from a feminist perspective, they might be suspected as leading to a sexual practice of domination/subordination. "Forbidden practices" involve behaviors that are clearly adjudicated by most feminists as anthical to the empowerment of women (Ferguson, 1989, 210–11). Further on in this essay, these categories will be used in trying to establish some ethical guidelines for feminist health practitioners and activists who must make decisions about adolescent reproductive health. In the meantime, the discussion returns to the sociohistorical background in which reproductive decision making is to be found.

Norplant: The Pros and Cons

Public discourse about Norplant generally focuses on: 1) Bioethical and political issues of coercion versus choice in contraceptive methods, particularly in the U.S., which has a history of eugenic approaches to birth control for poor and minority women; 2) contraceptive safety issues, made salient by historical realities of the marketing and widespread use of unsafe reproductive drugs (namely, DES and thalidomide, even after their deleterious effects were known); 3) lack of data about the long-term effects of hormones on adolescents; 4) a conservative anti-welfare political climate that situates health policy and practice within a political discourse of power, regardless of the intent of individual researchers or health providers; and 5) a social reality where health policy is often promulgated litigiously by lawyers and drug companies. These five issues cannot fail to have an impact on the Norplant debate and the relative positions of health providers and advocates as they struggle to provide the best choices to women for reproductive freedom.

Medical Issues

The benefits as well as dangers of Norplant have been documented in the medical literature, including some qualitative research surveying young Norplant users' experiences and reactions to the implants. Studies on Norplant use and its outcomes have been conducted in Texas, Baltimore, and Florida, but have generally been quantitative rather than qualitative, measuring the numbers and kinds of women who come to public health clinics to have Norplant inserted and the side effects they report. In studying adolescent use of Norplant, an emphasis has been placed on the numbers of births adolescents Norplant users have had, previous methods of birth control used, and protections used, if any, against sexually transmitted diseases, particularly HIV (Beilenson, et al. 1995; Berenson & Wiemann, 1995; Cullins, 1994; Weisman, 1993). Only a few studies have questioned the clinic patients in-depth as to their satisfaction and reaction to Norplant (Pies, 1995; Dabrow et al., 1995). Study methodologies have ranged from structured interviews with women using Norplant, to reviews of case records, to pregnancy outcome comparisons between women with Norplant and women using other contraceptive methods. Although there has been a plethora of women's health research since 1989 and the establishment of the NIH Office of Women's Health Research, there is a dearth of research in general where women's voices are heard, particularly poor and minority women. This is certainly the case in the burgeoning body of research, on Norplant, where study authors tend to be medical, academic, or clinical personnel who have minimal contact with study participants. This bias sometimes results in overly positive findings of Norplant efficacy and satisfaction. Women's concerns about side effects are sometimes labeled as "nuisance effects," by researchers who do not themselves experience them.

Providers as well as users assert that the major benefit of Norplant is its convenience and effectiveness as a contraceptive. The insertion procedure is relatively low risk and easily learned and need not require a physician. Once inserted, a woman no longer need be concerned about the possibility of pregnancy, and the inserts last for five years. Thus, many practitioners believe that Norplant is an excellent choice for adolescent and other women who have difficulty with the daily regimen of oral contraceptives or diaphragms and foam, the other most effective methods.

The deleterious physiological effects of Norplant inserts include the most often reported "side" effects: breakthrough bleeding; soreness or infection of the implant site; acne; weight gain; and depression (Pies, 1995; Zuber et al, 1992; White, 1996). In a 1995 study, Berenson and Wiemann commented that irregular menses was the most objectionable side effect of the Norplant users they surveyed. Another medical issue with Norplant is the difficulty of removal of the Norplant rods. The medical literature is increasingly reporting that removing implants is not as easy or straightforward as earlier thought and special training is needed for successful removal. The rods sometimes shift over time in the upper arm, and particularly in the African-American population, keloids may develop around the insertion site, further complicating removal.

Perhaps the most often cited negative issue with Norplant is the failure of most users to employ other means of protection against STDs and HIV infection. Because Norplant insertion is a one-time event and the contraceptive effect can last for five years, there is little incentive for users to return to clinics and health centers for follow-up care, particularly for detection and/or education about HIV and other STDs. In their study, Berenson and Wiemann reported that 31 percent of the Norplant recipients used condoms less frequently (Berenson and Wiemann, 1995). Most women visit health facilities in order to obtain contraception. However, once there, the the opportunity exists for comprehensive health screening and education. This opportunity is lost if women, particularly young women who might not see the need for health screening, no longer need return to health clinics or a provider's office to seek contraception. Because sexually transmitted diseases are an enormous health issue for young women, lack of follow-up care with Norplant can have serious and dangerous consequences. For this reason, many health activists who might otherwise be in favor of safe and long-acting contraception are hesitant to endorse the use of Norplant by adolescents—for example, the National Black Women's Health Network and the National Latina Health Organization (Scott, 1991; White, 1996).

Bioethical Perspectives

The major ethical issues that have been raised concerning long-acting contraceptives were summarized in the Special Supplement to the January/February 1995 *Hastings Report*. Surveying the issues of freedom and coercion in reproductive decision making, Ellen Moskowitz and her colleagues emphasize the social dimension of reproductive and contraceptive decision making. This point has been made by numerous feminist theorists, most cogently by Rosalind Petchesky in her 1980 *Signs* article on abortion and reproductive rights. This view holds that abstract arguments about absolute rights for freedom from coercion and free choice are irrelevant because there are never isolated, genderless, classless, and raceless "individuals" making choices about contraception. Reproductive decision making is a social act occurring within a web of social relations and within a historical context of social power. Absolute arguments "vastly oversimplify the complexity of contraceptive decision making in the real lives of women and men and the difficult choices often posed in a clinical setting" (Moskowitz et al., 1995, S1–8). This is an important point because sometimes both feminist health advocates as well as practitioners fail to acknowledge, or they remain unaware of, the social context in which both their points of view and those of their opponents are anchored. Moskowitz et al. discuss what they call the "sorry history" of U.S. social policy imposing forced sterilization on "socially marginalized, stigmatized or disabled people" (Moskowitz et al., 1995, S2). Thus, class and race issues are always involved in contraceptive policy and practice. The salience of the class issue in Norplant was underscored by the Nov. 11, 1993, testimony before the U.S. House Small Business Subcommittee on Regulation by Dr. Marc Deitch, medical director and vice president of Wyeth Ayerst, the U.S. distributor of Norplant. Responding to considerable criticism that Wyeth was pricing the drug too high, culling enormous profits, Dr. Deitch responded that a primary reason the price of the drug was kept high was "to prevent the drug from becoming known as a poor woman's drug, and thus perhaps be shunned by middle-class women" (Hilts, 1993, A19).

A Norplant insert costs about $16 to make and market. It is sold by Wyeth Ayerst for $365 per kit, but costs each woman from $500 to $1,000 for counseling, insertion, and removal. But Ayerst's strategy to market Norplant as a middle-class form of birth control backfired, and part of the irony is that many middle-class women, particularly those without health insurance, cannot afford the high up-front cost. Norplant was developed and brought to market with government research grants. The costs of Norplant are largely borne by the American taxpayer because the majority of women using Norplant are either Medicaid clients or women who receive it in publicly funded clinics. In a 1993 U.S. House of Representatives hearing on the costs of Norplant, Representative Ron Wyden, chair of the Small Business Subcommittee on Regulation, stated that "$17 million in taxpayers' dollars spent to develop the device, along with another $25 million from foundations, should have earned a lower price for at least public clinics" (Hilts, 1993).

Two additional issues are salient in the debate on Norplant. The first is the enormously high adolescent pregnancy rates in the U.S., particularly in urban areas. The lack of simple, foolproof, completely safe, and woman-controlled contraception makes fertility control problematic at best for poorly educated and poor young women. This social factor is the predominant reason that feminist health providers advocate the use of Norplant for many young women. In daily clinical practice feminist health providers often treat and counsel young women with high rates of unintended pregnancies whose life chances are severely restricted by their too early parenting responsibilities. A conglomeration of factors combine to make poor and urban minority young women at high risk for adolescent mothering. For these women, Norplant seems a good choice.

Hilde Nelson and James Nelson's 1995 article "Feminism, Social Policy and Long-Acting Contraception" raises an important point often missing from politio-ethical debates about contraception. They assert that the ethical discussion on reproduction must be "disaggregated" into two specific parties: the "birthgiver" and the "begetter." This is critical because in the U.S., as in most countries worldwide, women bear the major responsibilities for child-rearing and men are often absent as caregivers or financial supporters. Thus, the discussion about "reproductive responsibility" in the bioethical literature that is written by nonfeminist men or uses ungendered, classless, raceless categories of "persons," seems weak and unpersuasive. The fact that many women struggle alone to raise children is a central reality in the debate over reproductive control. It underscores the claims that women must have woman-controlled reproductive technologies and that women's decision whether to reproduce and under what conditions must be given heavier weight. Furthermore, male policy makers ruling on how and what reproductive methods will be available to women, and how and in what way women's reproduction should be "controlled," must be cognizant of this social dissymmetry and its requisite unequal burden on women.

Norplant in the Baltimore City School Health Clinics

A recent instance of the contest over long-acting contraception occurred in Baltimore in 1995, when a bill was introduced into the Maryland State legislature to prohibit the dispensing of Norplant in school-based and school-linked clinics. Baltimore is the only city that provides Medicaid-covered or low-cost Norplant implants to young women in public high school-based health clinics. From its inception, this policy has created much debate among practitioners, feminist health advocates and the African-American community. The student population of the Baltimore City Public Schools is more than 90 percent African-American, so debates about Norplant in school-based clinics impact disproportionately on this community. In an effort to stop schools from offering Norplant to Black teenagers, some members of the community, together with state legislators, drafted a bill prohibiting the dispersion of Norplant at schools. Arguments both in favor and opposed to this practice surfaced during the hearing on the bill. The logic of the debates on both sides during the hearing echoes some of the positions in the larger U.S. feminist community. Passionate arguments have been advanced in favor as well as against by a variety of contending parties, some in unusual alliances. In many other state legislatures and courts, bills have been introduced or decisions rendered to coerce Norplant use by poor and minority women, through cash incentives, punitive welfare policies, or court orders. The Maryland legislative initiative came from the other side: it was intended to prohibit the state health department from providing and encouraging Norplant use among urban adolescent women.

In Baltimore, the leading spokesperson in favor of the availability of Norplant, particularly for adolescent women, is Vannesa Cullins, an African-American obstetrician and gynecologist who is on the faculty of Johns Hopkins Medical School and is director of the Baltimore Health Department Division of Reproductive Health. On March 8, 1995, at the hearing in the Maryland legislature, Cullins testified in opposition to curtailing the provision of Norplant in school health clinics. She has conducted research on Norplant users at the Hopkins Bayview Reproductive Health Clinic, which she directs. A passionate advocate of long-acting hormonal birth control for poor, young, and minority women, the doctor believes that to withhold Norplant from this population curtails their freedom to choose birth control methods and would be a racist exclusion of a method that is freely available to white, middle-class, middle-age women. Her data from her study support her position that Norplant is an effective method for young women to control their fertility, thereby increasing their life possibilities. Cullins's view is that Norplant makes a difference in young women's lives since it is a more effective contraceptive for this cohort.

> At the Johns Hopkins Bayview Medical Center, 280 adolescents either delivered a baby or terminated a pregnancy between Jan. 1992 and January 1993. 33% chose Norplant postpartum or postabortal. 67% chose either no method or other reversible methods. Follow-up of 37 individuals who chose Norplant and 41 individuals who chose other methods revealed that after 1 year, 47% of oral contraceptive users had discontinued this method; only 16% of Norplant users had discontinued. Among the oral contraceptive group, 25% of the adolescents had experienced a subsequent unplanned pregnancy as compared to 0% of the Norplant Group. (Cullins, 1995)

Cullins's success figures are impressive and are borne out by interviews with young women at the Paquin School in Baltimore, a high school devoted to pregnant and parenting adolescent women (Goldstein and Valentine, 1993). While Cullins alludes to the side effects of Norplant, she does not detail either their nature or the incidence among her study population.

In the same testimony, Cullins used a strategic political tactic to support her argument in favor of Norplant. By citing the costs borne by the state in supporting single women and children on AFDC and children with disabilities, Cullins pitches her arguments to the conservative elements in the Maryland legislature. Here Cullins seems to abandon feminist arguments for reproductive control for women and takes on familiar eugenicist arguments about the "burdens to society" caused by the reproduction of children of the poor and "degenerate" classes. In the current political climate of conservatism and the use of women on AFDC as scapegoats for sociopolitical difficulties, Cullins's tactic seems inflammatory. At the bill hearing, Cullins's position was supported by members of Maryland Planned Parenthood as well as the state departments of education and of health.

Arguments against the provision of Norplant in school-based clinics have several rationales, some conservative, others progressive. Carl Stokes, a former Baltimore city council member and the father of two young daughters, testified in favor of prohibiting school-based dispersal of Norplant. Stokes, who considers himself a feminist, testified that the Baltimore Norplant policy is "both a social and medical experiment on our children" (Stokes, 1993). Citing the history of eugenicist practices of reproductive control in this country and the lack of long-term studies on the side effects of Norplant and the fact that previous studies on Norplant were conducted on adult women, Stokes argues against allowing school clinics to give Norplant to young women. In addition, he cites the fact that Baltimore city schools have a 50 pecent drop-out rate, so that medical follow-up on young Norplant users might be difficult at best. These arguments are similar to those made by other feminist health activists who argue against the use of Norplant by poor women who have difficulty receiving medical care.

Feminist Contentions: Providers Versus Health Activists

Anne Thompson, a certified nurse-midwife with an eight-year practice in adolescent reproductive health, is a fervent supporter of Norplant for young women. She is a feminist health activist who has been involved in the women's movement since her teens. Her professional ethic is to provide as many young women as possible with excellent, caring, feminist health care, complete with a full range of choices. Her vision is to empower young women to take control of their lives and their health. But, in her clinical practice, she is often discouraged by her inability to counsel young women successfully to postpone childbearing. In an interview, Thompson stated that in graduate school, she believed that adolescent pregnancy rates could be reduced by the provision of high-quality counselling, regular and comprehensive health screening, and a choice of contraceptive methods. However, after many years of providing care to multiparous adolescent women, she now believes the issue is more complicated, involving poor self-esteem, low life expectations, and patterns of sexual and physical abuse among many low-income women who sometimes respond to their desperate life situations by eschewing responsibility for their reproduction or not feeling empowered enough to take control. Moreover, her clinical experience has shown her that the young women she sees are not able to ensure that their partners use condoms and do not, in general, take precautions against STDs. Thus, in her view, Norplant and Depo-Provera are good reproductive choices because they provide young women with relatively safe, very reliable birth control that does not require continuous consciousness about contraception during sexual behavior. In this feminist nurse-midwife's experience, the health and life risks to young women of unplanned, unwanted pregnancy are far greater than any potential risks of long-acting contraception. She speaks with the fervor of a young Margaret Sanger and is angered by feminist health activists who are not involved in the daily lives of young women as they struggle with reproductive issues. She is particularly furious at lawyers and litigators, whom she feels intrude in women's lives in their search for money-producing lawsuits against wealthy drug companies.

Two important national feminist organizations are on the other side of the issue. The National Black Women's Health Project (NBWHP) and the National Latina Health Organization (NLHO) both advise caution in advancing the use of Norplant for young women of color (see the articles in the National Women's Health Network information packet on Norplant, 1994). Also citing the dearth of studies on young women, the lack of follow-up care and education for prevention of STDs, and the national history of eugenicist reproductive policies on women of color, the organizations believe that many women of color are not given sufficient information and are coerced into using Norplant. The NLHO in particular states that often Latinas are not given health information in Spanish and that providers are not careful to ensure that Latinas are making informed decisions about Norplant. In issuing its public position on Norplant, the NBWHP asserted that it remains apprehensive anytime government, the medical establishment or others target a particular group of women for one kind of contraceptive. . . . Rather than deal with the root cause of the problem, they seek simplistic solutions to complex issues. Public policies and programs are generally aimed at controlling the social behavior and fertility of women who usually have the least amount of power to question or resist. (National Women's Health Network Packet, 1994, 84)

Sharon Powell, an African-American health educator and activist in Chicago, Illinois, also argues against dispensing Norplant to adolescents. In addition to the above arguments, with which she agrees, Powell makes the point that the "convenience" of these methods of contraception are often more for the provider or the medical or social establishment than for the individual patient, who must cope with the side effects and the potentially deleterious long-term effects (Powell, personal conversation, May 1995).

Risky Practices: How Can Feminists Apply Ethical Principles to Seemingly Intractable Practical Debates?

We can search for some kind of ethical framework to adjudicate conflicts among feminist health activists/policy makers about long-acting hormonal contraceptives. The ethical dilemmas are now clear. 1) Advocating and/or prescribing Norplant can put one into unholy alliance with conservative or eugenicist political positions. 2) Feminist health practitioners, who often focus solely on the day-to-day issues of their patients, are in danger of occluding larger historical and sociopolitical perspectives in which the use of Norplant is embedded. 3) On the other hand, feminist activists/policy makers risk minimizing or overlooking the exigencies of adolescent women's contraceptive needs and the fact that no wholly safe and effective, woman-controlled method of birth control that both contracepts and protects against disease exists.

A return to the earlier discussion of feminist radical pragmatism suggests that feminists might advocate for a "mediated practice" that would allow for the provision of Norplant for adolescent women with the knowledge that it is a "risky practice." Such a practice would allow for the use of Norplant, or other potentially dangerous forms of birth control, in particular contexts. It would be mediated because it would allow for decision making *only after* careful deliberation and analysis of all of the factors involved. This would require those feminist policy advocates and/or activists who have little contact with daily realities of the women involved to become aware of these realities and be informed of the context in which reproductive decisions are taken. On the other hand, providers would have to understand the sociohistorical context in which individual decisions are taken and be aware that no individual circumstance or choice exists in a political or historical vacuum. Taking these factors into consideration in an analysis of the social, political, and individual risks versus the potential benefits of a potentially dangerous form of birth control could result in a mediated position, one that is cognizant of as many risks as possible.

Such a mediated position, based on a feminist radical pragmatism, might allow conflicting feminist groups to achieve consensus on the need for the short-term use of these dangerous methods, while advocating for safer methods that would not be designed to control the reproduction of marginalized, stigmatized groups of people, particularly minority and poor urban women. Furthermore, a mediated feminist position advocating or prescribing Norplant for adolescent urban women would require compensatory strategies to ensure that the practice is concordant with basic feminist values, including equality, control of reproduction, the right to bodily safety, and good health care. The strategies and practices required for the use of risky reproductive methods, particularly Norplant, in an ethical manner would include:

1. Rigorous follow-up care by feminist health providers to ensure that young women are protecting themselves from STDs and HIV.
2. Fully educating Norplant users to the dangers of long-term use; fully informing them of all possible side effects and being sensitive to the seriousness of women's experiences of difficulties.
3. Providing immediate, skilled, and free removal of the implants if young women are dissatisfied or report unwanted or dangerous side effects.

Furthermore, providers and advocates of Norplant must be constantly cognizant of the historical and sociopolitical conditions that make Norplant at best a risky form of contraception for poor and minority adolescent women.

Communication among conflicting viewpoints might be more possible and conflicts ameliorated if feminists could agree that a mediated ethical position can be applied to practical, concrete positions that demand at least short-term solutions. Women in general and young urban women in particular do not have the luxury of waiting for a totally safe, woman-controlled, low-cost form of contraceptive. The everyday realities of all our lives dictate that we make decisions and choices from available alternatives, even if imperfect and potentially dangerous. But we can argue, strategize, and advocate from an ethical position that allows us to choose ways of acting that conform to a mediated feminist pragmatism. This requires the sharing of research and data, as well as experience, analysis, and discussion of all factors involved, and principled debate when differences occur. This discussion and analysis must always be grounded in the experiences and knowledge of the women who are most effected by the policies and practices under debate. Such an ethics requires time and effort to see beyond one's personal, intellectual, political, or professional stance, to eschew the relative comfort of settled or unquestioned assumptions, and remain open to a continuous mediation of politics and practice, and experience.

Conclusions for a Mediated Feminist Ethics and Practice on Long-Acting Hormonal Contraception

The following conclusions are suggested as a beginning articulation of a mediated feminist ethic of policy and practice on reproductive health for the two different but overlapping feminist groups—health providers and health activists/policy analysts.

1. Feminist health providers, struggling to give the best possible reproductive care to young women, may forget or be unaware of the sociohistorical context of available contraceptive methods. They may overlook subtle coercive or eugenicist public policies advanced by people with a political agenda of control of the reproduction of certain groups: low-income women, women of color, and young women of all colors and classes.

2. However, the daily clinical realities of feminist providers are not experienced by many feminist health activists, who tend to have a more macroview of issues. Such activists are sometimes more aware of the medical literature detailing the controversies and dangers of long-acting hormonal contraceptives. Feminist health activists and researchers are often quite aware of the social and historical context of women's long struggle to gain access to and control over contraception. They tend to be deeply suspicious of new birth control technologies targeted to poor and minority women. Feminist health activists seem to be more concerned with coercive use of certain contraceptives than of coercive nonuse. More discussion addressing these contested issues ought to take place among feminist groups involved in contraceptive research, activism, and health practice.

The use of long-acting hormonal contraceptives, while it may be a "good method in a contraceptively imperfect world" (Thompson, 1995), is a risky practice, given the social context of racism, classism, and sexism in the U.S. In order to move toward a mediated ethical policy and practice on reproductive health, vigilance must be maintained and compensatory practices rigorously pursued. This includes careful education, genuine informed consent after extensive counseling, and extensive follow-up care of those choosing these questionable methods of contraception. In addition, providers and activists together must exert continuing political pressure on those controlling health research and resources, so that there can be progress toward developing safe, effective, easily accessible, and woman-controlled forms of birth control.

Acknowledgment

I would like to thank Ann Ferguson, whose theoretical and editorial advice as well as nurturance enabled me to complete this paper. She has been an intellectual inspiration, political comrade, and friend for many years.

References

Alan Guttmacher Institute. July 1993. "Norplant: Opportunities and Perils for Low-Income Women." *Special Report No. 2*. New York: Alan Guttmacher Institute.

Beilenson, P. L., Miola, E. S., Farmer, M. 1995. "Politics and Practice: Introducing Norplant into a School-Based Health Center in Baltimore." *American Journal of Public Health* 85, 309–11.

Berenson, Abbey and Wiemann, Constance. April 1995. "Use of Levonorgestrel Implants Versus Oral Contraceptives in Adolescence: A Case-Control Study." *American Journal of Obstetrics and Gynecology*, 172(4), 1128–37.

Bunch, Charlotte. 1983. *Learning Our Way: Essays in Feminist Education*. New York: The Crossing Press.

Correa, Sônia. 1994. "Norplant in the Nineties: Realities, Dilemmas, Missing Pieces," in G. Sen and R. Snow, editors. *Power and Decision: The Social Control of Reproduction*. Boston: Harvard University Press.

Cullins, Vanessa. 1994. "Comparison of Adolescents and Adult Experiences with Norplant Contraceptive Implants." *Obstetrics & Gynecology* 83(6), 1026–32.

———. March 8 1995. *Testimony on House Bill 511*. Annapolis, MD: Maryland General Assembly Ways and Means Committee.

Dabrow, S., C. Merrick, and M. Conlon. May 1995. "Adolescent Girls' Attitudes Toward Contraceptive Subdermal Implants." *Journal of Adolescent Health*. 16, 360-366.

Ferguson, Ann. 1983. "Sex War: The Debate Between Radical and Libertarian Feminists." *Signs* 10(1), 106–12.

———. 1989. *Blood at the Root*. London: Pandora Press.

———. 1996. "Radical Pragmatism, Risky Practices and Feminist Ethico-Politics." Draft manuscript.

Goldstein, Amy and Valentine, Paul. March 8 1993. "For Teens, Norplant Is a Personal Issue." *Washington Post*, A1.

Hilts, Philip. Nov. 11 1993 "Contraceptive Maker to Charge Clinics Less." *New York Times*, A19.

Holmes, S. May 3 1994. "Norplant Is Getting Few Takers at School." *New York Times*. A1.

Jones, J. 1981. *Bad Blood*. New York: Free Press.

Jonquil, K. S. G. 1994. "Was I a Good Midwife?" *Midwifery Today* 3, 19–40.

Kaiser, Henry J. Foundation papers from the November 1991 forum, "Dimensions of New Contraceptive Technologies: Norplant and Low-Income Women." Contact Sarah Samuels, Kaiser Foundation, Quadrus 2400 Sand Hill Road, Menlo Park, CA 94025 (415–854–9400).

Kolata, Gina. May 28 1995. "Will the Lawyers Kill Off Norplant?" *New York Times*. A. 31.

Moskowitz, Ellen H., Bruce Jennings, and Daniel Callahan. Jan./Feb. 1995. "Long-Acting Contraceptives: Ethical Guidance for Policymakers and Health Care Providers," in *Long-Acting Contraception: Moral Choices, Policy Dilemmas*. Hastings Center Report, Special Supplement, S1–8.

National Women's Health Network. 1994. *Packet on Norplant*. Washington, D.C.

Nelson, Hilde Lindemann and Nelson, James Lindemann. Jan./Feb. 1995. "Feminism, Social Policy and Long-Acting Contraception." *Hastings Center Report*, Special Supplement, S30.

Petchetsky, Rosalind. 1980. "Reproductive Freedom: Beyond "A Woman's Right to Choose." *Signs* 5(4), 661–85.

———. 1990. *Global Feminist Perspectives on Reproductive Rights and Reproductive Health*. A report on the special sessions held at the fourth International Interdisciplinary Congress of Women, Hunter College, New York. New York: Hunter College.

Pies, Cheri. 1995. "Norplant Use by Adolescents: Viewpoints of Three Stakeholder Groups." *Journal of Adolescent Health* 16, 405–11.

Powell, Sharon. May 1995. Personal conversation with author.

Reilly, Philip. 1991. *The Surgical Solution*. Baltimore: Johns Hopkins University Press.

Scott, Julia. 1991. "Norplant and Women of Color," In Sarah Samuels and Mark Smith, editors. *Norplant and Poor Women*. Menlo Park: Henry J. Kaiser Family Foundation.

Stokes, Carl. March 1993. *Testimony on House Bill 511*. Annapolis, MD: Maryland General Assembly Ways and Means Committee.

Thompson, Anne. May 12 1995. Personal interview with author.

Wajcman, Judy. 1994. "Delivered Into Men's Hands? The Social Construction of Reproductive Technology," in G. Sen and R. Snow, editors. *Power and Decision: The Social Control of Reproduction*. Harvard Series on Population and International Health. Boston: Harvard University Press.

Weisman, Carol. Sept./Oct. 1993. "Comparison of Contraceptive Implant Adopters and Pill Users in a Family Planning Clinic in Baltimore." *Family Planning Perspectives* 25(5), 224–26. New York: Alan Guttmacher Institute.

White, Evelyn. Nov. 1996. "Depo Povera, Norplant, and BGH: Are Hormones Hazardous to Teen Health?" *Soujourner: The Women's Forum*, 14.

Women and Pharmaceutical Project, Women's Health Action Foundation. 1993. *Norplant Under Her Skin*. Delft, Netherlands: Eburon. Distributed in the U.S. by the Boston Women's Health Collective, Somerville, MA.

17

Recovering Public Policy
Beyond Self-Interest to a Situated Feminist Ethics

Nancy D. Campbell

Situated Ethics

Theorizing that feminist ethics means something beyond advancing feminist "moral frameworks" for social policy, this essay argues that moral normativity does not a politics make. Feminist ethics can be used to "de-moralize" (Friedman, 1993) specific political arenas by calling into question the universal applicability of the moral judgments embedded in social policy. No arena stands in more need of "de-moralization" than the political regulation of illicit drug use by women, until recently considered a problem so minor it deserved little attention. Women appear in drug policymaking discourse as "exceptional addicts" in two senses—as exceptions to male rules, and as more perniciously addicted, and hence degraded, than men. The claim that women are rarely but exceptionally addicted limits inquiry into the specific structural and discursive conditions under which women use illicit drugs.

Both foreign and domestic drug policy differently impact particular communities of women. For instance, First World drug supply interdiction has led to environmental devastation in agrarian producing areas and detainment or incarceration of Third World women serving as drug couriers for economic reasons. Such efforts have been unsuccessful in interrupting the global flow of drugs; domestic U.S. drug policy has been mainly a matter of curbing individual demand through policies that oscillate between criminalization and medicalization. Obviously, the social effects upon women in producing nations, women who participate in drug trading, and women who are drug consumers differ but are significantly linked despite cultural divides and social stratification. Outside the structures of social inequality that produce drug use and trade, women's drug use is politicized largely in relation to addicted babies, and the *in utero* and neonatal effects of maternal drug use. Connections between relative integrity or destruction of communities due to the disparate impacts of drug policy or the culturally uneven effects of drug use have less often been drawn; only rarely have feminists engaged the topic despite the starkly negative and disparate effects of drug policy upon women's lives. For instance, adequate nutrition and actual access to prenatal care mitigate against Fetal Alcohol Syndrome (FAS) among upper- and middle-class white women alcoholics' children. Actual access to economic resources is little present for Native American women. Whereas illicit drug use rates are similar between white women and women of color, drug policy more negatively affects communities of color. Thus the ethical dimensions of drug use differ among communities of women. The question becomes, which policy mechanisms produce actual differences in women's means to reduce the harm of drug use and traffic in their lives and those for whom they care.

Public policy may maximize or minimize the harm done by drug use and traffic. Opponents of harm reduction policies pitch their objections to harm reduction as "moral values": to distribute clean needles or free condoms condones "deviance" or "immoral" behavior in contrast to the moral framework of "zero tolerance" or abstinence. Advocates point out that harm is the exercise of power upon particular bodies; what counts as "harm" depends on where you look, the political position from which you document harm done. The situated ethics of harm reduction allow communities to state politicized rather than individualized claims of injury— whereas an ethics of care that slides into a prescriptive moral framework of normative behavior does not.

Harm reduction was propounded as a "third way" out of the polarized drug policy debate (O'Hare et al., 1992). Harm reduction has an explicit utilitarian goal to reduce moralism in policy discourse so "more pragmatic interventions" interrupt the risks associated with drug use and traffic. Harm reduction advocates resist moralism; they consider it marred by medical or religious paternalism. They are less likely to construe drug use as a moral issue than to broach its global economic or "planetary consequences" (O'Hare et al., 1992). Harm reduction advocates neither politicize "harm" nor designate how to assess it—they do not address who should do so on behalf of whom. They assume we know harm when we see it; this, coupled with the political neutrality of harm reduction discourse, is part of its appeal in a highly charged policy arena. Harm reduction discourse asserts that victims are produced as collateral damage by the "war on drugs," extending a version of "care" to domestic partners, children, or the communal social fabric. This claim of collective community damage control becomes the basis for extending public responsibility through social policy. Whereas a Rawlsian might argue that abstract principles of justice apply equally to all individuals regardless of whether or not one "cares" about them, a harm reductionist would emphasize the withholding of abstract principles of justice and specific rights once participation in drug use or traffic is ascertained.

Harm reduction is little supported in the United States, a nation slow to recognize that measures short of "zero tolerance" might accomplish more than punitive "drug war" policies.[1] The war on drugs has had devastating effects upon women, particularly in communities of color. Feminists are aptly positioned to attend to the uneven distribution of relative social power and vulnerability in accordance with—rather than in resistance to—normative concepts of morality. Morality is governed by deeply gendered norms of "appropriate conduct, characteristic virtues, and typical vices . . . incorporated into our conceptions of femininity and masculinity, female and male."[2] A feminist avoidance of morally compromised women does little to contest the public discourse that brands drug-using women as "immoral others" who stand beyond the reach of feminism.

U.S. drug policy relies upon empirical research that problematically emphasizes the pathological traits of drug-using persons. Drugs appear in relatively non-pejorative terms, often as tools used by users to mediate discrepancies between expectations and opportunities. Arguing that women addicted to heroin need "skills" education—not moral condemnation—ethnographer Marsha Rosenbaum advocates "affirmative action" and employer incentives (Rosenbaum, 1981). Yet "skills" function as equivalent to morals: addicted persons lack something that make them incapable of managing the social contradictions they inhabit. Ethnographies of female heroin and crack-cocaine users underscore the need for public policy to expand women's options for self-definition, yet question addicted women's competence to remedy their individual deficiencies. "Narrowness often accounts for a woman's inability to end her career in heroin: she simply knows no other options and does not fully appreciate her own circumstances" (Rosenbaum, 1981, 138). The work of Inciardi et al. dispels the claim that women have a special affinity for crack-cocaine, a belief policymakers evidently hold. Yet these researchers consider drug use an overdetermined reply to personal disturbances that disorganize thought and values, resulting in "deficiencies in educational, employment, parenting, and other social skills" (Inciardi, 1993, 145). Rather than fault U.S. drug policy, the researchers consider drug use "a disorder of the whole person: the problem is the person and not the drug, and addiction is but a symptom and not the essence of the disorder" (Inciardi, 1993, 145). Individual drug-addicted women appear as the source of individual drug problems; skills education or "sensitivity training" by expert-class professionals can remedy the trouble but individuals are ultimately responsible for their disorder. Analytic attention to how social subordination is differentially produced and distributed as an effect of public policy is lacking. Women's relative immunity or vulnerability to becoming targets of punitive drug policies is not a matter of personal "identity" but of political positioning.

Policymaking provides an institutional site for the production of statements less codified than law, but often more explicit than law in the intent to punish or further subordinate *particular persons* who already occupy positions of vulnerability. Punitive regulation was increasingly gendered during the "refeminization" of drug use that accompanied crack-cocaine's appearance in the 1980s. Not since before the Harrison Act (1914), which criminalized narcotics use and led to prosecution of prescribing physicians, had women's rates of recruitment into addiction exceeded men's. An influx of women—potentially or actually pregnant—into the ranks of addicted persons during the 1980s produced a policy discourse in which drugs were represented as the ultimate "enemy of nurture," and women addicts as "anti-women" or "anti-mothers." Given the gendered division of the moral and manual labor of nurture—and the racialization of drug problems—pregnant women of color who used drugs were rendered hypervisible. This heightened visibility obscured the social-structural conditions resulting from decades of decisions made in urban social policy. The disparate effects of drug policy and the range of responses invoked to "manage" women's drug problems are the outcome of an uneven distribution of social power and vulnerability facilitated by public policy.

Congressional committee hearings showcased the staging of performative identities constituted through self-identification with particular issues, interests, or ethical positions. Women were repeatedly called the "real addicts" in the hearings of late 1980s and early 1990s, a reference to their putative stubbornness, resistance to abstinence, and an uncaring attitude toward children. Women were the "hard cases," according to then drug czar William J. Bennett, a proponent of the zero tolerance program (U.S. Cong. Senate, 1989, 18–19). Rebuked by the rarity of treatment programs that accepted pregnant women, Bennett insisted on "the hard case"—pregnant

women who willfully refused treatment, not women who were refused it
on grounds that addiction was not a "women's problem," or that women
were more trouble to treat.

Women's stubbornness was reiterated by Michael Dorris, adoptive
father, writer, and activist, on the issue of Fetal Alcohol Syndrome (FAS):

> If there was a person who was walking her child across the street without
> reference to traffic lights and the first time she did it her child was killed
> and . . . each time the child was killed, is it the responsibility of society to
> simply stand on the sidelines and watch and bury the child? I don't think
> so. There has to be found some balance between the individual rights of
> the already living and those that are going to live because she has decided
> to carry to term. (U.S. Cong. Senate, 1989, 19)

The debate over how social policy should treat pregnant addicts is a
debate over women's competence to make autonomous decisions about
whether and how to reproduce. The strategic contradictions and social
inequalities familiar to feminists who have struggled to expand the exercise
of reproductive rights are embedded in drug policy debates. Women are
central to current drug policy because of their role in reproduction and
their culturally designated responsibility for child care. Dorris's discursive
strategy deflected the subcommittee from arguments about social responsibility on the part of physicians or policymakers, moving it toward the
familiar terrain of the addict's personal behavior. Repeatedly in the hearings, women who were judged incapable of care and lacking moral values
embodied "addiction"—they were paradigmatic addicts.

Policymakers believe vulnerability to drug use is the basic cause of
urban disintegration; but "families headed by women are at the base of vulnerability to drug use." According to Senator Christopher J. Dodd (R–
Conn.), "women seem particularly attracted to highly addictive crack
cocaine." Children were situated as innocent victims of women whose
"maternal instincts" were blunted or rendered unpredictable.[3] Domestic
activities, parenting, and scholastic environments were recontextualized by
Senator Joseph Biden (R–De.): "There are housing projects where more
parents tonight will be cooking cocaine than will be cooking dinner for
their children. . . . [T]here are schools in this country where the phrase 'the
iceman cometh' refers to the arrival of a methamphetamine distributor and
not a work of literature." The deadening of "maternal instinct" provided
coherence between the rhetorical registers of social discourse about
addicting drugs.

Crack was perceived as a "women's drug" by policymakers, who saw their task as determining when to criminalize "abuse and neglect by women who are unable to manage their child care responsibilities." Reed V. Tuckman, commissioner of public health in the District of Columbia, claimed "crack is a drug that women seem to enjoy." Women's insatiable appetite resulted in "absolute, extraordinary addiction" that occasioned a new historical condition—the "loss of the maternal instinct."

> We have never seen that, really, at this level of magnitude in the history of human experience with a substance that causes people to no longer care about being a mother, the most fundamental of drives that occurs. (U.S. Cong. Senate, 1989, 38)

Evidence for this was the "paradox" that pregnant women used crack to induce premature labor. Rather than read this as a lack of reproductive autonomy, the "paradox" was instead evidence of the loss of "maternal instinct." Pregnant addicts abused crack, thereby stalling historical progress, "blunting" human beings, inviting sexually transmitted diseases upon themselves, increasing maternal and infant mortality rates, and undermining women's duty to care for children. They were represented as fundamentally lacking the instinctive morality normally the province of their gender.

Crack-cocaine's effects upon culture were mediated through women's bodies. New York City mayor David Dinkins quoted a National Institute of Drug Abuse (NIDA) psychologist on the effects of prenatal exposure: "crack, seems to be 'interfering with the central core of what it is to be human.'" Dinkins warned that employment and relationship skills were impaired in the shell-shocked children of addicted mothers. Dorris, too, feared cultural "malaise" and a new type of crime that is "absolutely pointless, has no conscience to it and is habituated because people who have this problem don't learn from their mistakes" (U.S. Cong. Senate, 1990, 20–21). Suggesting that perinatal exposure dehumanizes children in turn demonizes pregnant women, who are held liable for the "loss of maternal instinct," future violence, and the loss of maternal moral agency.

The interpretive powers of legal categories, diagnoses, and differential processes of racial, sexual, and gender formation focused upon the bodies of culpable addicted women and innocent babies. Women were positioned as deserving exclusion from the benefits of "civilization," just punishment for refusing to serve as "civilizing influences." Discursive positioning serves as a site of historical experience; addicted women live out their subordination. Rather than using the person of the pregnant drug user as an abject figure to justify punishment—as policymakers do—or do much the opposite and claim moral high ground, why not demonstrate the likelihood of harmful effects upon persons in specific situations? A situated ethical critique would direct drug policy away from the individual focus to the context of social vulnerability structured by urban social policy.

Feminist Attention to Drug Policy

Women's differential vulnerability to the effects of U.S. drug policy is produced by the figuration of pregnant addicts as moral failures, and as sources of a monstrous generativity. A sign of frustration to drug policymakers, pregnant addicts embody all that is wrong with the addictive structure of U.S. drug policy, structured by repetitive dynamics of criminalization and medicalization. Clarence Lusane once exhorted feminists to "play a more active role in the struggle against drug abuse and the violations of the drug war":

> Racism and class biases have historically isolated the mainstream women's movement from the needs and issues of poor women and women of color. The drug issue, with its uneven impact on women of color, can be the bridge that unites. Much more investigation needs to be done on why women are becoming more addicted to cocaine, crack, and heroin in this period. . . . The powerlessness of women of color is becoming even more acute as a result of the drug crisis.[4]

According to NIDA, more than 3.6 million (approximately one-third the total) regular drug users are women. Demographic shifts in the HIV-infected population indicate that half of persons diagnosed since 1993 were infected through IV-drug use; another quarter via heterosexual transmission (70–80 percent of whom are women; Kolata, 1995). Drug policy is demonstrably a women's issue, although it has seldom been addressed by feminists, who have taken a prominent stand against other policies that affect the quality of women's lives.

Feminist policy studies remain constructed within the terms of liberal interest-group pluralism. Nonfeminist policy studies see women simply as one "interest group" contending on the pluralist playing field. Feminist policy studies should not repeat the error of constructing a politics based on coherent "identities" unified in pursuit of common and identifiable "interests." While traditional interest groups use government to gain rights and privileges, the state has responded to feminist demands in ways that often reward some women at the expense of others. The emergence of a feminist "ethic of care" proffers a model beyond self-interest; sadly, an ethic of care remains beside the point of public discourse in this liberal and capitalist state. Feminist attempts to go public with an ethic of care raise, but beg, the question, "Who cares for whom?" Is it in "the feminist interest" to align ourselves with pregnant, drug-addicted women? Whereas "feminist ethics" cannot be reduced to an "ethics of care," an "ethics of care" can arguably respond to limit the punitiveness with which public policy is conducted:

> The United States has been in a period of conservative retrenchment when all forms of publicly supported service provision have been curtailed. We have been moving away from a caring orientation toward needy people. Social problems like poverty and drug abuse have been growing as a result, creating the punitive response toward people with such problems that we see exemplified in some policies toward pregnant addicts. (Young, 1994, 42–43)

A model of social obligation based on recognizing differential vulnerability to coercion or harm concretely applies feminist ethics to drug policy.

Feminists demand an "accountable" public policy; we evaluate proposals by whether we think they are "good" or "bad" for "women," assuming women constitute a group for whom identity and interest coincide. These beliefs obscure a politics of abandonment embedded in "identity politics" as practiced in liberal pluralist democracy. If identity is the basis for shared interests or caring relations, those with whom we do not identify or for whom we do not care are categorically excluded. Experiences we cannot comprehend or moral decisions we cannot condone become a basis for cultural "othering." Political contentions grounded in an ethical attention to how power and vulnerability are distributed—and the role public policy plays in that material and discursive process—might connect a feminist plurality more ethically than a politics of identity based upon a series of exclusions. We do not need a prescriptive ethics or a reiteration of maternalist morality. Can an "ethic of care" be structured so as not to presume unifying claims of normative identity? Feminism seemingly lacks an ethical discourse that does not collapse on the normative ground of identity/difference. Our failure to theorize connections not based in "identity" or particularized "care" is a liability in the application of feminist analysis to policy studies.

Social policymaking requires political commitment to both abstract principles of justice and concrete situations of care. Care will not necessarily be for someone to whom you are personally committed, nor for someone whose habits, sensibilities, or aspirations you admire, share, or even wish to include in the polity. An ethic of care must take into account positions

considered morally and socially problematic. Disidentification, Judith Butler maintains, is crucial to ensure that political mobilization in democratic
politics is not reduced to moral-psychological form (1993, 113). Political
identity need not come at the cost of complexity or the cruelty exacted by
the requirement of coherence:

> The contemporary political demand on thinking is to map out the inter-
> relationships that connect, without simplistically uniting, a variety of
> dynamic and relational positionalities within the political field. Further, it
> will be crucial to find a way both to occupy such sites *and* to subject them
> to a democratizing contestation in which the exclusionary conditions of
> their production are perpetually reworked (even though they can never
> be fully overcome) in the direction of a more complex coalitional frame.

An argument against the appropriation of those who occupy the "abject
zones within sociality" to an "all-consuming humanism" (1993, 243), Butler's political vision contrasts with a humanist-feminist ethic of care formulated within the normative confines of a dichotomy between "care" and
"justice." Similarly, Marilyn Friedman advocates moving "beyond *mere* caring dissociated from a concern for justice" implied in the moral-psychological framework promulgated by Carol Gilligan and assumed in empirical
psychology. Positions that locate political possibility in non-normativity—
or what Friedman ironically calls "de-moralized" ethical positions not confined to normative behavior—are attractive because they dis-identify
gender from political position.

Not all feminists see gender normativity as a liability. Some, such as
Monique Deveaux, link care to the humanist commitment to "reorder[ing]
social and political priorities to reflect the central role of care in all our
lives" (Deveaux, 1995, 117). Feminists have contested humanists long
enough that we should resist defining politics as evacuated of contestation—as "care" or the "harm" of not caring—because of the dangers carried by paternalism or maternalism as political positions that justify
relations of domination. Care is a normative naming of "our relatedness" in
Deveaux's formulation—"how we can and should live together." Need
"our relatedness" be normative? Need "how we can and should live
together" be delimited in advance? In the feminist domain, relatedness has
become (or remains) seductive: "care" overcomes a pervasive sense of
fatigue, a response to the seemingly endless series of claimants to feminist
identity. Is "care" the symptom of our political malaise?

Mine is an argument for a reconfiguration of what counts politically as a
"women's issue" by "de-moralizing" feminist politics. Instead of basing

feminist ethics in moral-psychological innocence or guilt, caring or not-caring, let us base them in political claims about how power and vulnerability are produced by and unevenly distributed through policy.

Who Cares What Harm Is Done?

The public discourse of "care" bridges individualism and communitarianism: caring individuals, although autonomous, seek to minimize harm. The convergence of "care" and "harm" is a suggestive political terrain. Recent feminist writing on the "ethic of care" took an explicitly antiessentialist turn in Joan Tronto's *Moral Boundaries* (1993), which asks us to abandon "women's morality," yet reconstruct an unabashed embrace of moral values "traditionally" associated with women. Her admirable question, "Who cares for whom?" unfortunately invites us to limit "care" to those for whom we care. The limits of "care" as a conceptual ideal for political life are masked by its bipartisan appeal. The finite and normative structure of care—who *should or must* or *ought* to care for whom—cannot be set aside. What is the politics of the interpretation of "care" in a political culture that genders care feminine, assimilating the activity of those who occupy "caretaking positions" to feminine identity?

To suggest an "ethics of care" as ground for a "normative conception of politics and policy" passes over the normative ground of care or the harm of not caring. How is "care" enacted and performed? By whom? What cultural presumptions lie beneath an "ethics of care"? Could there be a non-normative feminist ethico-politics without the presumptive normativity of "care"? Is drug treatment a "caring" response to addiction or not? We are talking about women who violate drug laws, after all. We can argue they are overdetermined to do it; their social-structural circumstances predispose them not to care about themselves or others. Such arguments carry little weight in "zero tolerance" climates. Who will persuade crime victims to "care" for offenders because that's the "moral" or "feminist" thing to do? Political claims will not be resolved by a return to the deserving/undeserving, fit/unfit dichotomy that undergirds the discourse of care. Care is contextual and concrete—and finite.

Feminist discourse resonates with harm reduction discourse. The actual harms of drug consumption are shaped by a gendered division of economic, sexual, and emotional labor that subordinates women's employment to men's and elevates women's responsibility for sexual and emotional labor. This is well documented in ethnographic accounts of women's drug use. Women's drug consumption is considered problematic in relation to women's responsibility for reproduction and caretaking. Gender and racial formation serve not as preformed moral-psychological "identities" but as political positions constituted by the practices of government as positions of relative immunity or vulnerability to taking the brunt of punitive drug policies. The difference between the underlying principles of the feminist ethic of care and the pragmatic ground of harm reduction lies in the different status of moralism in each approach. The feminist ethic of care is an attempt to remoralize public policy, while harm reduction seeks a de-moralization of the political sphere.

Social policy is constituted by both the discourse of government, and the sum of the actual practices of governance. One such practice is the emergence of state-level mandatory reporting laws when women who seek medical care test positive for drug use. Mandatory reporting would seem to yield a moral good—early identification of children potentially at risk for drug-related harm. Coupled with economic disadvantage, women are more vulnerable to policing and reporting, which compounds their increasingly realistic fears that *any* state involvement during pregnancy risks removal of their children. Mandatory reporting laws do little to encourage drug-addicted women's faith that social authorities "care"—they encourage much the opposite interpretation of the behavior of public officials. Limits on coercive public policy (civil commitment, birth control, sterilization, or child removal) should be proposed to assure women the state will not interfere—economically or ideologically—with access to reproductive choice or voluntary treatment. Where women are deterred from prenatal care, it is easy to see that drug-addicted persons who are pregnant are impacted by drug policy in ways different from non-pregnant persons. Pregnant women who voluntarily sought treatment for addiction have been not only denied it, but slapped with criminal charges, invasive surveillance, or court-ordered contraception. The case of "fetal harm" illustrates that what counts as "harm" depends upon who's doing the counting. Deirdre Condit points out that battering of pregnant women or male exposure to workplace toxins is not construed as "fetal harm," whereas most behavior of pregnant women is so construed in our current punitive climate. Like "care," then, "harm" is structured through racial and sexual economics; the "harms" to which we attend are political contingencies, and the result of politicized claims of injury to bodies larger than ourselves.

Feminist Ethics and the Ethics of the Pregnant Body

Political injury—the claim that harm results from the disparate impacts of state policies on subordinated classes—does not rest in individual identity. Harm is produced as an effect of policy decisions. The pregnant drug addict's person is a site upon which such injury is installed; she is a subject in need of "social management." Nancy Fraser argues that social welfare policy, as a textual and executive tool, translates needs into dependencies. This process of translation is neither innocent nor apolitical—it produces subordination as its effect. Who gets subordinated through policy—and how that subordination is justified—is the outcome of cultural contestation. We are reaching the limits of an impoverished interpretive framework that treats drug use as an attribute of individuals. A political injury strategy questions the tendency of U.S. policymakers to hold out for individual technical fixes—the promises of pharmacology, a "cocaine antagonist"—while retarding knowledge production about how conditions of social subordination produce drug use and traffic. A shift to political injury would redirect priorities and brook current impasses.

As a cultural attribution, "addiction" provides a diagnostic for subjects name individual failures of autonomy. For pregnant women, addiction triggers a *de facto* definition as uncaring "hard cases," unlikely candidates for rehabilitation. What does the person of the pregnant drug user embody for the feminist ethicist?[5] What forms of citizenship or personhood does she encode or activate? Patricia A. King argues that women's "biological and social roles as procreators and caregivers" have been ignored in drug policy. But most attention to women in policy discussions centers on reproduction, caregiving, and women's potential to abandon or harm those for whom they care. King finds that some policies prevent certain women from reproducing: "the belief that some individuals should not be permitted to be parents lies deep in our culture." She cites "legitimate distress about the conditions in which children live and the physical, emotional, and cognitive problems that they may suffer as a result of parental inadequacies," concern about costs, and a "persistent, pervasive, and highly discriminatory preference for homogeneity in parenting styles" (King, 1993, 307). Pregnancy is a condition not necessarily "chosen" that begs for an ethico-politics of moral obligation and connectedness—but also attention to the politics of social subordination. King argues the maternal-fetal "unit" is an intimate relationship marked by "a severe discrepancy in power." This "unit"—a complex relation rather than a "person"—embodies an uneven distribution of power and vulnerability, which public policy must acknowledge as an ethical relation. But public policy must also recognize that women differentially exercise the power to enact reproductive choices. Here feminists must connect ethics to politics, or risk obscuring our responsibility.

Arguments against criminalization are founded—and founder—upon the defense of civil liberties. An argument against invasion of bodily integrity is not persuasive—"invasion" is reconfigured as pregnant women "invading" uterine sanctity, using drugs as weapons of self- and other-destruction. There is no constitutionally protected right to engage in unlawful conduct, whether you're pregnant or not. There is little agreement about which fundamental rights criminalization denies. Legal scholar Dorothy Roberts argues the necessity to look past drugs to see the degradation of African-American women's fundamental right to choose motherhood rather than abortion. She argues that privacy doctrine—because of its "affirmation of the person" and freedom from government intrusion—should be linked to racial equality. But relying on nonintervention where the government has articulated compelling interests, where there are legal grounds for intervention in the best interests of a child, or asking frustrated and elected policymakers to buck the perceived consensus in favor of punitive sanctions seems precarious. Relying on privacy jurisprudence after *Bowers v. Hardwick* (1986) begs the question of government denial of fundamental rights. It is undeniable that the historical withholding of privacy rights and equal protection from African-American women is reiterated by current drug policy, as Roberts notes:

> The government's duty to guarantee personhood and autonomy stems not only from the needs of the individual, but also from the needs of the entire community. The harm caused by the prosecution of crack-addicted mothers is not simply the incursion on each individual crack addict's decisionmaking; it is the perpetuation of a degraded image that affects the status of an entire race. The devaluation of a poor Black addict's decision to bear a child is tied to the dominant society's disregard for the motherhood of all Black women. (Roberts, 1991, 1479)

However, we also have to look at what is historically new about the modality through which devaluation takes place. The move to criminalize pregnant women's drug use, advanced under the banner of "fetal rights," was made possible by doors left open in *Roe v. Wade*, and political opposition generated by that ruling. But criminalization is also the product of cyclic "law-and-order" campaigns that deflect attention from social-structural problems and project it onto the drug crisis. To focus upon the legal defense of pregnant addicts ignores the sad fact that even strong guarantees of autonomy and privacy may be insufficient to counteract this most political of personal problems if no attention is paid to the structural context.

A "shared interest" model that recognizes public obligation and personal autonomy was advanced by Dawn Johnsen, legal director of the National Abortion Rights Action League (NARAL). Pregnant women, she suggests, share state interest in healthy births; but women are better situated to assess potential harm. Drug use—both practice and discourse—undermines the "ideally better situated" pregnant woman that Johnsen constructs: if a pregnant woman uses drugs, she is not considered capable of "good" choices. Johnsen notes that "bad choices" don't mean women desire to give birth to unhealthy babies (Johnsen, 575). Rather, they are in the grip of strong dependencies. The appeal to "strong dependencies"—and women's predisposition toward them—overrides the fact that women often begin drug use and trade precisely because they are responsible for taking care not only of themselves but dependents (including adult men) with little or no economic or social support. Feminists are aptly positioned to make the case that women are not predisposed to dependency, but forced to make economic and reproductive decisions in the absence of a government that supports equality of access to health care or equal protection under the law. Policymakers seem relatively unaware of how gendered their assumptions about moral values and women's obligations are, and the extent to which they direct political responses by constituting, for instance, women's actions as criminal or pathological.

Feminist cultural studies provide a way to examine discursive constructions of morality, political conflict, and cultural othering in the political regulation of addiction, "criminality," and pregnancy. Public policy provides a prime site for the study of political culture and community in the late twentieth century. We cannot afford to ignore the state as one site where political identities are constituted and regulated, where determinations of whose interests count as "special" and whose do not are made, and where the link between identity and citizenship is forged to discount acts and persons "we" do not condone or include. While the state operates to exercise control over women who depart from recognized social norms, and to confine women to reproductive roles, the diversity of feminist interests should work to broaden what counts as a "women's issue."

Feminist policy studies should not be based in unifying moral claims but upon a "demoralized" politics focused on the structure of social rather than personal injury. Feminist insight into the constructedness of knowledge led to the recognition that "personal" experiences—including bodily experience—is never unmediated by political narratives. The moment has come to broaden this ethical and political insight to capture and critique the constitutive role of public policy in shaping social relations.

Notes

1. Because harm reduction relies upon a number of public health interventions widely understood to "condone" drug use—methadone substitution, clean needle distribution, or

education—it contrasts to abstinence-based models. Harm reduction advocates point out that conditioning social benefits upon maternal abstinence does little to address the differential distribution of vulnerability to drug use among women who inhabit certain social positions and ethical contradictions.

2. "Nothing intrinsic to gender demands a division of moral norms which assigns particularized commitments to women and universalized, rule-based commitments to men. We need nothing less than to 'de-moralize' the genders, advance beyond the dissociation of justice from care, and enlarge the symbolic access of each gender to the available conceptual and social resources for the sustenance and enrichment of our collective moral life" (Friedman, 1993, 271).

3. "Untouchable" newborns, handsome sons, and beautiful daughters transformed into horrifying crack addicts were characterized as a "lost generation." (*Impact of Drugs on Children and Families*, U.S. Senate Committee on Labor and Human Resources and the Committee on the Judiciary, 1989, 101st Cong., 1st sess. S. Res. 397. Washington: GPO.) Biden focused on the economic weighting of "the kite strings that draw our National ambitions aloft." Senator Dodd quoted "psychologists who tell me that children of substance abusers become emotionally blunted, callous at a very young age" (4–5).

4. During the 1980s, women's rates of incarceration for and recruitment into drug use outstripped men's; nearly 80 percent of women's crimes were designated "drug-related" (Lusane, 1991, 66).

5. Diprose (1994) defines ethics as the "*study and practice of that which constitutes one's habitat*, or as the problematic of the constitution of one's embodied place in the world" (19).

References

Butler, Judith. 1993. *Bodies That Matter*. New York: Routledge.

Chavkin, Wendy, and Stephen R. Kandall. 1992. "Illicit Drugs in America: History, Impact on Women and Infants, and Treatment Strategies for Women." *Hastings Law Journal*, Vol. 43.

Condit, Deirdre. 1995. "Fetal Personhood: Political Identity Under Construction." *Expecting Trouble*, ed. Patricia Boling. Boulder, CO: Westview Press, 25–54.

Deveaux, Monique. 1995. "Shifting Paradigms: Theorizing Care and Justice in Political Theory." *Hypatia*, Vol. 10, No. 2.

Diprose, Rosalyn. 1994. *The Bodies of Women: Ethics, Embodiment and Sexual Difference*. New York: Routledge.

Fraser, Nancy. 1987. *Unruly Practices*. Minneapolis: University of Minnesota Press.

Friedman, Marilyn. 1993. "Beyond Caring: The De-Moralization of Gender." *An Ethic of Care*, ed. Mary Jeanne Larrabee. New York: Routledge.

Inciardi, James A., Dorothy Lockwood, and Anne E. Pottieger. 1993. *Women and Crack-Cocaine*. Boston: Macmillan.

Johnsen, Dawn. "Shared Interested: Promoting Healthy Births without Sacrificing Womens Liberty." *Hasting Law Journal*, v. 43, March 1992, p. 575.

Kandall, Stephen R. 1996. *Substance and Shadow: Women and Addiction in the United States*. Cambridge: Harvard University Press.

King, Patricia. 1993. "Helping Women Helping Children: Drug Policy and Future Generations." *Confronting Drug Policy: Illicit Drugs in a Free Society*, ed. Ronald Bayer and Gerald M. Oppenheimer. New York: Cambridge University Press.

Kolata, Gina. 1995. "New Picture of Who Will Get AIDS Is Crammed With Addicts." *New York Times* 28 February: B6.

Lusane, Clarence. 1991. *Pipe Dream Blues: Racism and the War on Drugs*. Boston: South End Press.

O'Hare, P. A., R. Newcombe, A. Matthews, Ernst C. Buning, and Ernest Drucker, eds. 1992. *The Reduction of Drug-related Harm*. New York: Routledge.

Roberts, Dorothy. 1991. "Punishing Drug Addicts Who Have Babies: Women of Color, Equality, and the Right of Privacy." *Harvard Law Review,* Vol. 104.

Rosenbaum, Marsha. 1981. *Women on Heroin*. New Brunswick, NJ: Rutgers University Press.

Tronto, Joan. 1993. *Moral Boundaries: A Political Argument for an Ethic of Care*. New York: Routledge.

United States Cong. Senate. 1989. Subcommittee on Children, Families, Drugs and Alcoholism. "Drug-addicted Babies: What Can Be Done?" (hearings). 101st Cong. 1st sess. S. Res. 396. Washington, DC: GPO.

United States Cong. Senate 1990. Subcommittee, on Children, Families, Drugs and Alcoholism. "Children of Substance Abusers" (hearings). 101st Cong., 2nd sess. S. Res. 723. Washington, DC: GPO.

Young, Iris Marion. 1994. "Punishment, Treatment, Empowerment: Three Approaches to Policy for Pregnant Addicts." *Feminist Studies,* Vol. 20.

Contributors

KATHRYN PYNE ADDELSON is Mary Huggins Gamble Professor in the philosophy department at Smith College. She works as a volunteer at Wellspring House in Gloucester, Massachusetts.

BAT-AMI BAR ON teaches philosophy and Women's Studies at the State University of New York at Binghamton. Her primary theoretical and activist interests are in violence, though she escapes them often by pursuing other themes.

SANDRA LEE BARTKY is Professor of Philosophy and Women's Studies at the University of Illinois, Chicago, and teaches feminist theory, phenomenology, poststructuralism, and critical theory. She is the author of *Femininity and Domination: Essays in the Phenomenology of Oppression* (Routledge, 1990). She has served on the American Philosophical Association Committee on the Status of Women and is currently a member of the APA's Committee on the Status of the Future of the Profession. In addition, she is a founder of the feminist philosophical Journal *Hypatia* and the Society for Women in Philosophy, now an international network.

SARAH BEGUS is a feminist theorist, women's health researcher, and community activist who lives and works in Baltimore, Maryland.

NANCY D. CAMPBELL is Assistant Professor of Women's Studies at the Ohio State University. She teaches feminist policy studies, policy history, and feminist theory, and writes on the impact of licit and illicit drug policy upon particular communities of women. She recently received her Ph.D. from the History of Consciousness Program, University of California at Santa Cruz.

CHRIS J. CUOMO teaches philosophy and women's studies at the University of Cincinnati. She is the author of *Feminism and Ecological Communities: An Ethic of Flourishing* (Routledge, 1997).

VICTORIA DAVION is Associate Professor of Philosophy at the University of Georgia. She specializes in feminist philosophy, ethical theory, applied ethics, and social and political philosophy. She is the editor of *Ethics and the Environment* (JAI Press).

SUSAN DWYER is Associate Professor in the Philosophy Department at McGill University in Montreal, where she teaches moral philosophy, epistemology, and feminist theory. She has published in the philosophy of language, ethics, and epistemology. She is also the editor of *The Problem of Pornography* (1995) and coeditor (with Joel Feinberg) of *The Problem of Abortion*, 3rd ed. (1997).

DION FARQUHAR is a political theorist (Ph.D., New York University), cultural critic, poet, and prose fiction writer. Her first book is *The Other Machine: Discourse and Reproductive Technologies* (Routledge, 1996). She is currently working on a book on third-party gamete donation and changing kinship and family practices. She lives in Santa Cruz, California, with her partner and their twin sons and visits her home in New York as often as possible.

ANN FERGUSON is a socialist-feminist philosopher who is Professor of Philosophy and Director of Women's Studies at the University of Massachusetts at Amherst. She has written two books in feminist theory, *Blood at the Root: Motherhood, Sexuality and Male Dominance* (Pandora/Harpercollins, 1989) and *Sexual Democracy: Women, Oppression and Revolution* (Westview).

JANE FLAX teaches political theory at Howard University and is a psychotherapist in private practice. She is the author of *Thinking Fragments* and *Disputed Subjects* and of essays on psychoanalysis, politics, feminist theory, and philosophy. Her current project is a book on the politics of race and gender in the contemporary United States, focusing on transcripts of the Senate Judiciary Committee hearings on Clarence Thomas as a paradigm case.

LORI GRUEN has a two year visiting appointment at the Center for Applied Ethics at Stanford University. She has published on the ethics of human relations to nonhuman animals, ecofeminist philosophy, and most recently has edited a collection entitled *Sex, Morality, and the Law* (Routledge, 1997). She is currently working on the problem of moral alienation.

CHERYL HALL is Assistant Professor of Government and International Affairs at the University of South Florida and coeditor of *Hypatia: A Journal of Feminist Philosophy*. She is especially interested in feminist challenges to Western philosophies of reason, passion, and power, and is currently at work on a book about politics and passion.

RENEE HEBERLE is Assistant Professor of Politics and Women's Studies at the State University of New York at Potsdam. Her research and activism is primarily focused on the politics of sexual violence.

LISA HELDKE teaches philosophy and women's studies at Gustavus Adolphus College, St. Peter, Minnesota. She works in the area of pragmatist feminist epistemology, with an emphasis on the nature of objectivity. She also works on the philosophy of food, having coedited the anthology *Cooking, Eating, Thinking: Transformative Philosophies of Food* (Indiana University Press, 1992). Currently she is at work on a collection of essays with the working title *Let's Eat Chinese: Cultural Food Colonialism.*

BECKY ROPERS-HUILMAN recently received her Ph.D. from the University of Wisconsin at Madison. She is Assistant Professor of Education at Louisiana State University. She focuses her research on feminist teaching in higher education, implications of multiple theoretical approaches for methodological choices, and curricular issues as they intersect with opportunities for equitable and diverse practices. She is currently working on a book entitled *Creating a Poststructural Feminist Teaching Discourse: Knowledge, Power, Pedagogy, and Curriculum.*

MARÍA LUGONES teaches at the Escuela Popular Norteña, a center for radical political education for Latinas and Latinos, and directs the Latin

American and Caribbean Studies Program at the State University of New York at Binghamton. Her interests as a writer, an activist, and a grassroots educator center on the interlocking of oppressions and on resistance to interlocked oppressions.

HELEN WATSON-VERRAN is Senior Lecturer in the Program in the History and Philosophy of Science at the University of Melbourne, Australia. She has worked with the Yolgnu on many projects and has been adopted into that Aboriginal Australian group.

LAURIE ANNE WHITT is Associate Professor of Philosophy at Michigan Technological University. Her research deals with issues that lie at the intersection of indigenous studies, science studies, and legal studies. She is currently working on a book that focuses on the impact of intellectual property laws on the efforts of indigenous peoples to retain control of their genetic and cultural resources. She has been actively involved in various indigenous struggles in the United States, Australia, and Mexico.

Index